# About The Author

 Donald J. Ford, C.P.T., is president of Training Education Management LLC, a training and performance improvement consulting firm specializing in instructional design and human resource management. He has worked in the field of human resource development for over 20 years, first as trainer and training manager and then as consultant. His clients include public sector and Fortune 500 organizations in the auto, banking, utility, energy, electronics and aerospace industries in North America, Latin America, the Middle East and Asia. For these clients, he has developed custom classroom, self-study and web-based training, conducted performance and needs analyses, facilitated groups, managed improvement projects, taught courses in training, human resources, management, interpersonal skills and quality improvement and evaluated the results. Dr. Ford also teaches graduate courses in Organizational Management for Antioch University, Los Angeles, and has published 40 articles and three other books on topics related to training, education, and business. He holds a B.A. and M.A. in history and a Ph.D. in education, all from UCLA. Dr. Ford resides in Torrance, California.

**800 Pacific Coast Highway, Suite 8180**
**Redondo Beach, CA 90277 USA**
**info@trainingeducationmanagement.com**
**www.trainingeducationmanagement.com**
**1-310-316-2240**

PREVIOUS WORKS BY DR. FORD:
* *The Twain Shall Meet: The Current Study of English in China*. McFarland, 1988.
* *In Action: Designing Training Programs*. ASTD, 1996.
* *Bottom-line Training: How to Design and Implement Successful Programs That Boost Profits*. Gulf Publishing, 1999.

# Book Reviews

"Donald Ford has done it once again-a fabulous insightful resource for trainers and HR practitioners who really care about achieving what's most important for their client's success."

*Peter Chee*
*President and CEO*
*Institute of Training and Development*
*Penang, Malaysia*

This book provides in-depth explanations, examples and exercises that will help the reader distinguish different types of analysis such as performance analysis, job analysis, task analysis, skill gap analysis, learner analysis and the ubiquitous needs analysis. More importantly, this book continuously drives home the vital link between training activity and meaningful business indicators.

*Ethan S. Sanders*
*President and CEO*
*Sundial Learning Systems, Inc. and*
*Co-author of Performance Intervention Maps (ASTD Press)*

Dr. Ford's approach to training design helps the reader to understand the importance of taking a comprehensive and systematic approach to creating and implementing a training initiative from beginning to end. A major strength of his model is the rigorous approach to

front-end needs analysis and assessment that he recommends ... This book is a "must read" for any person considering the use of training for performance improvement in an organization.

*David D. Dubois, Consultant*
*Author of Competency-Based Human Resource Management*
*(Davies Black Publishers) and Competency-Based Performance*
*Improvement (HRD Press).*

I liked this book so much I bought a copy for each member of my training staff. Don's book covers all the basics of training and development. It's a must for any trainer's library.

*Richard G. Wong, Consultant and former Manager of Training and Organization Development Orange County Transportation Authority*

Where other books on instructional design offer principles and systematic approaches, this book goes beyond the ISD model to offer practical, down-to-earth guidance on everything from designing performance tests to negotiating maintenance issues with clients. I have used, and quoted from, line Training on numerous occasions. A must-have for every instructional designer's bookshelf!

*Carolyn Johnson Instructional Design Supervisor Southern California Gas Company, a Sempra Energy Utility*

Don Ford's book hits the nail on the head. It provides a clear introduction and explanation of the systematic training development process. At the same time, it never lets the reader lose sight of how important it is for all training activities to be designed to make significant contributions to organizational results, Bottom-line Training performs beautifully in both arenas, giving the beginner and the experienced developer alike fresh insights to our profession's business role and leaving them with a comprehensive set of design tools that will serve them well.

*John Stormes Past President International Society for Performance Improvement Los Angeles*

Don Ford's newest book on Bottom-line Training is the perfect mixture of strategy and techniques for implementing a systematic approach to training design and delivery. His examples, stories and models for bottom-line training are a great help to any trainer."

*Jean Barbazette President The Training Clinic and Author of Instant Case Studies and The Trainer's Journey to Competence*

# DONALD J. FORD

Ph.D., Certified Performance Technologist (C.P.T.)

# **Bottom**-line
## Training
PERFORMANCE-BASED RESULTS

# Second Edition

For order information or permission to use, please contact:

**Donald J. Ford**
**President**
**Training Education Management LLC**
**800 Pacific Coast Highway, Suite 8180**
**Redondo Beach, CA 90277 USA**
**1-310-316-2240**
**Info@TrainingEducatlonManagement.com**
**www.trainingeducationmanagement.com**

**ISBN No.** : 978-0-9763974-03

# Contents

# Dedication

*To the memory of my father; Kenneth A. Ford,*
*To my mother, Harriet L. Hurlburt and*
*To my two sons, Vincent L. and Steven L. Ford.*

# Preface

Over the past half century, the design of training programs has grown into a multi-billion dollar industry. With more organizations moving away from classroom lecture as the sole training delivery method, instructional designers have emerged as the new role model for training professionals.

Although much research has been conducted in how adults learn and how instruction can be designed to facilitate learning and maximize performance, too little of the cutting-edge knowledge in the field has made its way into the daily practice of training in corporate America. The majority of programs, especially those delivered in classrooms through traditional lecture, continue to be designed by subject matter experts who rely on their own intuition and experience to guide them, rather than a systematically applied theory of instructional design.

Though many fine programs are designed this way, a much larger number of these programs fail to help trainees reach the stated objectives and do not prepare them to apply what they learn on the job. Studies have found that as much as 50 percent of the training occurring today is not transferred back to the job, resulting in a monumental waste of resources.

All is not bleak, however. A growing number of training programs, especially those designed based on human performance technology, are developed using a systems model of instruction, so that the right content is taught to the right people at the right time. These training programs are the source of today's success stories in the workplace. It is this type of training that is transforming organizations around the world into high-performance, efficient, customer-focused firms that enjoy success in the marketplace. Increasing evidence supports the notion that investments in training and other aspects of human capital account for a large share of a company's financial success.

This book is aimed at working professionals in the field of training and development and those newcomers who wish to gain systematic knowledge and skills in the field. It is an easy-to-read introductory text that proceeds step-by-step through the process of creating and delivering outstanding training programs. It will make readers more effective trainers and more valuable to the people they serve.

*Donald J. Ford*
*Torrance, California*

# SECTION ONE
# **Analysis**

The first section of this book deals with the first phase of the results-based design model – analysis. In this phase, trainers investigate the need for training and uncover underlying causes for performance problems or new performance opportunities requiring new knowledge, skills or attitudes. This phase is also called needs assessment, needs analysis, opportunity analysis or front-end analysis – although technically speaking, they are not synonymous. This section will present knowledge in needs analysis and assessment, performance analysis, job analysis, task analysis, learner analysis, context analysis and skill gap analysis.

Each of these types of analysis provides specific kinds of information to the trainer that help determine whether training is needed at all; whether other interventions, such a job redesign, rewards and recognition, process reengineering, management or systems changes are required; and exactly what new knowledge skill and attitudes are needed to achieve the intended results.

Although any given project may not require all of these analytical tools, the accomplished analyst has them all available in the toolkit should they be necessary. The growth of analytical tools and methods is one of the most exciting developments in the field, for training design can never by better than the analysis that informs it. The following model depicts the analysis phase of training design as a learning map.

Figure: 1-1        **Analysis Phase**

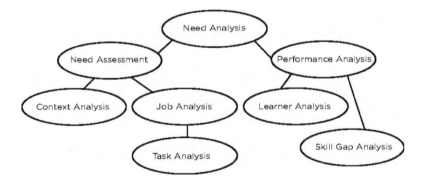

In the following seven chapters, you will learn about each of these types of analysis and how to use them to define training programs.

First, though, it is necessary to introduce the Bottom-line Training model to set the foundation for the chapters that follow. That is the subject of chapter one.

# Introduction to Bottom-Line Training Design

In this book, results come first. Why should a book on training design start with the results to be achieved? Because for too long, training and development has not directly tied itself to business results that matter to clients and customers. Is it any wonder, then, that when business turns sour, training is among the first things to go?

Put yourself in the position of a struggling business owner. Where would you put your limited resources when forced to choose: in production, service delivery, marketing or employee development? Of course, you would choose your products and services over the development of employees, unless you were certain that an effectively trained workforce that performs superbly on the job would boost your business' success. So, the first priority for anyone designing training programs today is to figure out how the proposed training enhances an organization's ability to deliver quality and thereby stay in business. Any result less than that will relegate training to the fringe benefit category of nice things to have – when the extra money is available to afford such amenities.

The book's organizing model is the most widely used instructional design system available today – the Instructional Systems Design (ISD) or ADDIE model, as it is sometimes known. It is illustrated below:

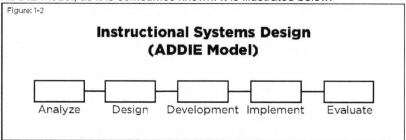

Figure: 1-2

**Instructional Systems Design (ADDIE Model)**

Analyze — Design — Development — Implement — Evaluate

### The Results-Based Model of Training Design

In order to focus on business results, designers must start with results and must constantly keep them in focus as they engage in their work. The following model illustrates how the training design process interacts constantly with the results being sought to keep training targeted on the things that will help a business succeed.

In this model, interactions occur in two directions. First, the design process is interactive as training proceeds from analysis to design, development, implementation and evaluation. Any one step in the process changes all other steps and may require rework of previous steps. Second, each step in the design process interacts with the results being sought. At every point in the design process, trainers must ask themselves if the work they are doing in that step supports the required results, or if changes are needed to properly address the results.

All this is well and good, but to use the model effectively, we must first define what results training design should seek to achieve.

*Figure 1-3*     Results-based Training Design Model

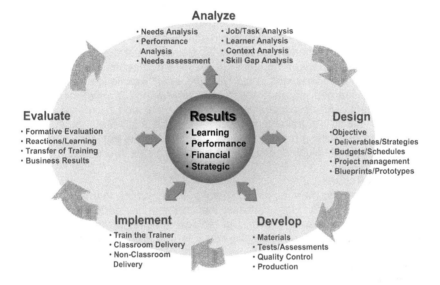

### The Results Trainers Seek

That training seeks to produce results is certainly not a revolutionary concept. Like any human endeavor, training and development exists to achieve valuable results. It always has and it always will. What has changed about training is the type of results being sought.

In the past, trainers were primarily concerned about producing one tangible result: learning. If they could demonstrate that trainees learned something of use in their classes, they were satisfied. If, in addition, trainees indicated they had enjoyed their learning experience, the class was declared a great success by all concerned.

Today, ensuring learning is still paramount; it's simply no longer sufficient. Instead, organizations expect training to produce something more valuable to the firm – performance. By this somewhat nebulous term is meant the ability to work up to the full expectations of a job and full capabilities of the worker.   Performance is the application of learning in a work context, and it is performance that organizations want and pay for when they request training.

## Performance Results

Thus, the first type of result organizations seek today is job performance. This may be categorized into several types of performance, among the most common of which are the following:

- Perform new job skills
- Perform existing job skills better, faster or cheaper
- Apply new knowledge to enhance performance
- Exhibit new attitudes or change old attitudes about performance

To achieve performance results, trainers must design training that simulates the job. Then, they must go beyond classroom learning into the workplace to assist trainees in applying the skills, knowledge and attitudes they have learned so that their job performance shows measurable improvement. This is exceedingly important work and represents a sea change in the role of training professionals. But it is still not enough. To be truly effective, training must go beyond performance to achieve even more fundamental and valuable results for the organizations they serve.

## Financial Results

If training has achieved results in terms of learning and job performance, then it ought to follow that the financial performance of the organization will also improve. But so few training programs are ever evaluated on their financial results that it is unknown at this point in time just how many training programs actually produce a positive financial benefit. Much of the problem is rooted in the archaic accounting practices of most firms, especially with regard to labor and human capital, which prevent many trainers from establishing a cause and effect link between training and the firm's financial performance. Adding to the difficulty is the typical confounding of various causes that contribute to a company's financial success, including such variables as: worker skills, product/service quality, research and development, technology, price, competition and market conditions. All of these factors interact in determining how well a company is doing at any moment in time.

All of these obstacles to measuring the financial impact of training have served to create cynics among both trainers and executives. Many simply declare that the financial benefits of training cannot be accurately measured and must be accepted on faith alone. This approach is a cop-out, and will impoverish the training profession if allowed to prevail.

Leaving aside for the moment the thorny issue of how training's financial impact should be measured (this will be revisited in the Evaluation section of the book), let us first enumerate some of the key financial results that well-designed training programs should achieve. They fall into one of four categories listed below:

- Avoid future costs by fixing a problem while it is still small and cheap
- Lower operating costs by saving on labor and/or materials

- Increase revenues by boosting sales of existing products/services or introducing new products/services
- Leverage capital investments in buildings and technology by ensuring that these investments are properly utilized by employees

Good training programs produce one or more of the results above, either directly or indirectly in combination with other factors. Measuring the impact that training had, and especially isolating the contribution of training as opposed to non-training interventions, is difficult, to be sure, but it had better be possible at least some of the time or else the training profession is in for a very rough ride in the years ahead.

## Strategic Results

As challenging as tying training to financial results can be, it is still not enough. One additional level of results must also emanate from effectively designed training – strategic results. These are results that not only improve job performance and financial results, but also enhance the organization's ability to compete and survive in the future. When training begins to influence strategic results, it then enters a whole new realm of importance and serves organizations in wholly new and indispensable ways.

Among the strategic results that training frequently contributes to are the following:

- Create new products and services and the means to deliver them to customers
- Improve the organization's ability to serve its customers, both current and future
- Open new markets for an organization's products and services
- Enhance organizational operations by redesigning processes and functions

When training establishes the ability to achieve strategic results on a regular basis, it no longer needs to justify its existence to skeptical executives. Instead, it moves from the fringe benefit list to the core of the business, because anything that helps a business grow and prosper over time is truly a critical core competency of the firm that needs to be nurtured.

### When Results Are Lacking: An Example

Having defined the kinds of results that training must achieve, let us now turn to an example of a trainer who failed to focus on results and the price she paid for this neglect.

Jane was the Training Manager for a medium-sized retailer specializing in children's and teen clothing. She had worked her way up from HR generalist to Training specialist to Training Manager, when the newly-created position opened up several years ago. Jane prided herself on hard work and good interpersonal skills. She always gave her best effort and tried hard to get along with everyone at the firm. People liked her and she seemed to have it made. Her small department of 2, consisting of a

Training Administrator and a Training Specialist, were also dedicated people trying to do their best to satisfy management and meet employees' needs.

Jane enjoyed facilitating learning more than any other aspect of her job. She loved getting up in front of a group of employees and helping them learn something new. It was a role she had discovered originally as a secondary school teacher and had developed over the years after she made the switch to corporate training.

She knew there was much more to training and development than classroom instruction, but her interests just didn't take her outside the classroom, where she felt most comfortable. She had taken a few workshops and attended conference sessions on needs assessment, instructional design and evaluation, but never really got around to implementing much of it at work. "No one would support me anyway," she told colleagues, "they just want me to put on some good training programs that employees will enjoy."

Her boss, the VP of HR, advised Jane to keep senior management happy and life would be good. He offered lip service to the importance of training, but Jane noticed that every time the HR budget had to be cut, training always took the biggest hit. She resented this, but could do little to stop it from happening.

At one point not long ago, the CEO, in a rare meeting with Jane, asked her about what kind of return on investment the company was getting from the nearly $500,000 annual expenditure on training. She stammered something about satisfied employees better able to do their jobs, but could not provide a single figure to back up her claims.

After that, she contacted a consultant specializing in evaluation, who gave her some advice on how to measure training results and demonstrate bottom-line results. She tried implementing a post-course survey, but found that most managers were too busy to complete it and send it back. Once she got data from a few managers, she wasn't too sure what to do with it. So, she quietly abandoned the effort after a few months.

When she got training requests from managers, she did her best to give them what they asked for. A senior VP asked her to find an executive leadership program not long ago and she searched through several online training databases to find him a great looking program at a local private university. A sales manager wanted to hire a consultant he knew as a sales coach and approached Jane to pay for it. She went to her boss and sold the idea after interviewing the consultant and determining that she was experienced at sales coaching.

Thus, her approach to analysis was to give requesters what they wanted to the best of her ability. She rarely questioned the requests she received and did little investigation on her own to determine whether the requests could legitimately be met with training solutions. Because of this, Jane sponsored many training programs that she knew would produce little long-term benefit. Her focus was on satisfying the immediate wishes of her superiors and clients.

Her approach to instructional design was also devoid of systematic process. She outsourced nearly all the custom design work that had to be done, often relying on off-the-shelf programs instead of custom design to save money. Her role in design was primarily that of a broker – searching for and hiring vendors to meet client requests. Her vendors rarely conducted a needs assessment or even talked to members of the target audience. Instead, the predominant approach was to meet with the requesting manager, get a list of the topics he wanted covered and find someone who could provide the training at the lowest cost.

For evaluation, Jane relied exclusively on learner reaction surveys. She collected these for nearly every class, summarized the comments and provided them to clients as proof of training's effectiveness. Other than the failed attempt to collect post-course survey data from managers, she did no evaluation of learning, performance, financial or strategic results. Deep inside, Jane knew she should be doing these things, but there never seemed to be any time for evaluation and besides, management never asked for such data anyways. They seemed content with what Jane was doing.

It was quite a shock then, when Jane was called in to see her boss unexpectedly one Friday afternoon. He sat down with gloom all over his face and broke the bad news: the Training Department had to be eliminated to cover a 25 percent decline in revenues over the last year. Jane and her staff of two were being laid off. When she inquired about who would take over all the training her department provided, she was in for a second shock: the little amount of training that would continue was being outsourced to one of her vendors! She couldn't believe what was happening to her.

### The Imperative of Results

The above case illustrates the perils of running training programs in a corporate world where things change at the speed of light and nothing is above the budget-cutting ax. It also speaks volumes about what happens to training when it loses its tie to key business goals – eventually it is jettisoned like so much flotsam.

To avoid this fate, Jane needed to take a results-based approach to training at each stage, starting with the request. Instead of simply giving management whatever it wanted, Jane should have insisted on conducting a needs analysis first, in which she collected data about the need for training and found out exactly what skills trainees needed to perform their jobs. Then, armed with this information, she could have directed vendors to develop a custom training solution that focused on producing superior job performance. She could also have utilized a variety of training delivery methods, including classroom, e-learning, self-study, coaching and a blend of all of these, to enhance trainees' learning and improved the chance of transferring skills to the job. Finally, she should have measured the results of training, including measuring learning through pre-post assessments, measuring performance and behavior change by following up with trainees and their managers 30 to 90 days after class and by linking key training programs to the organization's financial and strategic goals.

If Jane had run the training department like a business entrepreneur, with a profit and loss mentality, she would have seen the loss of management support materializing and would have been better able to show tangible benefits that the company received from its investment in training. She would have been able to show how training was saving the company money by improving productivity and efficiency and how it was contributing to corporate goals like increasing revenue and penetrating new markets.

Instead, training at Jane's company was viewed as a fringe benefit that was nice to have when times were good, but expendable when times were bad. Unwittingly, Jane played right into this image of training when she failed to question management's training wish list and neglected to apply systematic design and evaluation techniques to ensure that training made a measurable difference.

### The Changing Role of Training

With this little parable in mind, we can see that the role of training needs to change to remain relevant in the modern business world. The table below illustrates the vast changes sweeping the field as trainers are increasingly moving beyond learning to embrace workplace performance. Unfortunately, professionals like Jane, who focus on traditional classroom learning, are being left behind as the focus shifts to performance-based results.

In the analysis phase, trainers have traditionally focused on identifying learning needs without tying them to business results, or as Jane did, simply giving clients whatever they request. In the performance-based approach, trainers focus on identifying key gaps in job performance and investigate underlying sources of knowledge and skill that can contribute to closing the gap. Trainers also increasingly look at non-training factors, like motivation, process, resources and information, to determine the role they play in performance problems. In the design and development phases, traditional trainers focus exclusively on content, preparing an information dump primarily via lecture, or outsourcing design and relying on off-the-shelf programs, as Jane did. This typically involves getting a subject matter expert to tell everything he/she knows about the subject, without regard to whether it will help novice trainees perform better or not. In a performance-based approach, the design and development of training revolves around the tasks that trainees perform on the job and the missing knowledge and skills that they need to be successful performers. Anything else that clients may want included is nice to have but not necessary.

In the implementation phase, traditional trainers consider the classroom to be their kingdom, as Jane did. They focus all energies on making the classroom experience enjoyable and meaningful for participants. While performance-based trainers also attempt to make learning fun, they focus more on simulating work environments and providing lasting performance support to trainees after they return to the job. They do not consider the job done once participants leave the classroom; they consider the job is just beginning at that point.

**Changing Role of Training**

| TRAINING PHASE | LEARNING FOCUS | PERFORMANCE FOCUS |
|---|---|---|
| Analysis | Training Needs | Performance Gaps |
| Design | Content- driven | Performance- driven |
| Development | Information Dump | Task-Based Skills |
| Implementation | Classroom & Training Activity Focus | Simulation & Performance Support |
| Evaluation | Reactions & Learning | Behavior Change & Business Results |

In the area of evaluation, the focus is shifting from reactions via "smile sheets" and measuring learning through paper and pencil tests to following trainees back to the job and measuring changes in their work behavior and performance. Ultimately, performance-based training also focuses on measuring key business results produced by training, including cost avoidance, cost savings, revenue growth and strategic growth.

Whether trainers like it or not, the paradigm has shifted. We need to embrace this new world of performance-based training or see our role marginalized and outsourced, as Jane discovered the hard way.

### Book Layout

We will now explore the five phases of training design, periodically stopping to consider the results we seek. The first task is to analyze the need for training, presented in Section One, chapters two through eight.

Next we will deal with Section Two: Design, in chapters nine through thirteen. Third, we will cover Section Three: Development in chapters fourteen through seventeen. Fourth, we will consider Section Four: Implementation in chapters eighteen through twenty. Finally, we will discuss Section Five: Evaluation in chapters 21 through 25.

The book concludes with three Appendices: an extensive bibliography, a compendium of training design tools and job aids, and an index. The tools are also available on-line for download at trainingeducationmanagement.com.

# Discussion Questions and Exercises

1. Think back on the last training project you completed or the last training course that you took. How were the following bottom-line training steps handled?

Defining training results:

Analysis of training need:

Design of training solution:

Development of training materials:

Implementation of training:

Evaluation of training:

## Case Study: The New Product Launch

You've just received an e-mail from the Senior Vice-President of a consumer electronics company's largest division to request training for all of his 2,000 employees. His reason is that the company is about to launch a new line of wireless products and services and he fears employees will not be able to deliver these successfully without being retrained. Training needs to start in six months. The content must include: product features and benefits, sales techniques, customer service and a new customer information system being developed by the IT department.

*Your assignment is to determine what the Training Department's response should be to this request.*

# Chapter Two
# Needs Analysis and Needs Assessment

Although trainers often use the terms interchangeably, needs analysis and needs assessment are strictly speaking not the same thing. Needs analysis refers to an investigation into whether training or some other organizational intervention can solve a performance problem or enable a desirable new performance in the workplace. Needs assessment is the process of determining what knowledge, skills and attitudes (KSAs) employees need to perform their jobs. Typically, trainers start out with a needs analysis, also known as a front-end analysis, which broadly examines the problem or opportunity at hand and determines probable underlying causes. If a lack of knowledge or skill is indicated by the needs analysis, then a more detailed needs assessment is undertaken. If lack of knowledge is not an underlying cause of performance problems, then trainers should look at other issues, including management systems, tools and technologies, work processes, job design and performers' motivation, to find causes for the performance problem and recommend solutions. This broader look at all the possible underlying causes of performance problems has become known as performance analysis, to distinguish it from traditional training needs assessment.

A number of different methods and models for conducting needs analysis have evolved over time, including: Robert Mager's Performance Analysis model (Mager and Pipe, 1970), Geary Rummler's Organizational Systems model (Rummler and Brache, 1990), Allison Rossett's Needs Assessment model, (Rossett, 1987) and the author's own Analysis Process model, affectionately known as Ford's Model T (Ford, 1994). Each of these is a valuable approach that yields useful information in determining why performance is not meeting expectations.

### Mager and Pipe's Performance Analysis Model

Among the first systematic attempts to analyze work performance was Bob Mager and Peter Pipe's classic *Analyzing Performance Problems: Or You Really Oughta Wanna.* In this work, originally published in 1970, the authors present a flowchart based on a series of questions they pose when investigating performance problems. The underlying assumption of the model is that performance problems have two primary origins: the person doesn't know how to perform (lacks knowledge), or the person doesn't want to perform (lacks motivation). Of course, very often in the business world, the two causes are both present and interact with each other. It is well-known that a person who lacks knowledge will also typically lack motivation, since performing a task without the knowledge to do so leads to poor results and a lack of motivation to perform. However, Mager and Pipe point out that many performance problems are really disguised motivation problems, and no amount of skill training will solve a basic lack of desire or incentive to perform.

Mager and Pipe's performance analysis model is presented below:
*Figure 2-1:*

## Mager and Pipe's Performance Analysis Model

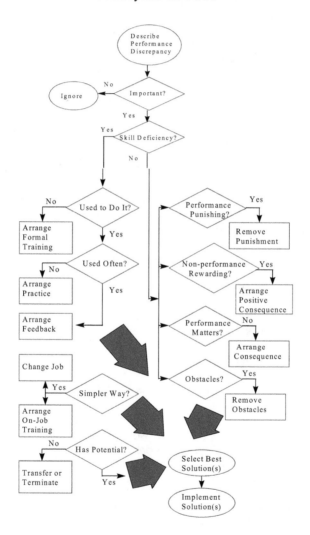

Mager and Pipe recommend starting the investigation by examining whether skill deficiency is a root cause of performance problems. The first question they recommend asking is whether the performer used to be able to perform the task in question. If the answer is no, then formal training in this skill is required. If the performer used to be able to perform, then the next question to be asked is how often they use the skill. If the answer is not very often or not for a long time, then Mager and Pipe suggest arranging practice in the skill, since this will help performers recall the knowledge they already have and will help achieve proficiency in performing the skill. If it turns out performers use a skill frequently but still exhibit a skill deficiency, then Mager and Pipe suggest arranging feedback on their skill problem and coaching to help them achieve the standards of the job. If all of these things do not solve the skill deficiency, then analysts should examine whether the individual possesses the potential to learn and perform the skill in question. If they do not have the potential, then transferring or even terminating the individual may become necessary.

Once skill deficiencies have been addressed, Mager and Pipe turn to motivation issues. They suggest that four conditions typically diminish motivation to perform a task and suggest ways to overcome the lack of motivation. The motivation obstacles and solutions are presented in the table below:

*Table 2-2:* **Motivational Problems and Solutions**

| Motivation Problem | Motivation Solution |
|---|---|
| Performance is Punishing | Remove Punishment |
| Non-performance is Rewarding | Arrange a Positive Consequence for Performing |
| Performance doesn't Matter | Arrange a Consequence for Non-performance |
| Obstacles Prevent Performance | Remove the Obstacles to Performance |

It helps to look at examples of each of these motivation factors, since some of them may not be immediately obvious. The first cause, that performance may be punishing, is one of the most common obstacles to motivation. One example would be a difficult, dirty task such as cleaning machinery in a factory. Because it is unpleasant, it is only natural to expect employees to avoid it. To motivate employees to perform unpleasant tasks, Mager and Pipe suggest either making the task less unpleasant, or increasing the rewards to make it more appealing.

A second example of performance being punishing occurs all too frequently in organizations. When an employee completes their assigned work quickly, or takes on more work than others, how are they typically rewarded for their extra labor? By being assigned yet more work to do. After a while, savvy performers figure out that the only reward for hard work is more hard work. This can cause even the most diligent performer to be tempted to slack off. After all, why rush through your work when the only reward waiting for you is more work?

A second common cause of motivation problems at work is that non-performance may have its own rewards, thus undermining the performer's motivation. This occurs when certain individuals get out of performing a task like say, cleaning up one's work area, leaving the job to someone else, or perhaps no one is required to clean up. When not performing a task has its own reward, then it is unlikely that someone will be motivated to perform the task, especially if it is unpleasant or difficult. To solve this motivation problem, Mager and Pipe suggest arranging a positive consequence to make the performance rewarding. For example, handing out a cash bonus or valuable prize to anyone who cleans their work area would make the performance of this task more desirable and non-performance less rewarding. Soon, performers would realize that they stand to gain from cleaning their work area and stand to lose if they do not, thus creating the underlying motivation to perform the task.

A third common motivation problem at work is that performance sometimes does not seem to matter. This is often true for trivial tasks like preparing routine reports that don't get read or acted upon. Once performers realize that no one reads the report, or that nothing is done with it, then they quickly lose motivation to perform the task. One example from a company I did work for was a mandatory monthly report of significant events and accomplishments required of all department heads. Although the President of the firm insisted he wanted these reports on his desk by the first of each month, managers realized over time that he did nothing with them, and they soon began to slack off. When several vice-presidents stopped turning in monthly reports and nothing happened, everyone else decided to abandon the practice too. In this case, the only way the President could motivate his managers to deliver the monthly reports to him was to arrange a consequence for department heads that refused to comply. He chose to withhold approval of their spending requisitions until he received their monthly report. Once a consequence existed, department heads were quick to comply with the monthly reporting requirement.

Finally, the fourth common motivation problem in the workplace is obstacles that prevent motivated performers from performing the task. Obstacles take many forms in today's organizations: managers and supervisors who undermine their own organization by erecting various barriers and obstacles to performance, inadequate tools and technology that prevent people from performing, workplace attitudes and culture that mitigate against performance, physical limitations and barriers in the workplace, safety and health concerns, lack of resources, competing priorities, etc.

When these obstacles appear, they must be removed in order to allow performance to take place. The barriers and obstacles to performance are a powerful force arrayed against trainers who seek to give employees the knowledge and skill to perform. When trainees return to the work environment, the new skills can be easily squelched by unsupportive supervisors, unbelieving co-workers, undermining organizational cultures, unavailable tools and resources and untold other barriers. This is why the removal of performance barriers has become an essential element of training design.

### Rummler's Organizational Systems Model

Geary Rummler has built upon the work of Mager and others and expanded trainers' horizons to look at the entire organization and see performance as a system. Though systems thinking has influenced instructional design from its infancy, Rummler is among the first to explicitly tie training to the organization's key business processes and results. He argues that needs analysis must look beyond the immediate job performer to capture the complexity of organizational performance. Specifically, he sees three descending levels of performance analysis:

**Table 2-3:** **Rummler's Organizational Systems Model**

| Level # | Scope of Analysis | Typical Needs Analysis Questions |
|---|---|---|
| 1 | Organization and Surrounding Environment | How does the job/performance under investigation affect the organization? Its customers? Its markets? Its strategy? What are the critical job outputs? |
| 2 | Process & Work Group | What tasks are required to perform the job under investigation? Which of these tasks produce critical results? Who is part of the work process and what are their roles? |
| 3 | Individual Performer | What competencies are needed to perform the job? What knowledge, skill and attitudes are needed? What training would enable these skills? |

Rummler describes four training assessment approaches that answer the questions posed above. These are:
1. Performance Analysis—Organization and Work Group Analysis
2. Task Analysis – Process and Individual Analysis
3. Competency Study—Individual Analysis
4. Training Needs Survey—Individual Analysis
These methods and others will be discussed throughout this section on analysis.

Of the four methods typically employed in needs analysis, performance analysis receives Rummler's endorsement for being the most powerful and complete method, because it clearly links training to performance outcomes sought by organizations, and considers both training and non-training causes of performance problems. At the same time, he admits that it is also the most time-consuming and difficult type of assessment, and because of this, other methods are often substituted.

My own experience with all four types of assessment discussed by Rummler leads me to believe that each has a place in the trainer's toolbox. We have yet to achieve the holy grail of a single best needs assessment method that is fail-safe under all circumstances. And we probably never will. So it is best to be able to use all four methods and more in the endless quest for organizational problems that training can and cannot solve.

A good meta-model for needs analysis is the following combination of the various methods.

Table 2-4: **Meta-Model for Needs Analysis**

| |
|---|
| 1. **Performance Analysis – Business, Process and Work Group Analysis** |
| 2. **Task Analysis – Process, Work Group and Individual Analysis** |
| 3. **Competency Study – Work Group and Individual Analysis** |
| 4. **Training Needs Survey – Work Group and Individual Analysis** |

### Allison Rossett's Needs Assessment Model

Allison Rossett's book on needs assessment has become a classic. She defines needs assessment as consisting of two kinds of activities:
- identifying gaps between what is happening and what should be happening (gap analysis)
- identifying causes for the gaps (causal analysis)

She also suggests three phases of needs assessment:
1. Planning
2. Doing
3. Using

During the planning phase, she suggests that trainers observe the work environment and read background materials to begin establishing a working hypothesis and focus on what to study. During the 'doing' phase, trainers should select an appropriate methodology to collect data and then gather data relevant to the problem under investigation. Finally, the 'using' phase consists of analyzing the data, identifying likely causes and making recommendations to solve the problem.

This approach can be used to analyze a broad range of issues, but it works best when preliminary needs analysis points to a performance gap that can be addressed through training or other skill-building. In this sense, Rossett's approach is a good follow-on to Mager and Rummler's more global analysis of performance problems in organizations.

Rossett offers a number of methods and sources for conducting skill gap analysis. Her methodology is summarized in the table below:

*Table 2-5:*          ***Needs Assessment Methods***

| Method | Uses | Sources |
|---|---|---|
| Interview | Identify optimals, barriers | managers, expert performers |
| Focus Group | Identify actuals, barriers | representatives of performers, customers and clients |
| Observation | Identify actuals | performers, customers, clients |
| Survey | Identify actuals, barriers, optimals | performers, managers, customers, clients |

She recommends identifying optimal levels of performance by interviewing key stakeholders and reviewing relevant company information such as job descriptions, policy and procedures, strategic plans, etc. and by benchmarking the function against leading firms. For actuals, she recommends observing performers at work, surveying performers, their managers and customers or conducting focus group interviews with performers or customers. To identify barriers to performance, she suggests using focus groups or surveys of performers, managers or customers.

The data generated from skill gap analysis typically will reveal deficiencies in one or more of the following areas:
1. skill/knowledge
2. motivation/attitude
3. environment
4. incentives

Only deficiencies in category one can be effectively addressed by training. Deficiencies in other areas are better addressed by changing the work environment, the management system, the reward/recognition system or the job itself. Of course, training may also play a role in enabling these changes, since managers and performers may require training on new or revamped workplace systems and may need help in changing their attitudes about the work they perform. But trainers must guard against the tendency to overprescribe training as a cure-all for performance problems. When trainers promise too much, they often underdeliver and cause irreparable harm to their own cause when recommended solutions fail to solve the problem.

### Donald Ford's Analysis Process 'Model T'

Not to be outdone by other model builders, I wish to close this chapter by offering up my own simplified needs analysis model, affectionately called Ford's Model T for my famous namesake, which was the essence of simplicity for its day. Not to take away anything from others, but the more complex needs analysis models become, the less likely that anyone will use them. So, in reviewing all the work done to date and reflecting on my own experience over the last three decades, I have found that, regardless of the assessment methodology or the problem at hand, needs analysis tends to follow a process involving four phases:

*Figure 2-6:*  **Ford's Needs Analysis Process Model**

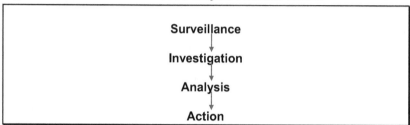

## Surveillance

Surveillance is the on-going process of reviewing vital information about an organization in order to understand the issues and problems it is confronting. It is akin to the ubiquitous video cameras in the workplace that record the movement and activities of employees and customers. The cameras provide a detailed record of daily life in organizations which can be reviewed when needed.

Likewise, trainers should be aware of the important events and information impacting the organizations they work for. Internal trainers accomplish a portion of this by simply networking and getting to know the people with whom they work. External trainers have to rely more on printed information and data searches to provide this background information. Other ways to conduct surveillance include:
1.  Have relevant company documents (periodic reports, senior executive memos, marketing information, position papers, etc.) circulated to you
2.  Stay abreast of current work performance policies, processes and standards
3.  Maintain effective networks of personal contacts in the organization
4.  Deepen one's knowledge of the key business issues senior executives are working on

The Surveillance Worksheet in Appendix Two, page 271 provides a more complete list of sources of information about organizations that can impact training. You may refer to this to see if your surveillance methods include everything you need to be effective. Surveillance, while unfocused on a specific performance problem, provides the necessary background to begin a more specific investigation quickly. It often generates business for the training department as well, since good surveillance can alert the savvy trainer to upcoming projects and initiatives that require a training component.  Many trainers find that the way they get invited to participate in key organization projects is to maintain a wide network of contacts throughout the organization who will alert them when training may be needed.

## Investigation

The investigation phase begins when trainers are confronted with a specific performance problem or opportunity which requires data gathering.  Like a good detective on the scene of a crime, the needs analyst is searching for clues to solve the mystery of why employees are not performing as required.  Clues can take many forms and require multiple methods to uncover.

The three most common methods used in needs analysis are:

- interviews
- surveys
- observation

Each has a specific purpose and unique strengths and weaknesses which are discussed in subsequent chapters of this section.

## Analysis

Once data has been collected, the analysis phase begins.  This is the most challenging phase, requiring the highest levels of skill and knowledge.  Many methods of analysis are available and the key challenge is to choose a method suitable for the data at hand.

Two basic analytical methods are:

- quantitative
- qualitative

Quantitative methods include statistical analysis, numerical summaries, graphs, charts, tables and related methods to analyze numbers.  Qualitative methods include summaries of interviews, field notes, ethnographic reports, work samples, video or audio tapes, content analysis and other methods to analyze non-numeric data such as people's words and actions.  More will be said about these analytical methods in later chapters of this section.

## Action

When trainers and managers begin to make decisions based on the data they have collected and analyzed, the action phase has begun.  The imperative to take action distinguishes needs analysis from pure research, where creation of knowledge is the end-product.  For needs analysis, even the failure to take action is, in itself, an action, since that means the organization has decided to live with a problem or forego an opportunity.  In most cases, though, some useful action results from needs analysis.  Among the typical action outcomes of needs analysis are the following:

- new performance skills and training content are designed and developed
- existing training content is updated or changed to meet new skill needs and new audiences
- alternative training and support is provided on the job through structured on-the-job training, electronic performance support systems, manuals, Internet, etc.
- changes occur to the job itself, the work process flow, the personnel, the technology, the compensation and rewards, the management or the entire organization which solve a performance problem without training
- an organization adopts a combination of new training and changes to the job and related systems in order to solve a performance problem
- an organization decides to live with an existing problem or forego a new opportunity because the costs appear to outweigh the benefits

### *Summary*

In this chapter, we have examined four different approaches to analyzing performance problems and assessing training needs. In each of these approaches, the emphasis is on establishing causal links of inadequate job performance and categorizing these as either skill and knowledge deficits that training can solve or motivational or organizational problems that require other interventions. Once the need for training has been established, techniques to assess the job, the content of training, the audience and the work environment come next. These are discussed in the following chapters of this section. The following chart summarizes the typical steps that designers follow in the needs analysis and needs assessment phase of training design.

Figure 2-7:

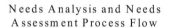

Needs Analysis and Needs
Assessment Process Flow

# Discussion Questions and Exercises

1. Conduct a skill gap analysis on yourself, using the standard of a Training Professional who can analyze, design, develop, implement and evaluate performance-based, bottom-line training.

   **Desired State: (What you and your customers want to see)**

   **Actual State: (What you are currently doing and achieving)**

   **Skill Gap: (The difference between desired and actual)**

2. Discuss the pros and cons of each of the four analytical models presented in this chapter. Which ones are you most inclined to use? Why?

**Case Study: Fast Food Franchise**
*Read the case below and decide how you would go about analyzing the management problems the firm is having.*

A rapidly growing fast food company with a franchise business model has begun to experience problems with some of its newly opened locations. Up to 20 percent of them are failing within a year at a huge cost to the company. The reasons for failure seem numerous, from poor location and advertising, to poor leadership and work planning, to untrained, unmotivated employees.

You have been asked to investigate the leadership and management problems at the failing franchise to see if better management training might help turn the businesses around. Currently, new Franchise Owners receive a one-week orientation to the business prior to opening their restaurant and periodic refresher training at company management retreats. They are selected primarily based on financial qualifications and past business experience.

# Chapter Three
# Performance Analysis

This chapter is devoted to a presentation of the basic theory and techniques behind human performance technology (HPT), the term used to describe a myriad of methodologies for studying and analyzing job performance. It will focus on ways that HPT expands upon traditional systems approaches to instructional design, especially in the area of motivation and organizational systems. Cutting edge approaches to dealing with non-training related interventions and ways to make training design more robust will also be discussed with illustrations from companies applying this emerging approach to training design.

Human performance technology has evolved over the past decade as a powerful new system for addressing performance issues in the workplace. It grew out of many existing disciplines, including education, anthropology, psychology, quality assurance, human resources, organizational development, information technology, sociology and political science. Among the impetuses driving this new approach were the quality improvement movement and global competition which has forced businesses to adopt new ways of serving their customers and controlling costs.

It has been embraced by many instructional designers because it offers solutions to non-training issues that have vexed trainers for years. As a systems approach, HPT looks at all the elements affecting job performance and prescribes comprehensive solutions to problems that address skill, knowledge, motivation, management and organizational issues. Historically, trainers have addressed knowledge and skill deficits through instructional design, but largely left to line managers the job of motivating employees and creating the organizational structure and support needed to sustain performance on the job.

The results have not been encouraging. As much as 50 percent of the learning in corporate classes has not been transferred to the job, according to a recent book on the topic (Broad and Newstrom, 1992). The main reason for this is a lack of management support for training in the workplace. Other reasons include a mismatch between what is learned in training and what is practiced on the job, inadequate organizational systems and resources to support trainees, and the trainees' own lack of motivation to try out new skills at work. HPT addresses all of these issues, whereas traditional training addressed only mismatches between training content and the job. Because of its comprehensiveness and focus on improving performance, HPT enables solutions to complex performance problems that training alone has failed to address.

Human Performance Technology offers the possibility of addressing many of these obstacles to training transfer by directly addressing organizational and motivational issues along with skill gaps. By encompassing a comprehensive approach to solving performance problems, HPT holds the promise of solving more performance problems than training can alone and also broadening the outlook and contribution of trainers who embrace the HPT approach.

### Human Performance Technology Defined

A single definition of HPT does not exist. Even the name itself is not universally agreed upon. Some people call it HPT, while others prefer Human Performance Improvement, and still others refer to it as Performance Consulting or simply Performance. Although no single definition of HPT exists, several working definitions have emerged. One of the most influential is the definition developed by the International Society for Performance Improvement (ISPI) which coined the term in the early 90's. According to their handbook, human performance technology is a "set of methods and processes for solving problems – or realizing opportunities – related to the performance of people. It may be applied to individuals, small groups or large organizations" (Stolovitch and Keeps, 1992).

Another influential definition appears in the American Society for Training and Development's *Models for Human Performance Improvement* (Rothwell, 1996):

Human Performance Improvement …[is] a systematic process of discovering and analyzing important human performance gaps, planning for future improvements in human performance, designing and developing cost effective and ethically justifiable interventions to close performance gaps, implementing the interventions, and evaluating the financial and nonfinancial results.

### Human Performance Technology Models

Like its definition, the process of conducting human performance technology lacks a single, unified model at present. However, several influential models currently exist, and they all agree on some of the basic activities of HPT. Two of the more complete models are presented here. The first comes from Rosenberg and Deterline, who formulated the model to explain a series of case studies on the use of performance technology in the workplace (Rosenberg and Deterline, 1992). They see HPT occurring in five major stages:
1. Performance Analysis
2. Cause Analysis
3. Intervention Selection
4. Change Management
5. Evaluation

Their model is depicted below:

### Performance Analysis

The performance analysis phase, also sometimes referred to as "front-end

Figure 3-1:

## Human Performance Technology Model

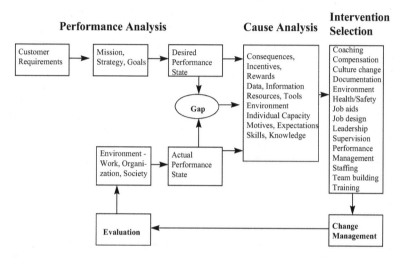

analysis", centers on analyzing an organization's performance requirements and capabilities in order to identify gaps between actual performance and desired performance. The tools of performance analysis include assessment of customer needs and requirements, organizational mission and strategy, organizational capabilities and key competencies, and measures of current organizational performance. This data forms the basis for defining an organization's current performance capacity and identifying gaps between current performance and desired performance in the future.

An example of the application of performance analysis is a financial services company that decided to introduce a new product line in annuities, a fast-growing retirement investment strategy. As executives considered the strategy they wished to pursue in this new market, they realized that the current workforce might be unprepared to sell and support the new product line. To investigate this aspect of the new product launch, they employed a human performance consulting firm to conduct a comprehensive performance analysis of the firm's capabilities to sell and service annuities to its customers.

The consulting firm began its work by examining the financial services company's strategy and goals for the new product line, including reviewing all existing written documents and interviewing senior managers to understand their thinking in depth. They then conducted focus groups and surveys with a sample of current and target customers for the new product to determine what customers needed from a financial services firm offering annuities. They also conducted benchmarking studies of several competitors who had already entered the annuity market to better understand the unique challenges and needs of this market. Based on this data, the consultants developed a detailed portrait of the competencies and skills required to be successful in the annuities market, including risk management, selecting annuities to offer for sale, marketing plans, sales strategies, customer service requirements and even legal and ethical issues.

This portrait of the ideal performance state represented a vision of what it would take for the organization to make a successful entry into the annuity marketplace. The next step was to investigate the organization's current work environment and workforce to determine the extent to which its actual performance matched the previously-identified performance requirements for the new product line. This phase of the analysis used employee surveys, direct observation of employees and interviews with key decision makers to identify existing workforce competencies related to annuities. Additionally, a custom-designed test of annuity product knowledge that was administered to a random sample of the target workforce measured the current workforce's knowledge of this product line. The data revealed that the organization's current ability to design and deliver annuity products was limited by a lack of knowledge about annuities, and confusion among many employees about why senior management wanted to embark upon this strategy in the first place. The analysis did find bright spots, however. The company's ability to provide customer service and follow up for these new products was very strong, based on existing customer service capabilities. Furthermore, nearly half the sales force had some experience with selling annuities from previous employers and education. The biggest weakness was the firm's ability to design annuity products that would perform competitively in the marketplace while providing a solid return to the organization. This area was then targeted for intensive development and skill-building to ensure a successful entry into the market. The important piece of information regarding employee confusion over this new initiative also became a valuable input to the causal analysis phase of the project.

### Causal Analysis

Causal analysis is the process of examining all the possible underlying causes for a performance gap in order to design a comprehensive intervention that will address all the causes. It is the key step in the human performance technology model, since the correct identification of causes for inadequate performance is essential to solving the problem. Among the causes for performance problems, the following occur frequently:

- no consequences (or even positive consequences) for poor performance
- lack of incentives or rewards for good performance
- lack of information required for good performance
- lack of resources, tools, equipment, etc. to enable good performance
- an environment that does not reinforce good performance
- individuals' capacity to perform up to standards
- lack of individual motivation to perform
- lack of knowledge and skill needed to perform

Though this list is by no means exhaustive, only one of the causes (the last) can be directly addressed by training. The others would require additional interventions. Of course, the reality in complex organizations today is that performance problems are often a combination of factors, requiring multiple interventions to fully resolve. In fact, the ability to see performance as a system and address causes systematically is one of the key competencies for good performance causal analysis.

Thomas Gilbert developed one of the most comprehensive methodologies for cause analysis (Gilbert, 1978). Using a modified behavioral engineering model, he identified six key factors that influence job performance, as illustrated in the model below:

Figure 3-2:    **Organizations and Performance**

| Resources | Structure/Process | Information |
|-----------|-------------------|-------------|
| **Organization** | | |
| Capacity | Motivation | Knowledge |
| **Individual** | | |

The first three factors – resources, structure/process and information – are primarily the responsibility of the organization. The last three factors – capacity, motivation and knowledge – are primarily individual employee issues.

Returning to our example of the financial services firm about to launch an annuity product line, the consultants found a number of underlying causes for potential performance problems. First, they identified a need to provide knowledge and skill to at least half the existing sales force on annuities as an investment tool and the sales strategy needed to compete in this marketplace. They also identified a critical need to train underwriters, risk managers and others in the in-depth design of annuities.

Having addressed the skill gap issue, the consultants turned to other underlying causes of potential performance problems. The widespread confusion and skepticism about the new product launch was correctly seen as a key obstacle to success. Further analysis revealed that many employees had a poor impression of annuities, finding them less 'sexy' than the other investment tools currently offered, and feared that the company would siphon resources away from other product lines and thus damage the firm's overall health. Among the sales staff, concerns about the annuity product line centered around the compensation package that had been proposed. Many sales people felt there wasn't sufficient incentive to sell this new product, tempting them to stick to existing product lines instead which had a proven sales track record. Finally, a third major cause of potential problems surfaced with regards to the computer systems that would support the sales and marketing of annuities. The information systems department was running behind schedule in developing new databases and financial software to support the product launch. This could seriously threaten the success of the entire venture.

### Intervention Selection

Once underlying causes have been identified and confirmed, the third phase of HPT is selection of appropriate interventions to address all the causes. An intervention is simply any conscious action designed to mitigate or eliminate a cause for inadequate performance. The list of possible interventions would be quite lengthy indeed, among the most common of which might be:

- training
- on the job coaching
- culture change
- teambuilding
- management systems
- information systems
- tools and equipment
- environmental engineering

Anything that addresses an underlying cause of performance problems is a good candidate for inclusion as an intervention.

In the financial services company's case, the interventions were narrowed down to three major initiatives: training for all affected employees on annuities, an internal public relations campaign to convince skeptical employees of the merits of annuity products and a decision to delay product launch until the necessary supporting software systems were available. These three interventions addressed the three most important underlying causes of potential performance problems and taken together, helped to build a critical mass of support for the annuity product launch.

### Implementation

The fourth phase of HPT is the implementation of the previously-selected interventions. Implementation may be as simple as designing and delivering training or as complicated as changing the entire culture of an organization.

Whatever the implementation strategy is, it helps to have a clearly defined change management process to drive the implementation and help everyone involved to move from resistance to acceptance of the change. If the implementation involves training, it is important to provide reasons for employees to participate, especially those that pertain to what's in it for them personally. If changes are proposed to compensation or other human resource systems, these must be carefully explained to employees to reduce resistance. Changes to facilities, systems and equipment will likely require communication, training, planning and adequate resources to be a success. A key ingredient in reducing opposition to change is to involve people in the change. The more involved people are, the less likely that they will resist.

In our financial services example, the implementation of training, public relations and information systems were carefully planned and sequenced to build upon each other. It was decided that first attention should go to the information systems bottlenecks, since they had the longest timeline. A thorough review of the upgrade project revealed a number of management deficiencies that were immediately addressed. Additionally, extra resources were devoted to the project to speed up implementation. Second, the firm turned to an aggressive public relations campaign to help its employees understand why the firm was moving into the annuity market. The campaign also served as a kind of pilot test for the upcoming customer marketing campaign the firm intended to launch in advance of the new products. The campaign stressed the potential for business growth, and the new career opportunities that would flow from this new product line, and explained how existing products would continue to be supported as in the past. Finally, training was custom-designed for each of the employee populations who would need it: underwriters, sales people and customer service representatives. Training was timed to occur just before employees needed to use the new skills, so they would not be forgotten from disuse. As employees saw that the firm was aggressively solving the information system problems, and learned about the benefits and features of this new product, their resistance diminished, thus enabling the company to move ahead with its planned launch knowing it enjoyed the support of a majority of the workforce. A handful of vocal opponents to the new product line left the firm, so that they would not be able to undermine the effort from within.

### Evaluation

The role of evaluation in human performance technology is no different than the traditional role of evaluation in training. It is important to determine whether the interventions selected and implemented are having the desired impact. To do this, the four-level evaluation model developed by Kirkpatrick (Kirkpatrick, 1975) can be applied. First, reactions from employees, suppliers and especially customers can be collected by survey or interview. Second, evidence of new skills and knowledge can be gained from training tests, self-ratings or supervisor ratings. Third, evidence of behavior change on the job can be found through job observation, interviews or surveys of employees and their managers. Even better, the organization may be able to examine existing metrics to spot trends that indirectly demonstrate new job behaviors, such as increased sales, lower operating costs, lower absenteeism and turnover, etc. Fourth, and most important, firms should evaluate the results of performance interventions to determine if the business' performance and all-important bottom-line have been positively impacted. A return on investment should be calculated for major initiatives.

Increasingly, performance evaluators are questioning the adequacy of Kirkpatrick's four-level model. There are tow major problems with using the model when evaluating performance improvement:

1. Focus on learning interventions
2. Lack of formative evaluation

The first problem is that Kirkpatrick's model is a training evaluation model that does not work well for non-training interventions. Although some have argued that level two (learning) can simply be dropped for non-training interventions, the model's underlying logic starts to break down when levels are removed. Moving directly to level three (behavior) does not check whether the intervention produced its desirable results or met its objectives. Improved performance could be due to other factors.

The second problem is more severe. Kirkpatrick's model assumes that evaluation is summative, occurring after the training event and summing up the end results. In HPI interventions, however, the majority of resources are frontloaded on analysis and design of interventions. Because of this, it is important to engage in formative evaluation of the HPI process and collect real-time data about how the intervention is going. This can avoid disaster by identifying problems with interventions before they are fully implemented so that corrective action can be taken to maximize the end result. To address these and other problems with Kirkpatrick model, I have developed an HPI Evaluation Model, depicted in the figure below (Ford, 2004).

The evaluation baseline phase includes indentifying and developing measures for the business goals and the performance gaps identified during analysis. This baseline allows pre-post intervention comparisons to isolate the effect the interventions have had. The formative evaluation phase looks at the root cause analysis to ensure that the correct root cause has been identified. This can be done through a variety of qualitative methods, including:

- Expert review (like getting a medical second opinion)
- Peer review (having colleagues uninvolved in tan HPI project review the analysis to judge its quality)
- Pilot tests (running small pilot studies can help to verify whether root causes can be adequately addressed by proposed interventions)

Figure 3-3:                          **HPI Evaluation Model**

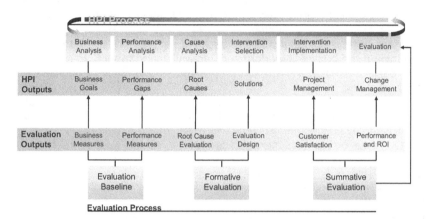

The summative evaluation phase, like Kirkpatrick's model, focuses on measuring reactions to the interventions (customer satisfaction with how interventions are being implemented), behavior change (job performance pre and post-interventions) and results (impact on performance gap and business goal, ROI).    By conducting HPI evaluation in three phase performance consultants gain the maximum advantage from their evaluation efforts.

### Richard Clark's Human Performance Technology Model

A second influential model for HPT has been developed by Richard Clark at the University of Southern California (Clark, 1995).    Like the previously discussed HPT model, Clark also divides HPT into five phases, though they differ in detail from ISPI's model.   Clark's model is presented below.

### Initiating Event

The initiating event for HPT intervention is often a business problem that cries out for a solution.  But HPT is not merely meant to be a reactive approach to business problems.   It can be used with equal or perhaps even greater effect, by those who are more proactive in addressing performance issues.  Thus, it is an ideal companion to business and strategic planning processes and to performance management systems.  Whether proactive or reactive, HPT may be initiated whenever evidence appears to suggest that human performance is not reaching its full potential.

### *Opportunity Analysis*

Clark prefers the term 'opportunity' for the front-end analysis phase of his model because HPT is ultimately about seizing opportunities to maximize human performance.

*Figure 3-4:*

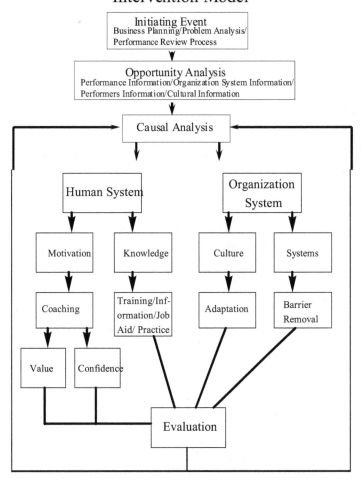

# Human Performance Technology
# Intervention Model

Initiating Event
Business Planning/Problem Analysis/
Performance Review Process

Opportunity Analysis
Performance Information/Organization System Information/
Performers Information/Cultural Information

Causal Analysis

Human System

Organization System

Motivation

Knowledge

Culture

Systems

Coaching

Training/Information/Job Aid/ Practice

Adaptation

Barrier Removal

Value

Confidence

Evaluation

To analyze a potential opportunity, he suggests collecting four kinds of information:
1. performance information
2. performers information

3. organization system information
4. cultural information

Performance information includes data about the activities, processes and results that an organization currently obtains and wishes to achieve in the future. Performers' information includes data about the aptitudes, knowledge and motivation of employees currently performing a job or set of tasks. This is akin to learner analysis.

Organizational systems information includes data about the organization's structure, processes, markets, customers, competitors and other key components of its business. This information helps to identify any system-related sources of obstacles or problems impeding performance. Cultural information includes data about the values, beliefs and norms of an organization which shape its world view. This information is critical to understanding why organizations behave in certain ways and how they need to change in order to enhance performance.

### *Causal Analysis*

In Clark's model, causal analysis is a process of isolating symptoms of performance problems and assigning them to one of four possible root causes: motivation, knowledge, culture or systems. The first two are characterized as belonging to the human system while the last two belong to the organizational system. Proper diagnosis is essential since each of these sub-systems requires different solutions.

Clark suggests starting with the human system first, since it is typically easier to address. Within the human system, the first priority is to determine if lack of knowledge is causing or contributing to a performance problem, because knowledge is prerequisite to performance. Second, the motivation of performers should be examined, with particular attention to two facets: value and confidence. Value refers to how much performers are engaged and committed to the tasks they perform, while confidence refers to their sense of self-confidence with regard to the tasks at hand and directly affects the amount of effort they are likely to expend.

Once the human system issues have been analyzed, the organizational system is then examined. System components like management, information technology, production, research and development, sales, customer service, etc. should be analyzed to determine if any of these are creating obstacles to performance and if so, for ways to remove these barriers. Cultural information like values, beliefs and norms are analyzed to determine if they support or undermine performance. Where organizational culture impedes performance, a change effort to adapt the culture to performance requirements is recommended.

### Implementation

Once a thorough analysis has been performed, a suggested course of action emerges. Clark suggests the following remedies for common causes of performance problems:

### Evaluation

The final phase of the HPT Intervention model is evaluation. Like the ISPI model, Clark adopts Kirkpatrick's four-level evaluation model. He recommends that each implemented solution have its own evaluation plan to

**Table 3-5:     Performance Cause and Solution Matrix**

| Cause | Solution |
|---|---|
| Poor Motivation | Coach performer to increase their buy-in and adjust their confidence level in the assigned tasks |
| Lack of Knowledge | Design training, provide information, job aids or arrange practice in the tasks |
| Cultural Barriers | Adapt the culture to remove or mitigate the barriers to performance |
| Systems | Remove barriers to effective performance or build new systems to enable performance |

measure the extent to which each of the contributing factors to performance problems are reduced or eliminated by the proposed intervention. The results of evaluation studies can be used in a formative way to improve the HPT process while also providing summative evidence of the success of a given HPT project. The key to evaluating HPT interventions is to find ways to translate evidence of success into concrete business results that really matter to an organization. A second key point is that evaluation data often helps to analyze future performance problems and so feeds directly back to the causal analysis phase.

### Example of the HPT Intervention Model

To see how the HPT Intervention model works in practice, consider a case involving a large corporation in the transportation industry. They were experiencing rising costs and delays in repairing vehicles that triggered an opportunity analysis by the firm's Performance Consulting group in Training and Organizational Development. The management of the Vehicle Repair Center believed that the problems were caused by poorly-trained mechanics who were not repairing vehicles properly every time. Because of this suspicion and the fact that knowledge is prerequisite to performance, the consulting group first examined the knowledge and skill levels of the 50 mechanics who were responsible for keeping the company's fleet of trucks on the road. The analysis revealed some weaknesses in the training system for these employees, especially in the area of updating their skills when new vehicles and systems were added to the fleet. It also found that newly-hired mechanics, although extensively trained before being assigned to work, were nevertheless much more likely to make errors that caused vehicles to be returned for additional service. This suggested to them that the transfer of newly-learned skills needed to be strengthened for new hires.

Besides these two weaknesses, however, the consultants could not find a major deficit in mechanics' skills. Most were highly trained and capable employees, with many years of experience, who were able to troubleshoot and repair most vehicle problems without difficulty. This then led them to investigate other aspects of the performance system for underlying causes. They turned next to study the motivation of repair specialists. They found that nearly all of them were highly interested in their work and took pride in doing a good job. Most had been working on cars and trucks for years and found great pleasure in repairing them. So, they appeared to sufficiently value the work they did. Regarding their confidence level, the consultants found a different picture. The veteran employees in the department tended to be highly confident in their ability, sometimes even over-confident. This caused some problems for them when they ran across a particularly difficult repair job. They tended to rely too heavily on tried and true solutions that had worked in the past, instead of putting in the effort to thoroughly troubleshoot the problem and examine all possible causes before taking action. This meant some repairs were incomplete or did not fully solve the problem. New hires, on the other hand, had a different motivation problem. They were often under-confident in their newly learned abilities and so they had a tendency to give up too easily in confronting tricky troubleshooting problems, or to misdiagnose problems based on an incomplete analysis of the problem. The consultants realized that department supervisors needed to do a better job of providing individual coaching to employees to help the more senior ones realize that some of the jobs they were assigned were more difficult and required greater effort than they had been giving, while helping new hires build up their confidence level so that they did not give up on difficult repair jobs or reach hasty conclusions. The consultants also suggested that all repairpersons receive more regular feedback on how they were performing, by reporting how many vehicles were returned for repair, for what reason and who had worked on the vehicle originally. By providing this detailed performance feedback for the first time, repairpersons were able to see how their own performance compared with the group norm and were able to adjust their effort level if needed to match the performance of the group.

The consultants then turned to the organization system to see if any systems or cultural components were contributing to performance problems. With regard to the system components, the consultants found two potential problems. One was the way the department handled new information about vehicle repair, such as when new vehicles were introduced to the company or changes in repair procedures were adopted. This information was typically communicated in a weekly bulletin that all repairpersons were supposed to read. The consultants found that few of them read this material, and even those who did complained that it was often confusing and unhelpful. Since repair problems were greater on new vehicles, the consultants determined that the department needed a better system to alert employees to changes in repair procedures, especially with new vehicles. They recommended the department start holding mini-training sessions on new vehicles and new repair procedures, conducted by some of the senior technicians, so that everyone would have the same knowledge of these systems.

A second systems problem that was uncovered was a new computer database that had been implemented to track repairs and the parts used. The new system still had some bugs that prevented it from capturing all the necessary repair data. Further, many employees had received inadequate training on the new system, and so were not using it efficiently. The consultants recommended that the bugs in the new system be fixed and that everyone receive adequate training and guided practice in using the new database. They emphasized the value of providing a quick reference card as a job aid that summarized the major functions and commands of the new system and suggested that this be incorporated in an electronic performance support system that would provide just-in-time learning about the system as employees used it.

Turning finally to cultural issues, the consultants found two areas of concern. One was a tendency for department management to keep valuable performance information to themselves instead of sharing it with employees. For example, the new database had sophisticated cost and inventory reports that told management how much it cost and how long it took to perform nearly every repair operation in the department. Yet, none of this crucial performance information was being shared with employees, because management had historically not trusted employees with such data. The consultants convinced managers that information about how employees were performing could help them adjust their own effort and see where they had weaknesses. Since the data could be tracked to the individual mechanic, it could provide important input for individual coaching.

Secondly, the consultants noted a second cultural problem with regard to compensation and rewards. Since the mechanics were unionized, they had traditionally placed more value on seniority than performance. Pay systems were based almost exclusively upon time in the job. The consultants realized that this system did not provide sufficient incentive to perform outstanding work. To address this problem, they recommended that a certain percentage of the mechanics' total compensation be based upon performance, with the rest determined by seniority. Although the union did not like this idea initially, they were eventually persuaded to accept it when management guaranteed that no employee's existing salary would be cut. Instead, they created a bonus system where mechanics who performed outstanding work could earn extra money on top of their regular salaries.

When all these changes were combined into a single solution, the repair department began to see immediate results. Better trained new hires were paired up with journeymen mechanics so they could get up to speed faster on the job. The new communication systems that opened up dialogue between supervisors and employees helped to identify weak areas of performance and ensure that employees' skills were up-to-date with rapid changes in technology. The fully-implemented computer tracking system allowed both managers and employees to quickly identify problem areas and address them before they caused major problems, and the new electronic performance support system ensured that employees used the database properly. Finally, the cultural change management effort helped to promote better teamwork between management and employees and the new compensation system gave employees the incentive they needed to give the extra ten percent when needed. Any one of these interventions, by itself, would not have solved the department's problems. But all of these things taken together, reduced rework by over 50 percent, and brought the total repair costs for the organization down by nearly 15 percent. These savings were then used in part to fund the new bonus system and to allow the company to cut its prices and therefore capture more market share.

*Summary*

Human performance technology, or performance analysis for short, has taken the world of instructional design by storm. It is not hard to see why from the examples we have looked at in this chapter. This systems approach to human performance problems offers a more robust set of tools to address the myriad underlying causes of performance problems in the workplace. Increasingly, complex problems defy a simple training solution. Instead, like the soaring repair costs of the fictional transportation company, the answers to performance problems are often found in a combination of training, motivation and rewards, systems and culture change. Those who can bring such comprehensive solutions to bear on today's organizational problems will reap the benefits of improved performance and profitability in the new economy.

# Discussion Questions and Exercises

1. Compare the HPI model and the ISD (ADDIE) model. What similarity do you see? What are the key differences?

2. What are the key differences between the Rosenberg & Deterline HPT model and the Clark model?

3. Think of an example of a training design project you worked on that could have been improved by taking an HPI approach. How would you

have acted differently?   How would the results have turned out differently?


## Case Study: Utility Facing Deregulation

- Profile: GasCo is a 135 year old firm, the largest natural gas utility in the U.S., with $US 1.3 billion annual revenue, 16 million customers and 10,000 employees. It is facing market deregulation as a result of legislative action.   The Public Utilities Commission is allowing competitors to enter GasCo's market for the first time.   These competitors are offering lower prices and quicker customer response time and threaten to erode GasCo's market share, especially with lucrative commercial and industrial customers.
- Business Goals: Gas Co executives have identified the following high priority goals for the organization:
  - Reduce costs by 10% ($75 million/yr.) to enable price cuts that will keep the company competitive.
  - Increase customer satisfaction by 10%, especially with regards to customer response time,
- Performance Goals: A preliminary analysis by a performance consulting firm indentified the following key performance goals to support the business goals above:
  - Reduce customer response cycle time from an average of 2.5 days to 1 day. This will increase customer satisfaction and discourage customers from switching to the competition.
  - Increase labor productivity 10% by reengineering field service work to make it more efficient and customer friendly.

1. How would you go about conducting a root cause analysis of this case?

2. What are some likely interventions that you would look at to solve the business and performance problems?

3. How would you apply the HPI evaluation model to this case?   What would be some key measures you could use to track the business and performance goals?

# Chapter Four
# Job Analysis

Job analysis is the process of determining how work should be organized and performed. It includes activities such as determining the optimal organizational structure, management reporting relationships, divisions of labor, job roles and responsibilities, job descriptions, required knowledge, skills and attitudes, compensation and rewards. This chapter will discuss all of these aspects of job analysis, summarizing the literature in this field and providing practical guidance.

### Origins of Job Analysis

Once upon a time, life was much simpler and work got done primarily by individuals or small intact groups, such as families. Then the industrial revolution came along and changed all that forever. Work became a collective endeavor involving thousands of individuals. To make factories run in those days, work was broken down into the smallest possible units and jobs were created to perform each discrete task. As the factory system spread and evolved, management experts became more skillful at breaking work into its most basic building blocks so that it could be easily monitored and controlled by management. Henry Ford's introduction of the automobile assembly line hastened the move to a highly articulated division of labor, and management experts at the time like Frederick Taylor, father of scientific management, fine tuned the assembly line factories of the day with detailed time and motion studies to determine the optimum melding of man and machine.

Another early development in job analysis was the company organization chart, which showed how a company was organized and who was in charge. Most industrial corporations took the basic work flow process of manufacturing – design, build and sell – and turned it sideways with a President at the head to create the modern organizational chart, represented by the example below.

*Figure 4-1:*     ***Typical Company Organization Chart***

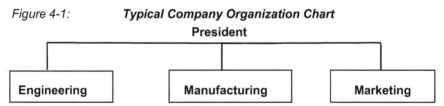

Over the years, as corporations grew and became more complex, organization charts reflected this by getting larger and more elaborate. Today, some large companies have organization charts that take hundreds of pages to display in detail. I encountered one large firm that chose to place every single one of its 10,000 person work force in their respective place on the company's organization chart, an effort that took over 250 pages of charts to document.

Recently, organizational development experts have begun to question the value of the traditional organization chart, claiming that it fails to capture how work gets done in organizations and that it can actually impede the work flow by encouraging the development of silos, or isolated fiefdoms, represented by the major departments of a corporation, who often treat each other like the competition, or worse. Modern management experts like Tom Peters argue that traditional organizational structures result in bureaucratic behemoths who cannot respond quickly enough to the pace of change in business today (Peters, 1987). Instead of these antiquated structures, Peters and others argue for a more nimble, team-based organizational structure that allows companies to quickly respond to issues and opportunities in the marketplace by forming and disbanding rapid response multifunctional teams to meet business challenges. Unfortunately, many organizations today have simply layered cross-functional teams on top of existing functional management structures and created a matrix organization in which employees have many masters and little sense of direction or priorities.

All of this background helps us understand that job analysis is a highly political endeavor, in that it addresses the basic structure and values of an organization and very often threatens all those who have a stake in the status quo, and in most businesses, that is just about everybody.

Job analysis may be conducted on many levels and with many purposes in mind. Richard Swanson (Swanson, 1994) has identified three basic types of job performance analysis:

1. Present performance problems
2. Performance improvement opportunities
3. Future performance requirements

The first is the most typical scenario, in which a performance problem has occurred that is causing enough pain to the organization to be addressed. Examples of this type of problem are:

a) increase in billing errors in an insurance company

b) increase in scrap costs in an automobile factory

c) decrease in on-time deliveries at a shipping company

d) increase in turnover and absenteeism in a retail store

The usual approach in these situations is to look for recent changes in the job or incumbents that might be causing problems and to fine tune the existing training and workforce. Rarely do such problems result in a complete redefinition of the job. When they do, it is often due to a host of problems, not just one.

The second level of analysis, performance improvement, typically looks beyond the current job performance to seek incremental improvements in the future. Here the opportunities for job analysis are greater, since clients are often willing to entertain more wholesale changes to the job in order to obtain performance improvements. Often, such improvements include upgraded technology and equipment, which translates into new training needs. The biggest difference between this type of analysis and the first, however, is in the point of view of the analyst and the client. In the first case, both are concerned with a problem. In the second, both see an opportunity. Beyond mere semantics, orientation towards an issue affects the way it is investigated and solved.

The third type of performance analysis – future performance requirements – is where job analysis really becomes crucial. This is because many future-oriented analyses are able to start with a blank slate and design the job from scratch. With this approach, it is even possible to go beyond analyzing jobs to look at the structure of the entire organization, or large company processes to see if redesign would help.

### A Job Analysis Model

Many excellent job analysis models exist (Campbell and Campbell, 1988, Hammer and Champy, 1993, Dunnette and Hough, 1991, Nadler, Gernstein, Shaw, 1992, Swanson, 1994). To present them all here would be beyond the scope of this work, but it will help to have a generic working model of job analysis as a basis for seeing how this fits into other types of needs analysis. Whether working with an existing problem or a future greenfield site, job analysts typically work through a process like the following:

**Figure 4-2:**     **Job Analysis Process Model**

| |
|---|
| 1. **Define the Job Outputs** |
| 2. **Define the Job Duties** |
| 3. **Define the Job Boundaries** |
| 4. **Define the Job Behaviors & Competencies** |
| 5. **Define the Compensation Plan** |
| 6. **Define the Career Path** |

Each of these elements will be briefly described in the following section.

The outputs of a job are the right place to begin an analysis for the same reason that the results are the right place to begin a training design. We should always focus first and foremost on the results we seek. Job outputs may be described in many ways, depending on the type of work involved. Some key characteristics of job outputs include that they are specific, measurable, important to the organization, and a direct result of one's labor. Examples of outputs might be:

a) taking a customer's order over the telephone
b) assembling a piece of furniture
c) soldering a printed circuit board
d) publishing a marketing report
e) writing a computer program

Although these could certainly be made more specific, they represent the type of outputs that define the results achieved by employees on the job.

From outputs, job analysts would then turn to defining the duties of the job. These are typically encapsulated in a job description that eventually will include other information, such as standards and hiring criteria. The list of duties is often broadly written, since a more detailed description emerges from the task analysis phase to be discussed in the next chapter.

Typical job duties found on a job description might include:

a) answer customer telephone calls
b) produce marketing information and reports
c) develop new computer application programs

The list of duties may be quite exhaustive, or include only the most frequently performed duties. Like fashion trends, job descriptions seem to go through cycles of brevity and expansion, depending on the prevailing mood of the day. Current practice is to define the job clearly, with major duties spelled out in detail, but most job descriptions have that infamous escape clause called 'other duties as assigned'. Employees know it is those 'other duties' that will usually cause the biggest headaches. Indeed, some firms have gone so far as to ban the job description altogether, claiming that they need the flexibility to ask employees to do whatever is needed.

Once the duties of the job have been defined, it is a natural progression to the boundaries of the job. By this is meant the way the job fits within major organizational processes and structure. At one end of the boundary should be the inputs the job receives from others, either within or outside the organization. All jobs work with inputs, whether they are parts moving down an assembly line or a request from senior management to perform a special task. These inputs are akin to a supplier who provides the raw materials with which an organization works to produce a final product. At the other boundary, the job produces certain outputs that then become inputs for another person's work. The outputs should have already been outlined in the first step, but some additional outputs may also be identified at this stage when they are incomplete or require another person to process.

Examples of job inputs and outputs for a customer service representative might include those in table 4-3.

It is important to establish the boundaries of jobs so that employees know where their job begins and ends, and even more crucial, know where

Table 4-3: **Examples of Job Inputs and Outputs**

| Inputs | Outputs |
|---|---|
| Telephone Call from Customer | Completed Order for a New Service |
| E-mail Request from Customer | Completed Change of Address |
| New Telemarketing Sales Campaign | Completed Order from a New Customer |

their work comes from and where it goes after they are done. By having this understanding of the work process, and not simply their own set of duties, employees can see the big picture and can better focus their efforts on what really matters.

The next step in job analysis is to specify the behaviors and competencies required to perform the duties contained in the job description. Behaviors are the observable actions that employees take in the course of their work. For example, a key behavior for a customer service center representative is to answer customer phone calls. For a computer programmer, a key behavior is writing programming code. Competencies are the underlying capabilities, knowledge and attitudes required to perform jobs, and are not always directly observable. For a customer service representative, a key competency might be empathy for customers. For a computer programmer, a key competency might be troubleshooting faulty code. Both of these competencies are critical to the job, but not easily observed directly. To establish competencies for jobs, analysts rely on direct observation of work, interviews with incumbents, especially those recognized as star performers, and increasingly, on survey research in which experts or job incumbents rate and rank lists of competencies to determine those most applicable to a particular job. Competency studies have become particularly popular to document managerial and professional jobs that do not easily lend themselves to traditional task analysis (Dubois, 1993). For a corporate executive, the competencies required to perform the job might include the following:

- strategic vision
- customer focus
- decisiveness
- communication abilities
- perseverance
- emotional intelligence
- analytical abilities
- credibility

The next step in the job analysis process is to define the compensation plan for the job, including base pay, bonuses, promotional raises, rewards and non-cash compensation such as health benefits, life insurance, etc.

While a complete treatise on compensation is beyond the scope of this chapter, a number of good reference works can shed more light on this topic. (Milkovich and Wigdor, 1991; Chingos, 1997; Lawler, 1990; Rock and Berger, 1991).

Within the context of a job analysis, a compensation plan may simply tweak existing policy or may involve a complete overhaul. Typically, the compensation plan would start by examining any existing compensation plan or policy. Radical departures from past practice must be justified by confirmed benefits that outweigh the ever-present risks of messing with someone's pay check. No matter how rosy the light that illuminates it, employees view any change in compensation as an attempt by the company to take something away from them. Furthermore, the impact of changing compensation for one job often has unintended consequences for other jobs as well.

Once a vision for the compensation plan has been defined, the next step is to look at market labor rates for similar work. This is done through salary surveys or the use of wage survey data already available. Once the market rate has been set, a range of salary around this rate should be constructed. It is popular these days to use broad salary bands rather than narrow salary ranges to allow greater flexibility and better differentiation between key performers and those who don't contribute as much. Whatever the choice, it is important to allow for growth in salary within the job, unless it is clearly meant to be entry-level.

Once salary ranges have been set, pay and promotion policy come next. Employees appreciate knowing when they are eligible for raises and the criteria for granting them. These things should be spelled out in simple language and communicated to the workforce.

Finally, the compensation plan should look at non-monetary rewards and benefits, since these are increasingly valued by employees and often provide greater motivation than one's regular salary. Aside from the usual health, dental, pension and life insurance benefits, companies are using a host of rewards to motivate employees, including:

- compensatory time off
- bonuses
- gifts
- public recognition
- free trips
- parties and celebrations
- awards
- special assignments

All of these things are effective if they genuinely reward excellent performance and are meaningful to employees.

The final step in the process is to define the career path for the job, including where the job fits within the organizational hierarchy, what jobs feed into it, and what jobs it might prepare incumbents to be promoted into.

Again, the scope of this step depends upon the nature of the job analysis. It may change little or radically.

Some thought to career development is essential to an effective job analysis and design. Though traditional career development focused exclusively on upward mobility, career development today recognizes that most moves are lateral, rather than up (Kaye, 1997). If the job is part of a progression, it is important to look at the entire job family, rather than at a single job in isolation. This not only conserves valuable resources by allowing analysis on a broader scale, but also ensures that jobs mesh with one another and that a clear system of hiring, development and promotion exists.

A first step is to define minimum requirements to enter the job. If it is entry-level, identification of the source of good candidates must be made. If a bidding or job posting system is used, employees need to understand how it works and how to prepare themselves for jobs.

Second, placing the job in the context of other positions helps employees see how the job fits in with other related work and defines a career ladder or perhaps a lattice for employees to follow. This may have been partly done during the compensation phase, if salaries of related jobs were looked at for comparable worth.

Finally, it is important to define the development needed to fill the job and keep employees' skills updated. It is popular nowadays to place most of the responsibility for career development upon employees, since it is felt that they have the greatest stake in their own careers. Corporations no longer want to take on the paternalistic obligations of the past either. But it is critical to provide the resources that employees need to develop themselves and remain valuable for their organization. Without adequate career resources, exhorting employees to look after their own careers looks like empty, self-serving rhetoric on the part of business owners.

## Summary

In this chapter we have briefly examined the specialized field of job analysis. The scope and nature of the field have been defined and the typical process steps have been described and illustrated with examples from various professions. The field draws from many disciplines, including industrial psychology, compensation, benefits, career development, quality assurance and human resource development. Highly complex job analyses are generally conducted by a team of specialists from each of these disciplines.

# Discussion Questions and Exercises

1. Using you own job as an example, conduct a brief job analysis covering the following points:
   a. Job Outputs

   b. Job Duties

   c. Job Competencies

   d. Compensation Plan

   e. Career Path

**Case Study: Defining a Newly Created Job**

A small business has grown sufficiently to afford a Marketing professional for the first time. The business buys and sells advertising time on local radio and television stations for large consumer clients. The Marketing professional will develop new business opportunities and expand the market for the firm's advertising services.

*How would you go about design a job analysis for this new position?*

# Chapter Five
# Task Analysis

Task analysis is the process of breaking a given job down into its component tasks, discovering the relationships among the tasks, and the prerequisite knowledge and skills required to perform the tasks. It is often done in conjunction with job analysis, but does not have to be. Task analysis is typically used by training designers to determine the knowledge, skills and attitudes that must be learned in order to perform the job under investigation. This chapter will describe several common approaches to task analysis and give detailed instruction on how to perform a task analysis. Techniques will be illustrated using different types of jobs.

### Importance of Task Analysis

Training on job-specific skills is nearly always based on a task analysis of the job. For this reason, it is one of the core skills of training design. Besides providing the detailed content for job skill training, task analysis also serves as a map of the job and the skills needed to perform it. It can often provide useful information to incumbents, managers and human resource professionals about the nature of the job and the people best suited to perform it. It often serves an additional purpose as well; designers use it to gain the approval of managers and clients to move forward with a design project. For all these reasons, a task analysis should be a prerequisite step to any skill-based training.

### A Task Analysis Process Model

Task analyses vary in scope from a single job duty to the consideration of thousands of jobs and duties. Despite this variation, a standard approach to task analysis is usually followed. This is presented in the chart below.

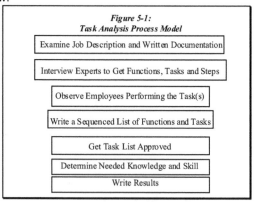

Figure 5-1:
Task Analysis Process Model

Examine Job Description and Written Documentation

Interview Experts to Get Functions, Tasks and Steps

Observe Employees Performing the Task(s)

Write a Sequenced List of Functions and Tasks

Get Task List Approved

Determine Needed Knowledge and Skill

Write Results

Each of these steps is discussed in detail below.

The first step is to examine any existing documentation about a job, starting with the job description. If this information is unavailable or outdated, then chances are the investigation must begin with a job analysis first. If documentation exists, be sure to find out how current it is and what portions may be out of date. A well-written job description constitutes a great starting point for task analysis.

The next step is to determine the job's primary functions, tasks and steps. To understand this step, it is necessary to define the relationship among job title, functions, tasks and steps. These may be considered as a hierarchy, with each descending level representing greater detail. The following chart illustrates the relationship.

*Figure 5-2:*
## *Relationships Among Job Elements*

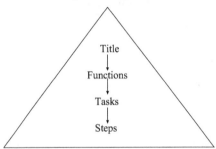

The job title is the most general of the four elements. It provides a general classification of the job and its role in the organization, but little else. For example, the job title "PC Support Specialist" tells us that the job involves specialized knowledge of personal computers and the role is to provide support and service to end-users. Beyond that, we know little of the job's specific duties. Likewise, the job title "Vice-President of Sales and Marketing" informs us that this is an executive-level position having broad management responsibility for an organization's sales and marketing functions, but little else.

When we turn to the functions of the job, we begin to define the major parts of the position that require the performance of multiple tasks, or that represent core responsibilities of the position. For a PC Support Specialist and a Vice-President of Sales and Marketing, the following functions might apply:

*Table 5-3:* **Sample Job Functions**

| PC Support Specialist | V.P. Sales and Marketing |
|---|---|
| Provide technical assistance to PC end-users | Develop marketing plans |
| Troubleshoot end-user PC problems | Hire and train sales staff |
| Handle PC software upgrades and enhancements | Handle key accounts |

These functions help to define the scope and responsibilities of the job and differentiate it from similar jobs within and outside the organization. Defining the functions of a job like Vice-President of Sales and Marketing helps us see how this job differs from one organization to the next and the specific requirements of the position.

From functions, the analyst then turns to tasks. A task is a single work activity that can be completed in a series of steps. One function may require multiple tasks. For the sample jobs and functions above, the following might be some of the tasks required.

*Table 5-4:* **Sample Job Tasks**

| Job Title | PC Support Specialist | V.P. Sales & Marketing |
|---|---|---|
| **Function** | Provide technical assistance to PC end-users | Develop marketing plans |
| **Task One** | Answer end-user questions about Personal Computers | Conduct market research |
| **Task Two** | Train end-users on new PC software | Present marketing plans to executive decision makers |

The task level of analysis usually translates nicely into the major topics and objectives of training programs. To take the PC Support Specialist job above, the two tasks listed under the function "provide technical assistance to PC end-users" could be translated into the following course objectives:
1. To answer common PC technical questions posed by end-users
2. To train end-users in the functions and operation of new computer software programs

These two objectives, in turn, would form the basis for two modules in a training program for PC Support Specialists.

Finally, the functions of a job may be further divided into the steps required to perform each function. Steps may be thought of as the detailed procedures and processes required to perform a task. These would form the content of a training program, just as the functions of the job suggest the objectives of training.

To illustrate this, the PC Support Specialist function of answering end-user questions about PCs might be broken down into the following steps:
1. Receive the question (phone, e-mail, in person, etc.)
2. Analyze the question
3. Research the answer
4. Present the answer to the end-user
5. Check for understanding

These five steps would form the detailed content of a module on answering end-user PC questions. It would also help to define the policies and procedures of the job, if they did not already exist, and would provide a uniform methodology for PC Support Specialists to employ in answering questions. Of course, exceptions to this method might have to be noted for simple questions that require no research or complex questions that require extensive troubleshooting, but such exceptions would help to define the boundaries of the job's functions and tasks.

### Sequencing Job Functions, Tasks and Steps

Once a detailed job map consisting of the title, functions, tasks and steps has been developed, the next thing is to sequence this information in a logical way so that it may be easily learned. A number of different sequencing principles may be used, depending on the content of the job and the previous knowledge of the trainees. The following sequencing rules are often used in task analysis:
1. Order tasks like they are performed on the job
2. Easy tasks come before difficult tasks
3. Frequently performed tasks come before infrequent ones
4. Tasks for which trainees have prior knowledge come before those that are brand new

Of the four sequencing rules, the best is to follow the order in which the job is performed, unless one of the other rules compels the designer to rearrange the natural order. An example of this would be the job of a Training and Development Specialist. If one developed training following sequencing rule one, then the first topic would be needs analysis, since it occurs first in the training process. But needs analysis is typically one of the most difficult training job functions to learn, and it is not generally the most frequently performed task, so starting with it violates two of the other sequencing rules, namely the easy to difficult rule and the frequent to infrequent rule. In this case, then, it might be better to start out a course for Training and Development Specialists with another topic, such as classroom delivery and facilitation, and introduce needs analysis later in the course when trainees have developed knowledge and skill in other areas.

In addition to the tasks and steps themselves, it is useful to collect other information about the task for later use in the design of training. This information often includes:
- reason task is performed
- initiating and concluding events
- equipment and materials used
- standards

The inclusion of this kind of information provides further background that trainees are likely to need to know in order to perform the task well. Let's look at each of these in turn.

The reasons a task is performed a certain way or performed at all helps trainees understand the importance of the task and the problems and dangers of performing it incorrectly. The initiating and concluding events of the task, also known as the task boundaries, help trainees understand what must happen to start a particular task and what constitutes its successful conclusion, often including a hand-off to someone else. The equipment and materials used in performing the task are obviously just as important to know about as the task itself, and may be more complicated to learn. For example, the task of typing a simple memo is arguably easier than the prerequisite word processing skill needed to operate the software used to write memos.

Finally, the standards of the task, including things like quantity, quality, time, cost and safety standards, are critical to being able to perform the task successfully at work. Of course, few training programs promise to turn out fully proficient, experienced performers. The practice time required to develop that level of expertise is generally unaffordable in training classes. Instead, most training programs set out to meet minimum performance standards only, knowing that trainees will improve with more on the job practice and coaching.

### Task Analysis Methodologies

Now that we have defined what task analysis is and the general process of performing a task analysis, we need to describe the methodologies available. Methodologies for conducting task analysis are not fixed, since the nature of such analysis varies enormously from one job and organization to another. Indeed, the hallmark of effective task analysis is to come up with a methodology suited to the job under investigation, rather than apply a cookie cutter to all the jobs one encounters. A second key consideration in this process is the level of knowledge that the analyst possesses about the job under investigation. Where the analyst possesses expert knowledge of the job, the process presented below may be dramatically reduced, since he won't need to rely so much on subject matter experts (SMEs) to provide the technical details. On the other hand, when analysts do not know the job in question intimately, they must rely on experts to provide much of the information required.

The following techniques are most frequently employed in task analysis:

- interviews with subject matter experts, incumbents, decision makers, etc.
- observation of experts at work
- surveys of job incumbents and subject matter experts

Of these three, interviews are the most common and the richest data collection technique for job analysis. The interview format is open and allows both the analyst and the expert being interviewed to explore a large terrain. Sometimes interviews are recorded on audio or video tape to help document complex tasks, or copious notes may be taken by the analyst or third party. The best sources of information are the recognized experts at the job in question. Additionally, it is customary to interview key managers and decision makers so that their views are reflected in the analysis. An effective approach to interviewing subject matter experts is to draft a list of questions and distribute them in advance of the interview to allow both sides to prepare. Then, once the interview starts, use the questions as a guide, but allow the subject to elaborate and diverge where necessary so as to acquire a complete picture of the job and tasks.

Observation is the second most popular task analysis technique, and it is often combined with interviews. Direct observation of the work being performed under actual conditions is often the only way to fully understand and document complex tasks, especially those that are highly technical. Observations are usually recorded on a form, but free-form notetaking may also be employed. Once again, the use of recordings, particularly video tape, helps the analyst preserve a detailed record of the job for subsequent analysis. An example of a task analysis observation checklist is contained in Appendix Two on p. 272.

Finally, surveys may be used for very large scale task analyses when it is desirous to obtain the input of all jobholders and key experts. For example, if one was undertaking a task analysis involving a manufacturing assembly job performed by thousands of workers, it would be helpful to survey the entire population or a representative sample to discover how they perform the task. This of course would have to be followed up by interview and observation to fully document the tasks.

### Discovering the Underlying Skills and Knowledge

Once a detailed task analysis has been completed, sequenced and approved, the training designer must move on to a consideration of the underlying skills and knowledge required to perform the tasks. This is where some good detective work and a solid background in educational psychology come in handy.

Although the needed knowledge and skill for a rote task like changing a tire appears simple and straight forward, this is only because it is so familiar to us. Let's take a brief look at some of the underlying knowledge and skill required to change a tire. First, here's the complete task analysis, with procedural steps and equipment:

Now that is quite a procedure, once you write down all the steps. But let's stop and consider the kinds of knowledge and skill that are required to perform these sixteen steps. Let's start with knowledge, defined as the higher order understanding required to learn specific skills. First of these is the ability to read, since the tire changer is going to have to consult his owner's manual to find the location of his equipment. Our changer will also need to identify a host of tools and automobile parts. Finally, he or she ought to know a bit about automobile tires in order to purchase a new one or have the flat one repaired. Now let's look at the skills needed, defined as the manual or psychomotor abilities required to physically change the tire. Here we encounter a host of physical skills, including:

- turning a wrench
- assembling and raising a jack
- removing and replacing hub caps
- removing and replacing tires

*Table 5-5:*          ***Task Analysis: Changing a Tire***

| |
|---|
| **Equipment Needed:** jack, tire arm, tire wrench, spare tire<br>**Steps:** |
| 1.  Put car in Park and apply parking brake.<br>2.  Remove jack, tire arm and wrench from where it is stored (usually the trunk – see automobile owner's manual for exact location)<br>3.  Using tire arm, pry off the hub cap on the flat tire.<br>4.  Using the tire wrench, unloosen the lug nuts on the flat tire.<br>5.  Insert the jack in the proper position under the bumper or frame of the vehicle (see owner's manual for exact location)<br>6.  Insert the tire arm into the jack lever and begin to operate the jack using an up and down motion (or circular for some jacks). The vehicle should slowly lift off the ground.<br>7.  Continue raising the jack until the flat tire is off the ground.<br>8.  Remove the loosened lug nuts from the wheel and store in a safe place.<br>9.  Remove the flat tire from the vehicle.<br>10. Place the spare tire over the lugs on the vehicle's brake drum.<br>11. Screw on the lug nuts and tighten using the tire wrench.<br>12. Lower the jack using the reverse motion for raising.<br>13. Check that all lug nuts are securely fastened.<br>14. Replace the hub cap by positioning it in place and firmly rapping it with a clenched fist.<br>15. Put the flat tire and tire equipment back in the trunk.<br>16. Drive to the nearest tire dealer for a new tire. |

To a complete novice who has never before changed a tire, this is a daunting amount of knowledge and skill to master. Perhaps that's why so many people prefer to rely on a towing service when they have a flat tire.

This example illustrates the complexity of discovering the underlying knowledge and skill needed to perform a task. To perform most work tasks successfully, performers rely on a basic knowledge of language, mathematics and science, an understanding of concepts and classifying objects, cause and effect analysis of events, objects and people and the memorization of complex sequences of actions and decisions. That's quite a lot to simply get the job done, but it is what happens in the minds of performers. Capturing this information in a useful way is difficult, but it is the heart of good instructional design. We will turn to this topic in more depth in the section on Design (see Chapter 13).

*Summary*

In this chapter on task analysis, a process model was presented that serves as a guide for conducting task analysis. This was illustrated with several different job examples. Some common data collection methods of task analysis were presented, including interview, observation and surveys. Finally, we discussed the underlying knowledge and skill needed to perform tasks and noted the complexity and difficulty of precisely documenting this, even for a routine task like changing a tire.

# Discussion Questions and Exercises

1. What are the key steps in performing a task analysis?

2. Using you own job as an example, develop a task analysis for your most important job duty.

**Case Study: New Marketing Position (same as Job Analysis, chapter 4)**
A small business has grown sufficiently to afford a Marketing professional for the first time. The business buys and sells advertising time on local radio and televisions stations for large consumer clients. The Marketing professional will develop new business opportunities and expend the market for the firm's advertising services.

*How would you go about conducting a task analysis of the major duties of this position?*

# Chapter Six
# Learner Analysis

Learner analysis is the investigation of the current and future audience for training. It is conducted in order to understand the prerequisite knowledge, skill and experience of the training audience so as to better target the intended training. It also includes examining the culture, learning styles, background, values, and beliefs of the audience so as to match the training design and methodology to the audience. This chapter will provide a number of different strategies for learner analysis and use a variety of examples to illustrate useful techniques. As one of the newest needs assessments methodologies, learner analysis will be treated in depth.

### Importance of Analyzing the Learner

In this age of individualized instruction, it seems obvious why designers would want to focus on the learners. But such was not always the case. Much traditional instructional design was based on the premise that anyone could be taught to do anything. Therefore, analyzing the learner seemed like a waste of time. Most courses assumed the learner was a blank slate, *tabula rasa* waiting to be filled with knowledge and skill.

The advent of cognitive psychology and the demands of business leaders have prompted a complete change in that thinking and brought learners to center stage, much as customers now occupy center stage at many progressive businesses. Cognitive psychologists have long argued that learning takes place in the human mind through the active participation of learners. What learners do mentally in learning new knowledge and skill is at the very heart of learning and so studying how learners learn is a crucial component of training design. Business leaders have spurred this shift too, by demanding more efficiency from their training function. It is no longer acceptable to run hordes of people through generic training courses, whether they need it or can apply it or not. Instead, the current focus is on customizing learning for the individual through the use of computer-based training, individual learning contracts and custom training designs targeted to very specific populations. This cannot be successfully done without analyzing the learners to discover their individual needs.

### What We Need to Know About Learners

Learner analysis typically takes two forms: general studies of the learning styles and preferences of learners and specific investigation of the needs of particular training audiences. Both of these play a useful role in informing designers about the needs, interests and learning styles of the audiences they are trying to reach. General studies of learning styles and preferences help designers provide a variety of learning activities and opportunities that appeal to all styles. Studies of specific training audiences provide valuable information about learners' current knowledge, their motivation to learn and their attitudes toward the subject and work. This kind of information can make or break a training program.

## Learning Styles

A great deal of research has been done on preferred learning styles of both adults and children. Educational psychologists have identified three primary learning preferences: auditory, visual and kinesthetic (Filipczak, 1995). The auditory learner learns best through hearing. These individuals love to listen to lectures, 'war stories' and discussions, finding that they can identify key points and synthesize information primarily by listening. The visual learner learns best through seeing. Some researchers suggest that the majority of Americans are visual learners, and that they enjoy watching videos, seeing demonstrations and observing first-hand. From this, they can deduce the information they need and see exactly how to apply it. Finally, kinesthetic learners tend to be hands on, needing to physically interact with content in order to learn it. These learners like to be active, and to touch and manipulate physical objects in a laboratory setting.

Aside from these general characteristics of all learners, researchers have also investigated the differences between how children and adults learn. Malcolm Knowles was among the first researchers to recognize that adult learners were different from children and required a different approach, which he dubbed andragogy, to distinguish it from pedagogy (Knowles, 1984). He identified the following general characteristics of adult learners:

- self-directing
- motivated by self-interest
- life-centered and pragmatic
- change is primary driver to learn
- rely on experience to learn

Knowles believes that trainers and instructional designers can capitalize on these traits to create more effective training programs. He offers the following examples of how training can accommodate the learning styles of adults. To address adults' need to be self-directing and in control of their learning, he suggested the use of individual learning contracts in which learners decide up front what they want to learn and how they wish to demonstrate mastery of the content. To address adults' reliance on their rich reservoir of experience, he suggested a participative classroom setting in which learners are encouraged to share their experiences with peers. He also cautioned that when a learners' past experience contradicts the content of new training, particular attention must be paid to helping the learner unlearn the old habits before they can successfully master new ones. To address adults' desire for life-centered, pragmatic learning, Knowles suggests designing training that can be immediately applied to the job, so that adults see the relevance and deepen their learning. Finally, to address adults' tendency to become ready to learn when a change occurs in their lives, he suggests that training programs be timed to coincide with major changes, such as: starting a new job, getting a promotion, moving to a new company, etc. It is at these times, along with major changes in one's personal life like marriage, divorce, death in the family, etc., that create the ideal teachable moment for adults, since we seem to understand that our survival in a new situation depends on learning new knowledge and skill.

Another researcher who has studied the learning styles of adults is Ned Herrmann, whose work on whole-brain learning has identified four primary learning styles: (Herrmann, 1989)

1. Theoretical
2. Structural
3. Discovery
**4.** Sharing

These four happen to coincide with four of the most influential schools of thought in educational psychology:

1. Cognitivism
2. Behaviorism
3. Experientialism
4. Humanism

Herrmann posits that theoretical or cognitive learners tend to like theory and logic and use analysis, especially quantitative approaches, to learn new things. These are individuals who tend to do the best in traditional educational settings that stress theory and logic. Structural or behavioral learners tend to gravitate toward highly organized learning, with plenty of drill and practice and frequent evaluative feedback. These are learners who like the structure of computer-based training. Discovery or experiential learners value the freedom to explore and discover for themselves. They like to creatively conceptualize new ideas and synthesize existing knowledge with the new. These learners tend to do best in a self-study or laboratory setting, where they can exercise total control over what and how they learn. They tend to do the worst in traditional education classrooms where they have little control. Finally, sharing or humanistic learners tend to learn best in small group settings where they can share feelings and emotions with others and learn together. They may also be highly kinesthetic learners, needing to move about and experience learning hands on.

Although this information about adult learners is fascinating, it is often difficult to know how to apply it to effective instructional design. After all, if learners are so different, how can one accommodate all the various styles? Herrmann's answer is that good training must teach to all four styles, by using a variety of activities and methods that appeal across all four major learning styles. For example, a course on performance appraisals could include the theory of performance management, guided drill and practice, self-discovery exercises to identify one's own communication style and small group exercises in which participants share performance appraisal experiences. Such a course would offer something to each of the four learning styles.

### Content-Specific Learner Analysis

Although the research on general learning styles helps designers to be aware of the need for variety, it still does not provide a great deal of specific information for a given course or subject matter. To get at this kind of information, it is necessary to conduct a learner analysis of the identified audience for a given training program. Increasingly, such analysis is included as part of the needs assessment that is conducted to identify the objectives and content of a course.

Such analysis typically looks at the following elements of the learners:

- knowledge and skill levels
- attitudes
- motivation to learn and perform
- basic skills, including literacy
- tool and equipment skills
- cultural and diversity issues

The key issue for designers is the current knowledge and skill levels of the target audience. This forms the prerequisite foundation for the course. Anything beyond current levels must be learned in training or on the job. A second consideration is the learners' aptitude and past experience with the subject matter. For the sake of simplicity, learners can be classified, with regard to any subject, as either experts or novices. Experts are those who have previous experience in the subject area and who have a demonstrated aptitude for learning about the subject. They often have taken previous classes on the subject or ones closely related to it. Experts learn quickly and easily, in some cases without formal instruction at all. These learners may get what they require from a job aid or reference manual. Novices, conversely, are newcomers to the subject matter, or those who possess little aptitude for learning it. Those without any prior exposure will require very detailed and thorough instruction that leaves out nothing relevant to the performance of the job. Those with poor aptitude will need extra practice and coaching to help them overcome their natural barriers to learning the subject. Novices invariably require more time than experts to learn the new subject.

Where possible, it is best to separate expert and novice learners, and to present two versions of a training program uniquely geared to each. The reality of life, however, is that trainers frequently deal with both experts and novices in a single class. What to do then? It is essential in that case to meet the needs of novices, since they will be unable to perform if they do not learn the skills. Of course, this risks boring the experts, but a skilled facilitator can often include their expertise in the classroom by inviting them to share it in discussions or work with slower individuals. If instruction is aimed at the experts only, the consequences for novices are dire. They will not learn enough to be able to perform on the job, thus wasting the investment in their training.

Attitudes and motivation to learn are equally important considerations as knowledge, for without the proper motivation, little knowledge will be learned. Motivation to learn can be triggered by both intrinsic and extrinsic sources. Learners may have an inherent interest in the subject matter, they may have a strong achievement ethic, or may simply enjoy learning because of past successes. These are all intrinsic motivators. In business settings, learners have powerful extrinsic motivators also, such as obtaining or maintaining their jobs, winning promotions, getting raises, rewards or recognition, and earning the respect of peers. It is important to understand these motivations and how they impact a given training program in order to ensure that the pre-conditions of learning are present.

Two other very powerful drivers of motivation to learn are self-confidence and engagement. Learners who possess sufficient self-confidence in their ability to learn are much more likely to make the right amount of effort and to succeed in their learning. If learners lack confidence, they are not likely to try hard enough or long enough to learn. On the other hand, learners who are overly-confident may also fail to learn because they make too little effort. Learners' engagement refers to the value and importance they place on the subject matter. This is obviously a key determiner in the amount of effort and attention they devote to the subject. Those who value the subject highly, either for intrinsic or extrinsic reasons, are much more likely to attend to the training and put forth the effort required to succeed.

Basic skills, including literacy, numeracy and computer literacy, are obviously key foundation skills for all learning. And yet recent U.S. government studies demonstrate that up to 40 percent of adults possess inadequate basic literacy skills to meet the current needs of their jobs and daily lives (U.S. Department of Labor, 1991). This translates into two of every five adults, and chances are good at least one of those five will be sitting in the training program you are designing. Knowing this in advance, a savvy designer will make use of graphics, photos, video and other non-print media to help those with weak literacy skills learn the content. But beyond these band-aid solutions, society must invest more in adult basic skills to ensure that everyone has the foundation needed to learn new job skills in the future.

Depending on the type of training program, tool and equipment skills and manual dexterity may be important areas to investigate. If the training includes use of computers, machinery or industrial equipment, hand tools, laboratory equipment, etc. then attention to learners' manual dexterity and previous experience with such things is essential. In fact, much technical training these days is in reality training in the operation of equipment.

Cultural and diversity issues must also be addressed with regard to the learner population. This is especially true for global training programs designed to be used in multiple countries. Experts in this field recommend involving members of the target countries and cultures as subject matter experts in the design of the training, so as to better reflect cultural sensitivities and ensure the learning activities and teaching strategies are suited to the local environment. In some cases, it may be necessary to develop alternative activities for different cultures, to reflect their values and ensure learning occurs.

### Methodologies for Learner Analysis

Learner analysis lends itself to interviews and survey research. In-depth interviews with a representative sample of the target audience, or focus groups with this audience allows for a full exploration of the backgrounds, attitudes, skills and cultural norms of the target audience. These may be followed up, if need be, by survey research with a larger segment of the population. The surveys may range from sophisticated learning styles analysis to simple checklists of skills, attitudes and behaviors relevant to the proposed training. An example of such an instrument is located in Appendix Two, p. 278.

An additional way to reflect the voice of the learner is to involve a small number in the design process itself, either by making them subject matter experts or forming a review board that can be periodically convened to review the design and development process at key junctures. Just as it is imperative to gain the approval of decision makers at each point in the training design process, it is equally critical to ascertain that learners will find the training suitable to their interests and needs. The larger the stakes and the more diverse the potential audience, the more crucial it is to seek out the voice and opinions of the target audience.

### Summary

In this chapter, we have examined some of the ways that designers can analyze the characteristics and needs of learners. We have noted that research on general learning styles of adults suggests that they learn in different ways, using different strategies based on personal preferences and past experience. To accommodate these diverse styles, designers should use a wide variety of learning activities and teaching strategies, including multisensory approaches to content. Analysis of specific learning populations should focus on their prerequisite skills, their motivation to learn and any diversity issues that may impact learning.

The more that designers know about the target audience for training, the better they are able to customize the training to suit the unique needs of learners. This is something that makes a great deal of sense both from the point of view of designers who want to see successful learning take place, and from the point of view of business decision makers who want to see training targeted to maximize its impact and efficiency.

## Discussion Questions and Exercises

1. Using the Learner Analysis worksheet in Appendix Two, conduct a brief learner analysis of the participants in the course you are currently taking or last took. What are you key conclusions about the audience?

2. How would you describe your own learning style?  How does your style impact the way you like to learn?

### Case Study: The Reluctant Learners

You have been asked to design a refresher training program on ergonomics safety for a group of computer programmers who have been suffering increasing repetitive motion injuries.  The programmers are skeptical about the need for this training and tend to view repetitive motion injuries as a job hazard that cannot be avoided. They have voiced opposition to the plan to attend a class, claiming they are too busy and won't learn anything they don't already know.  They prefer to receive a job aid or online reference.

*How would you go about conducting a learner analysis of this target audience?  What are some key learning style issues you will need to address?*

# Chapter Seven
# Context Analysis

Context analysis examines the environment in which trainees will learn. It includes considerations about whether training should be delivered in a classroom environment, on the job, via computer or other technology and the characteristics of the chosen environment. Attention is also given to any barriers that may prevent learning and ways to remove or mitigate these. Additional issues to be considered in this chapter are:
- size of groups to be trained
- the facilities available for training
- audio-visual aids and equipment available
- the availability and skill of trainers to deliver the program
- the frequency of course delivery
- the cost of training delivery and who will bear it
- the match between the training environment and the work environment

Since this is a rather new area of needs analysis, it will be treated in some depth, with illustrative examples provided in the chapter and a job aid in Appendix Two.

### Why Context Analysis Matters

In today's training environment, designers are increasingly asked to provide training in a host of settings. Gone are the days when learning occurred only in classroom settings of 15-25 participants, led by an expert instructor. Today, learning may be conducted in groups large or small or even one learner at a time, using sophisticated multimedia software or a simple flip chart. So analyzing the context in which learning occurs, including consideration of all the various ways in which a given training may be delivered, has become a key component of training design. Without such analysis, trainers may find themselves lacking the options they need to fully address the needs of learners and clients.

### Elements of Context Analysis

The following are some of the key factors to be considered in a context analysis:

Figure 7-1:     **Context Analysis Factors**

| | |
|---|---|
| * Training group size | * Training length |
| * Training facilities | * Training delivery costs |
| * Presentation method | |
| * Training frequency | |
| * Training transfer strategies | |

The overall size of the training audience is one key starting point for context analysis. This includes both the immediate audience for training, which is usually known in advance of design, and the potential future audience for training over the lifetime of the course. This latter audience is harder to predict, but some estimates should be made early on. When training is aimed at a large audience, typically at least a thousand people, then this presents a number of options regarding delivery of the program that smaller audiences do not justify, including use of multimedia, distance learning and multiple class sites. Conversely, training that will only be presented to small numbers of learners, especially when the numbers are below 100, calls into question the amount of time and money that an organization wishes to invest in designing and delivering training for such a small group. The per capita costs really begin to skyrocket when numbers dip below 20. At that point, individual tutoring and on-the-job coaching may make more economic sense than a full-blown formal training program.

A related consideration is group size for delivery of training. Aside from the total numbers to be trained, additional constraints on group size are the nature of the content to be taught and the existing delivery resources of the organization. Content that requires intensive individual or small group practice to master should be delivered in small group settings of no more than 20 people. An example of this would be Presentation Skills, which typically includes several opportunities to present sample material, often accompanied by videotaping and detailed debriefing. Obviously, such methodologies do not suit themselves to large lecture hall audiences. But an overview of an organization's new benefits package, for example, may be delivered by a skillful presenter to audiences of hundreds or even thousands, since it is largely an informative lecture with little hands-on practice.

A third key issue is availability of instructors qualified to present the training. If instructors are not available, a plan to hire from outside or train internally must be developed. The number of instructors needed is a function of the content, group size and the delivery schedule. When trainers are unfamiliar with the content, a train the trainer session will need to be developed and delivered, usually by the training designers. If novice trainers, such as line managers, are proposed, a more detailed train the trainer course that includes basic presentation and facilitation skills may be called for. If outside contract instructors are to be used, a reliable source must be identified and a train the trainer program implemented to be able to deliver the content within the context of the organization.

An offshoot of the group size and instructor issue is consideration of whether training might be delivered individually, using either print-based or computer-based tutorials. This approach is increasingly favored by organizations that have difficulty assembling groups of people for classroom training, either due to logistic or time constraints. For example, a shipping company with hundreds of small, local offices can ill afford to assemble large groups of employees for centralized training sessions.

Instead, they are better off providing computer-based training at each office or using self-study or small training modules that can be delivered on-site by existing management personnel. Contrast this situation with the classic large manufacturing facility that has thousands of workers all needing similar training. In this case, classroom delivery in larger groups ensures that training is delivered quickly and relatively cost-effectively.

The point of this discussion is that designers must know the organization well enough to consider all these delivery options before they begin the design and development of training. Otherwise, they risk creating training programs that cannot be easily delivered, and therefore will not be utilized to their full extent.

If formal training is to be conducted, availability of facilities should be an early consideration. While some companies are blessed with ample training facilities, most must share space with other functions, or even rent space in hotels or other venues for large-scale training programs. In some cases, it may be desirable to move off-site, to cut down on disruptions and allow participants to concentrate on the content and interact more intensively with each other. Some organizations simply consider it a perk to attend training in an attractive off-site locale, although cost considerations must be factored into this. When dedicated training facilities exist, the designers can generally assume a full coterie of options and equipment will be available. For programs using rented or borrowed space, no such abundance can be assumed. In fact, it may be necessary to rent or ship the instructional equipment that must be used to deliver the program.

An even more complicated situation arises when training involves computers or other high tech equipment. The availability of the equipment will then dictate class size, since it is inadvisable to have more than two people share a piece of equipment such as a computer, and ideal for each person to have their own.

A related issue to group size is the preferred presentation method to be used for training. If a classroom delivery method has been chosen, it will be important to decide early on which instructional strategies will be employed in order to estimate ideal group sizes. Hands-on practice often determines maximum group size, as well as the organization's ability to release groups of individuals to attend training on company time. If a non-classroom method such as CBT or on-the-job (OJT) training has been chosen instead, then availability of computers and OJT coaches will affect the total number of trainees who can learn simultaneously.

The frequency and length of the proposed training program are key considerations in planning delivery strategies. If a program is a one-shot deal, as many are, then designers must ensure that the single opportunity that they have with the learners covers everything they will need to know to perform effectively. On the other hand, when training programs involve multiple sessions that meet over a long period of time, consideration must be given to issues of continuity, drop out rates, make up schedules and the like, since the longer a training course takes to complete, the more learners are likely to drop out along the way.

The length of training programs obviously affects a number of design and delivery issues. The typical one-day training program has a certain rhythm to it due to its length, including time to get acquainted in the morning, presenting most of the heavy content before lunch and planning the bulk of practice exercises for the afternoon, when the audience's attention begins to wane. The increasing popularity of short one or two hour modules of training present their own challenges to quickly engage learners in the subject matter and afford opportunities to practice outside of class, since the practice time is often cut to fit the shortened time frame. Finally, those who design longer training programs that take weeks or even months to complete are confronted with the need to build learning over time, usually by carefully sequencing content, and by frequently reviewing past material to ensure that it is not forgotten.

Although instructional designers are not always accountable for training delivery costs directly, they must pay attention to the ways in which their training design impacts delivery costs. The most elegant training design in the world is of little use if it cannot be delivered within the budget of the organization. Knowing up front what the limitations are helps designers to make sound instructional choices while honoring the organization's capability to deliver the content.

Delivery costs are typically a function of the following major cost drivers:
- instructor salaries
- participant salaries while in training
- instructional equipment used
- instructional materials used
- facility costs
- food and ancillary costs

These costs need to be identified as part of the context analysis so that they may be included in planning for instruction. They may also become part of a cost/benefit analysis to determine whether training is a cost-effective alternative to address performance issues.

One method of comparing delivery costs between courses and organizations is to add up all the potential costs and then divide by the total number of learners to arrive at a per person cost of training. This can even be further standardized by dividing per person costs by the number of days of training to arrive at an average daily cost of training per person. One organization which did this found that its average per capita daily cost of training delivery varied from as little as $50 to over $500. Most of this variation was due to class size, since larger classes create significant per person cost savings over smaller ones. High tech classes cost more too, due to equipment costs. Though they could not identify a single ideal cost per day for training, they were able to identify target ranges for various kinds of classes, including: instructor-led seminars, large group lectures, laboratory-based classes and computer-based training. Budgetary issues will be dealt with in more depth in Chapter 11.

A final key consideration of context analysis is the training transfer strategies that will be employed to ensure skills learned on the job are put to use in the classroom. One part of this is ensuring that classroom learning matches as closely as possible the conditions under which employees will perform on the job. A second issue is how to ensure that skills learned in training will be transferred and reinforced back on the job.

To ensure a good match between the training and the job environments, a thorough task analysis must be undertaken. The task analysis will identify the tasks and procedures and the equipment and tools used on the job. This information can then be used by the designer to ensure that the same procedures, equipment and tools are taught in class. Practice sessions are a particularly important opportunity to simulate the job environment. If learners use a particular piece of software or tool on the job, it should be utilized in practice sessions too. If practice involves solving an on the job problem, as many management training programs do, then allowing participants to come up with their own practice scenarios makes the training more relevant and the application more immediate. If homework assignments are given, they should focus on job applications for the material being taught. When cost considerations make it impossible to exactly simulate the work environment, close approximations should be developed instead, stressing tips and techniques for dealing with the real situation on the job.

To ensure that newly-learned skills transfer to the job, designers should consider how to employ the assistance of supervisors and mentors back at work. Research suggests that the single most important factor in transferring skills to the job is the learners' direct supervisor, who often either makes or breaks a training program by his actions once learners return to work. Supervisors who are familiar with the content of the training themselves, and who support employee learning are in a better position to coach and reinforce learning on the job than those who take little interest in training. Designers can help busy supervisors by preparing executive summaries of the content of training to share with them and by creating job aids and other materials designed to be used by supervisors in their on the job coaching assignments. Also, requesting regular feedback from supervisors of trainees helps to forge a strong link between training and line managers. Finally, executive support for training can translate into management pressure on supervisors to give employee job training the importance it deserves. From there, it is up to designers to create training that is relevant to the business and that clearly makes a difference in the performance of employees. When supervisors see first-hand that their trained employees perform better, they are likely to support more training. Conversely, if they can see little or no difference in their employees' performance, they are likely to question the value of future training programs.

**Summary**

In this chapter on context analysis, we have considered a number of elements of the learning and the performance environment that impact training design and delivery. Among the issues we have explored are the following:

- size of groups to be trained
- the facilities available for training
- audio-visual aids and equipment available
- the availability and skill of trainers to deliver the program
- the frequency of course delivery
- the cost of training delivery and who will bear it
- the match between the training environment and the work environment

By analyzing each of these variables up front as part of the needs assessment, designers ensure that they create programs that can be delivered cost-effectively by the receiving organization. Moreover, they also pave the way for successful transfer of training to the work environment so that training will achieve its intended benefits.

## Discussion Questions and Exercises

1.  Using the course you are currently in or the last one you took, conduct a brief context analysis, identifying the following key context issues:

    - Group size?
    - Training facility?
    - A-V and learning technology?
    - Trainers?
    - Course frequency?
    - Delivery costs?
    - Match between training and work environment?

## Case Study: Alternative Learning Contexts

A global consumer products company has been delivering all of its training in classroom settings for many years. Now that is has expanded to over 70 locations in 30 different countries, it is looking for some cheaper and more effective alternatives to delivering training.

*Using the context analysis model presented in this chapter, analyze the key contextual issues facing this company and identify some possible alternatives to classroom training delivery.*

# Chapter Eight
# Skill Gap Analysis

Skill gap analysis is a specialized form of needs assessment that examines and documents the gap between employees' current skills and the skills needed to perform successfully. It is an appropriate follow up analysis technique when needs assessment has proven that employees are not performing as well as they must due to a lack of knowledge or skill. It is especially used when the basic skills of employees appear inadequate for the job they hold. Through practical examples and job aids, this chapter will assist readers to master this important analytical skill. Although skill gap analysis is rarely conducted in isolation of other needs analysis, it is treated separately here to highlight the importance of this form of analysis and to present specific techniques to measure and document skill gaps.

### The Importance of Skill Gap Analysis

Few needs assessment topics are of greater important than skill gap analysis, since it goes to the heart of training assessment. Unless a significant gap exists between the current performance of employees and the desired or required performance, it is unlikely that training will be pursued. By measuring current skills and comparing them to current or estimated future skill needs, training designers clearly demonstrate a need for training that can be compelling to decision makers.

Another reason why skill gap analysis is so crucial is that it drives much of the design phase of training, which often focuses on skill gaps in the formulation of objectives and content of training. It also suggests what level of skill trainees need to reach by the end of training to be proficient. This in turn influences the amount and kinds of practice that are provided and the strategies to transfer newly-learned skills to the job.

### A Skill Gap Analysis Model

Skill gap analysis is essentially a comparison between the current state of skills and some desired or future state. The model below reflects this fundamental nature of skill gap analysis.

Skill gap analysis usually proceeds from existing skills to desired skills, but it may also be initiated by an anticipated change in the future that drives organizations to look at existing skills. Whatever prompts an organization to examine skill gaps, it is essential that both current and desired skill levels be investigated. The strategies for each differ and will be presented separately.

*Figure 8-1:*
# *Skill Gap Analysis Model*

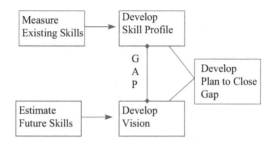

### *Documenting Existing Skills*

Designers may use a number of techniques to document the existing skills of their workforce.  Among the most common are:

- tests
- performance appraisals and documents
- quality assurance data
- customer feedback data
- self-perceptions

Although some firms are reluctant to test incumbents, fearing resistance or even litigation over the issue, testing remains the most reliable way to measure existing job skills, presuming a valid test can be located or designed.  Current labor law and judicial guidelines require that any test used to make employment decisions must be demonstrated to have a direct link to job duties and performance.  Thus, a generalized I.Q. test which measures intellectual aptitude  would not be considered job-related, whereas a test that measures the ability to assemble a piece of machinery would be job-related for machinery assemblers.  Tests of basic skills such as English and mathematics are considered job-related if it can be shown that ability to speak, read and write English and perform mathematical computations are essential to job performance.  In most cases, such a case can easily be made, but probably not for unskilled labor that does not require any literacy.  Quite often, organizations use basic skills tests such as the Test of Adult Basic Education (TABE) or the Test of Adult Literacy (TAL) as a baseline measure, since these tests have already been validated and shown to be job-related in most cases.  This baseline can then be compared to the estimated future skill requirements to determine the extent and nature of a skill gap.

Although basic skills tests are useful measurement tools, they are only a starting point for more advanced job skills often required at work today.  Someone with adequate basic skills may still be unable to perform a complex job successfully. In this case, a custom test, created for the specific jobs in question, needs to be developed to supplement the basic skills tests. In some professions, standardized vocational tests exist, but other more specialized jobs cannot be measured by existing published tests.

A second measurement strategy is to rely on existing performance documentation, such as appraisals and supervisor ratings of employees. Such documentation can give a general impression of the quality of the workforce, but suffers from its subjectivity and lack of differentiation among employees. Most organizational performance management systems only distinguish among exceptional, average and problem performers. To document a skills gap, a more finely-tuned performance management system is needed. This may require the creation of skill gap surveys, or the observation and documentation of skill gaps as they occur and manifest themselves in the workplace. Some organizations regularly survey both employees and supervisors to determine the existing skills of the workforce and track development over time. These organizations also put in place individual employee development plans that can be monitored to measure how much employees are learning and developing themselves.

A third method to measure existing skills is to rely on quality assurance data or customer feedback to determine how well employees perform on the job. Most organizations collect quality assurance data that measures how well work is performed, usually in terms of the number of errors made on the job. These errors result in rework, scrap, rejected merchandise, warranty claims, customer dissatisfaction and loss of market share. By tapping existing quality data and tracking it over time, trainers can learn a great deal about the skills of the workforce and target areas of the business that are causing the greatest number of problems. The added appeal of customer feedback is that this directly impacts an organization's bottom line. When customers express dissatisfaction with products and services, it is certain that this will hurt a business if uncorrected. Business executives are keenly aware of the importance of customer satisfaction and will be likely to act upon any skill deficit that can be directly linked to customer perceptions of the quality of the business. The difficulty with this data, however, is in directly locating a cause and effect relationship between poor quality and employee skills. Quite often, quality problems are a combination of many elements, including skill gaps, inadequate quality control, poor management systems, defective materials and equipment, etc. Nevertheless, this data can be a very powerful ally to trainers attempting to sell a skills gap solution to decision makers.

Once a measurement system has been developed, it is important to use the data to create a profile of the firm's capabilities. This includes both individual employee skill profiles and overall organizational skill capabilities. The leading companies who take skill development seriously create a systematic approach to employee skill development. They carefully document each employee's existing skills and plan to develop additional skills over time. They tie pay, rewards and selection systems to skill needs, so that employees have the proper incentives to develop themselves and so that selection and promotion decisions are based on skill needs, and not serendipity. Some go a step further and develop an organizational profile of the skills and competencies of their workforce, using sophisticated human resource databases to store and track key capabilities so that they can quickly respond to opportunities as they materialize and plan for future needs. This seems to be particularly important in high tech sectors of the economy where skills become obsolete so rapidly that they must be constantly replenished by updating work force skills.

### Estimating Future Skill Needs

If measuring current skills is challenging, then estimating future skills is an act of clairvoyance. And yet, it is important to look at future needs of an organization in order to develop the necessary skills before they are needed. Since skill-building is a long-term process, organizations who wait until the need is at hand find themselves in a mad scramble to locate employees with the necessary skills. Such firms often hire talent rather than develop it, but this can be a costly solution and one that does little to build future capacity.

Methods for estimating future skill needs include tapping data sources ranging from strategic plans, market research, information systems, future technologies and global economic trends. While all this information helps point the direction that a business is headed, it does not necessarily indicate what kind of workforce will be needed. For this part of the analysis, designers must rely on their ability to translate a future requirement into a concrete and finite set of job duties, tasks and skills. They may rely on any of the following techniques to identify future skills:

- literature search of future industry trends
- job task analysis
- interviews with subject matter experts
- benchmarking leading businesses
- process improvement analysis
- systems analysis
- behavioral analysis

Each of these techniques offers sources of data that can deepen the analyst's understanding of the future skill requirements of an organization. This information must then be synthesized into a comprehensive description of the future job and the knowledge and skill needed to perform it. This becomes the future vision that the organization embraces and uses to guide the development of the work force.

To illustrate this process, consider a very common future job requirement – the automation of an existing manually-performed task. Let's assume that the task in question is taking customer orders for office products. This common work process is performed currently at XYZ Corp. by telephone order takers who write down all the information on pre-printed forms and then submit these to the shipping department to fill and ship to customers. The future order-taking process will be done instead via the company's web site, where customers will be able to log on, peruse on-line catalogs and place orders by completing fill-in-the-blank forms which are automatically sent to the shipping department.

The analysis of this future job requirement might begin with a comprehensive literature search of internet-based marketing and sales techniques that could identify the major elements of a successful sales strategy. Next, one might conduct a benchmarking study of a successful internet-based marketing company to determine how they set up their web site and how it operates. Third, interviews with key decision makers and subject matter experts who came up with the new strategy would help the analyst understand the rationale for the change and the business' goals. Fourth, the new order-taking process would need to be documented in detail, including the role of computer systems and human interactions. Fifth, a detailed behavioral analysis of the tasks, knowledge and skills required to perform each step in the order-taking process would need to be developed. This could then be compared to the existing process to identify major changes and their skill implications.

The result of all this analysis would be a clear picture of how the new process will be performed, how it differs from the old process, and the new knowledge and skill needed to perform the process. In this example, the new order-taking process might be diagrammed as follows:

### Figure 8-2:
## *Internet-Based Order Taking Process*

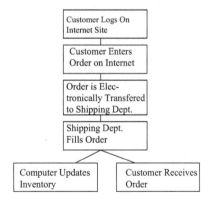

Key differences between the old telephone-based order taking process and the new automated process might be:
1. no direct interaction with customer
2. creation of computerized product database
3. link between web site and shipping department and between shipping department and inventory system

4. computer skills to retrieve orders from database
5. troubleshooting skills to solve problems with computer systems

The knowledge and skills needed to perform the new work process would include:

- computer keyboard and mouse skills
- database entry, search and retrieval skills
- Internet browser and e-mail software skills
- computer system troubleshooting skills
- customer service problem solving skills (for orders incorrectly handled by the computer and for customers who need help with the new system)
- knowledge of Internet web sites, computer database concepts and principles, problem solving and troubleshooting principles
- knowledge of the English language, ability to read and write at an eighth grade level at minimum

From this analysis, it is clear that the existing workforce of telephone order-takers would need substantial retraining to be able to operate the new Internet-based order system. In fact, it might be concluded that so much training would be required that it would be more cost effective to hire a different set of workers to handle this new process, though that would have to be weighed against the cost of laying off or reassigning existing workers. In any event, this procedure leads clearly to a link between the new work process and the knowledge and skills required to make it operate efficiently. Just imagine for a moment the chaos that would result if such a radically new work process were implemented without any retraining of the existing workforce. Telephone order takers and shipping clerks would be immediately overwhelmed by the complexity of the new computerized system, orders would be incorrectly filled and customer complaints would skyrocket. Despite this bleak scenario, companies introduce radical new computer technologies every day in the United States without the slightest thought for the impact this will have on the existing workforce and their ability to perform. Is it any wonder that many computer investments never demonstrate a positive return on investment? Only by training people to use new technologies can the full benefits of automation be realized. And the training designer is in an ideal position to help organizations reap the benefits of technology.

### Closing Skill Gaps

As alluded to in the above example, strategies to close documented skill gaps include retraining of existing workers, or hiring new workers who possess all or most of the new skills sought. The decision of whether to go with the existing workforce or hire new employees is a difficult one for organizations and is influenced largely by the magnitude of the gap, the estimated cost and time to close the gap, and the availability of trained workers in the business' labor pool. Even when companies decide to hire new workers to replace existing ones, some training in the new system as well as orientation to the new organization will be necessary to ensure a smooth transition.

### *Summary*

In this chapter, we have examined a skill gap model that involves measuring existing employee knowledge and skill, estimating future skill needs and planning to close the gap through training, hiring or a combination of the two. Various methods to measure workforce skills and estimate future requirements have been presented. A case study involving automation of customer orders illustrates the complexity of issues that designers must confront in conducting successful skill gap analysis. It also shows that when a thorough skill gap analysis is conducted, it greatly enhances the chances of future success, while failure to address future skill needs is a sure ticket to disaster.

# Discussion Questions and Exercises

1. Assume that you have just been offered the job of your dreams. Conduct a skill gap analysis on yourself to identify the key training that you will need to succeed in your new position.

## Case Study: The New Call Center

A large bank has decided to consolidate all of its customer service and billing functions into a single call center, to e located outside the U.S. They need to identify the skill gaps of the new workforce to be able to provide the necessary training. They anticipate that their new labor market will have a large number of recent college graduates who are the target audience for the new jobs. These people are bright, but lack business experience.

*How would you design a skill gap analysis for this company? How would you measure future and current skills? How would you propose to close the skills gap?*

## Section One Conclusion: Grounding Training Analysis in Results

In concluding the analysis section, let's spend a moment reviewing the key theme of this book—that training must always be firmly grounded in business results. Recall that the four types of results that training can produce are:

- **learning**
- **performance**
- **financial health**
- **strategic growth**

The analysis phase of training is crucial to achieving these results. During needs analysis and performance analysis, trainers determine the root cause of the performance problem or the critical enablers of a new business opportunity. They should be looking broadly at all four of the results above in order to determine how training can contribute to the solution, and what other interventions may be needed.

If a knowledge deficit is identified during the needs analysis, a more detailed training needs assessment is undertaken, using techniques like job task analysis, learner analysis, context analysis and skill gap analysis. Although the primary purpose of these analyses is to identify the learning objectives and content, attention must also be given to performance issues and how the training will produce financial or strategic results. The task analysis and learner analysis helps to determine the performance requirements and the specific needs of trainees. The context analysis looks, among other things, at the match between training and the job and ways to enhance skill transfer. These are all important performance issues.

Finally, the analysis phase should identify clear financial and strategic benefits from conducting training. The skill gap analysis can help to quantify the extent of a skill gap and translate this to dollars and cents. The performance analysis should identify key financial and strategic goals of the business that have prompted an investigation into a performance problem or opportunity.

If the analysis cannot pinpoint an important performance, financial or strategic objective for training, then it makes little sense to continue with the design effort. This is why analysis is becoming such a key component of training design and one that is increasingly occupying more organizational time and resources. If we can't clearly identify the cause of performance problems and link their solution to important business results, we are unlikely to get clients to step forward with money to pursue training. Though training professionals are often disappointed to see no training emerge from a needs analysis, it is far better to recognize the limits of training at the outset than to promise solutions that training cannot deliver.

# Section Two

# Design Phase

The book's second section covers the design phase of training design, which, as the name implies, is the heart of the process. Because of the loose way in which trainers use the term 'design', sometimes meaning a specific phase of the training process and sometimes using it as a shorthand way of referring to the entire process, I will carefully define the term as I am using it here to mean the preparation of a blueprint for a training program, using the analogy of an architect who prepares blueprints for a building before it is constructed. This section encompasses five chapters: Training Objectives, Training Deliverables and Instructional Strategies, Budgets and Schedules, Project Management and Blueprints/ Prototypes. Each of these topics forms an essential element of an effective training design blueprint.

*Figure 9-1:*

# Training Design Phase

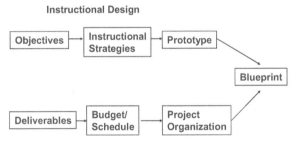

# Chapter Nine
# Training Objectives

The heart of the design phase is carefully crafted training objectives. These form the goals of the training design, and shape its content. This chapter will describe the elements of an effective training objective, give examples from successful training programs, and introduce the notion of a hierarchy of objectives based on prerequisites, enabling objectives and terminal performance objectives. Exercises and job aids will walk readers through the training objective process step by step.

### Where Do Objectives Come From?

As you saw in Section One, objectives come from a needs analysis of the performance problem or opportunity that training is supposed to resolve. A well-conceived training needs assessment should identify specific new skills, knowledge, and attitudes that trainees need to acquire in order to perform on-the-job. Objectives are statements of the specific outcomes to be achieved by training, stated from the point of view of the learner. An objective has been defined as a change in the behavior of the learner (Tyler, 1949). Behavior, in this case, is defined broadly to include thinking and feeling, as well as observable actions, although the latter makes for a much better learning objective, as we will see.

Sometimes, needs assessments are not crystal clear about the objectives to be learned, however. They may stop short of naming specific skills and instead focus on broad areas of knowledge such as: leadership or marketing or time management. In these cases, the instructional designer must investigate these broad knowledge areas and pinpoint exactly what tasks, procedures, concepts and principles need to be learned. These would then become the training objectives guiding the development of a program.

### Why are Objectives Important?

Objectives are not mere formalities or academic exercises. They ensure that training has a clear focus and purpose, and that it has measurable outcomes. Without clear objectives, a great deal of training goes on which lacks any apparent purpose. Without purpose, training cannot determine its outcomes and without outcomes, there is no purpose in conducting training in the first place.

Objectives satisfy several audiences and purposes. First, the designer writes objectives to determine the content and structure of the training program. Second, clients and sponsors review objectives to determine if the proposed training will meet the outcomes that they have in mind. Third, learners need objectives so that they can determine if the proposed training is going to help them learn something new and to focus their attention while learning. Finally, trainees' managers and training evaluators use objectives to determine whether learning has occurred and whether that learning has transferred to the job and is producing the desired results for the organization.

### Components of a Learning Objective

Training objectives have four main components. Two are required: a target behavior and content, while two are optional: conditions and standards.

As a bare minimum, an objective should have a behavior and some content. It often also contains conditions and standards. The four components are described below:

1. A statement of the target behavior in the form of an action verb.
2. A statement of the content, which is the task or topic upon which the trainee will act.
3. A statement of the conditions under which the trainee is expected to perform the target   behavior, such as environment and tools provided.
4. A statement of the standards that the trainee will achieve upon mastery.

We will now examine each of these components in more detail. Target behaviors are expressed as verbs and should be action-oriented and measurable. For example, contrast the action behavior in "type a paragraph" with the more abstract and passive "understand how to type". The former objective clearly states the outcome, and it is something measurable. The latter objective would be difficult to measure and does not produce a useful job-related outcome. When objectives do involve abstract knowledge, the measurement of such objectives requires an indirect approach, such as asking participants to apply concepts in a measurable situation. Of course, typing is a physical activity and is easily expressed as an action verb. When teaching a theoretical subject which imparts ideas or facts, it may be impossible to directly observe students performing an action. Instead, trainees can be asked to perform some activity that enables them to apply the ideas or facts being presented. For example, if a training session on safety rules in a machine shop was being presented, the following objective would require students to perform two actions:

*OBJECTIVE: To list and explain the safety rules that apply in a machine shop.*

In this case, the two target behaviors are clearly stated -- "list and explain", and the successful mastery of these two behaviors implies that a person would likely follow these rules in the machine shop.

The table below illustrates the contrast between common action verbs and abstract verbs used in training objectives.

*Table 9-2:*        ***Action versus Abstract Behaviors***

| Action Verbs | Abstract Verbs |
|---|---|
| To write | To know |
| To demonstrate | To understand |
| To define | To be familiar with |
| To solve | To perceive |
| To explain | To be aware of |
| To apply | To think about |

Setting a target behavior gives the trainer a readily observable basis on which to assess learning. A well-defined target behavior gives the trainees a specific goal, too. Trainees will know specific actions they must take to achieve the desired performance and trainers will clearly know when the objective has been learned. Target behaviors are also keys to good instructional design. If the target behavior is "to type", then the designer must focus on teaching participants to type and giving them ample opportunities to practice and develop this skill. If the target behavior is "to list", then the designer must focus on presenting lists of items and giving the trainees practice in listing things, either in writing or orally.

Even a subtle change in the target behavior can make an enormous difference in the content of training. Take for example the following two objectives:

*To identify key principles of diversity.*

*To apply key principles of diversity.*

In the first case, learners merely need to be able to pick out key principles from a list or a case study, while the latter objective requires them to apply these principles to solve diversity-related problems. Clearly, the second objective is a more meaningful one, and also much more difficult to learn. The content of training designed around the first objective would be significantly different from that of the second.

The second required element of an objective is a statement of the content. Since the content is the task or topic of the objective, it is expressed as a noun, often the object of the action verb. For example, in the objective:

*To write reports of monthly activity;* "reports of monthly activity" is the content that learners will be writing about.

The content element of the objective identifies the task to be performed, or the topic or area of work to which the behavior is applicable. Objectives which are clear and provide guidance in the development of training programs must include both the behavior element and the content element of the objective. For example:

*OBJECTIVE: To write clear and well-organized reports of monthly department activities*

This objective includes the kind of behavior sought (write clear and well-organized) and also indicates the content with which the writing must deal (reports of monthly department activities).

Likewise, the following is a complete objective:

OBJECTIVE: To identify dependable sources of pricing information

This contains both the behavior (to identify) and the content (dependable sources of price information).

It may be helpful to list the behaviors and content of a training program in a matrix (see Chart One) which can be used to match target behaviors with content areas. This is illustrated by displaying the behaviors and content for a Train the Trainer course.

Chart 9-3:     **Matrix of Objectives for a Train the Trainer Course**

**Target Behaviors**

| Content Areas | Identify | Describe | Design | Write | Apply | Decide |
|---|---|---|---|---|---|---|
| 1. Needs Analysis | X | X | | | | |
| a. Training needs | X | | X | X | X | |
| b. Job tasks | X | X | X | X | | |
| c. Costs/Benefits | X | | | X | | X |
| 2. Objectives | X | X | | X | | |
| a. Sources | X | X | | | | X |
| 3. Instructional | X | X | | | | |
| a. Principles | X | | | | | |
| b. Presentations | | X | | X | X | |
| c. Demonstrations | | X | | | X | |
| d. Discussions | | X | | | X | |
| e. Cases/ Role plays | | X | | X | X | |
| 4. Evaluation | X | X | | X | | |
| a. Designs | X | | X | X | X | X |
| b. Methods | | X | X | X | | X |

The matrix helps the designer to see which target behaviors go with which content topics. It also can serve as a checkpoint to ensure that all the objectives of a course cover the content and behaviors that have been identified by the training needs assessment. A blank objectives matrix is included in Appendix Two on p. 282 to assist you in developing program objectives.

Once behaviors and content have been identified, a training objective can be written. This may suffice by itself, but sometimes more information is needed. One of the things that is often added to an objective is a list of the conditions. The conditions component of a training objective describes the situations or environment in which the trainee is expected to perform. By including conditions in a training objective, trainees know what resources they will have and in what environment they can expect to perform. Stating conditions also helps the trainer determine what resources must be provided for the trainees. Listing all the conditions is not necessary, especially if they are self-evident. For example, including the condition "a table and chair will be provided" adds little to the effectiveness of a training objective.

Here are some typical examples of conditions:

*Given a standard set of gauging tools...*
*Without the aid of mathematical tables...*
*Using an electronic calculator...*
*Given a rapidly changing market...*
*Using a PC...*

Both the trainer and the trainees can visualize the objective once they know the behavior, content and conditions. However, they still don't know how well the objective must be performed. The optional standards component of the objective describes the desired level of performance after training.

Consider this training objective: "To type a paragraph". What constitutes satisfactory performance? Must a trainee type the paragraph without errors? How long can the trainee take to type it? How long is the paragraph?

To avoid these ambiguities, you may want to include performance standards in the training objective. Standards can be divided into three categories:

1. **Quantity**: How much will the trainee accomplish?
2. **Quality**: How well will the trainee perform?
3. **Time**: How long will the trainee have to complete the behavior?

Consider this example:

*To type a 100 word paragraph without error in two minutes.*

This gives a quantity standard (100 words), a quality standard (without error) and a time standard (in two minutes). Note also that setting the degree of difficulty helps to define the amount of time needed to achieve the desired standard. If the standards in this objective were lowered, trainees would require less practice to achieve it. Consider the same objective with different standards:

*To type a 100 word paragraph with no more than five errors and in five minutes.*

As a general rule, let the standard of quality accepted or desired in the work place determine the level of difficulty of the training objective. Sometimes, a "trainee" performance standard is identified that is somewhat below normal standards, recognizing that new learners will need time to develop the proficiency of more experienced employees.

Alternatively, it may be necessary to set standards after trainees have had some practice performing the behaviors. This is particularly true of new training programs. In these cases, the standards are determined by observing and measuring acceptable levels of performance of an experimental group and then adopting these for subsequent groups of trainees. It would be premature to set a precise performance standard in the training objective before trainees have had actual job experience.

## Sequencing Objectives

So far, we have considered objectives in isolation. In most training programs, objectives do not exist in isolation. Instead, there may be several objectives of differing importance and difficulty being learned. To help instructional designers sort out the many objectives of a complex training program, a hierarchy of objectives is sometimes constructed (Mager, 1975). The hierarchy typically consists of the following elements:

1. Prerequisite Objectives - behaviors that learners must have prior to beginning a given class, such as basic literacy in English.
2. Enabling Objectives - behaviors that learners must master first before they are able to perform the ultimate behavior being taught
3. Terminal Objectives - behaviors that learners will be able to demonstrate at the end of a training program. These are the ultimate goals of the program.
4. Performance Objectives – behaviors that learners will be able to exhibit on the job after they return from training.
5. Results Objectives – accomplishments that the organization will be able to achieve as a results of better training employees, including financial and strategic results.

## Example of Objective Hierarchy

Let's take a simple example to illustrate the hierarchy and relationship of various types of objectives. Consider the following terminal objective:

*To make a pizza*

What are some enabling objectives that would need to be learned in order to make a pizza? Here are some possible candidates:

- To use an oven
- To make pizza dough
- To make pizza sauce

These three skills would need to be taught first in order for someone to be able to make a pizza.

In order to learn the three enabling objectives, however, one needs to learn some prerequisite skills, which may not be taught in a pizza making class. Some of these include:

- To read a recipe
- To measure ingredients

These prerequisite objectives could be further broken down into even more basic prerequisite skills. For example:

*To read a recipe*

has its own prerequisite objectives, such as:

- To identify the meaning of words
- To decode abbreviations
- To identify facts
- To summarize main ideas

For most subjects, a hierarchy of objectives will exist. It is often useful to start by specifying the terminal objective first and then working backwards to enabling and prerequisite objectives, but it is not necessary to do this. One could also move the other way, from prerequisite to enabling to terminal objectives, or even conceivably start somewhere in the middle.

### Classifying Objectives

To classify objectives by type, it is helpful to ask two questions of any objective after writing it. These are:

1. Why do learners need to be able to do that?
2. What do learners need to know to be able to do that?

The first question helps move up the hierarchy to identify the truly meaningful skills that comprise terminal objectives. Keep asking this questions until you reach an objective that is undisputedly important to achieve.

The second question helps move down the hierarchy by identifying prerequisite and enabling skills that must be learned first. Once these skills have been identified, it is important to determine whether learners possess them already or not. If they do not, they must be learned prior to teaching the terminal objective.

### Selecting the Most Important Objectives

The needs analysis and preliminary design of objectives will often produce more objectives than can be achieved within a training program. Since a great deal of time is required to change the behavior of people, a small number of important objectives is preferable to a large wish list. Moreover, any list of objectives may contain some which are in conflict with other objectives. If objectives are not consistent, trainees may become confused by contradictory behaviors. For example, if one objective of a management development program is "to encourage independent action and initiative in employees" while another objective is "to tighten central control over the organization", trainees will likely become confused by these two contradictory objectives and will not achieve either.

One way to select a few important, consistent objectives is to screen a list of objectives in terms of values that are important to the corporation. Objectives which best serve the organization's philosophy and values should be chosen over those which contradict or do not support important values.

To use a statement of corporate philosophy as a selection criterion for objectives, the criteria must be stated clearly. The implications for training must be explicit. Once the criteria are selected and made explicit, every proposed objective can be examined to determine if it agrees, disagrees or is unrelated to the philosophy. Those objectives which agree with the corporate philosophy should be identified as the most important areas for training.

As an example, suppose one of a company's philosophical values is employee loyalty. What implications does this value have for training? It suggests that training programs which emphasize team building, organizational cohesiveness, and cooperation would support this value and should be encouraged while those programs which emphasize independent action, competitiveness and organizational conflict would tend to undermine the company's values and should be avoided.

Consider the list of company values espoused by a large company in the energy field listed below. What are the implications of these values for training? You may want to restate the values in a form that is most useful for training.

Figure 9-4:    **Company Vision**

| |
|---|
| 1. We place customers first. |
| 2. We will maintain profitability of the businesses we are in. |
| 3. We will use our core competencies to develop new revenue sources. |
| 4. We employ committed, competent people. |
| 5. We will be the low cost provider of energy. |

Now consider the list of objectives below from a hypothetical management development course. Which of the objectives agree with this company's values, which disagree and which are irrelevant? Those which agree with company values are the best candidates for planning a management training program.

Figure 9-5:    *Objectives of Management Development Training*

| | |
|---|---|
| Irrelevant | 1. To successfully manage relations with one's boss. |
| Disagree | 2. To reduce absenteeism. |
| Irrelevant | 3. To make important decisions as part of a team. |
| Irrelevant | 4. To respect the diversity of subordinates. |
| Agree | 5. To reduce the cost of customer operations below the industry average. |

| | |
|---|---|
| Agree and | 6. To make work assignments that improve productivity efficiency. |
| Disagree | 7. To provide the best benefits and salaries in the industry. |
| Agree | 8. To solve major cost, quality and productivity problems within one's department. |
| Agree | 9. To empower employees to make decisions at the lowest possible level. |
| Agree | 10. To document and terminate employees who are not making a productive contribution to the organization. |

From this exercise, we can see that the objectives that emphasize efficiency, productivity, cost control and empowerment have the greatest congruence with the company's values, while those emphasizing higher costs in the form of salaries and benefits and employee problems like absenteeism contradict company values. Finally, several objectives related to teamwork, diversity and management-employee relations are irrelevant to the company's values.

### Summary

If training is to have the desired outcomes, we must write clear and measurable training objectives. We start by analyzing the tasks of a job and describing these as behaviors. The behaviors become the sources for writing training objectives. A training objective has four components: target behavior, content, conditions and standards.

Individual learning objectives are typically arranged in a hierarchy when combined with other objectives. The hierarchy consists of prerequisites, enabling objectives and terminal objectives. It is important to sequence objectives properly in order to facilitate learning. Finally, objectives should be screened against key organizational strategies and values to be certain that they are congruent with the overall mission of the organization. Objectives which clash with prevailing values and mores are unlikely to be achieved without first changing the underlying cultural norms.

# Discussion Questions
# And Exercises

1. Examine the list of training objectives for a first-line supervisory financial training program and determine the hierarchy among them by assigning a level to each objective.
   Use the following scale: **P = prerequisite   E = Enabling   T = Terminal   PF = Performance   R = Results**
   ___ Interpret monthly budget reports.
   ___ Inform employees of key budgetary issues.
   ___ Produce high-quality, low cost products for customers.

    \_\_\_\_ Read a company budget report.

    \_\_\_\_ Manage department budgets within 5 percent of plan.

2. Consider the list of Management Development Training Objectives in Table 9-5. in light of your organization's culture and strategy. Which objectives agree and with your organization's vision and which disagree? Which are irrelevant?

**Case Study: Objectives for a Basic Skills Program**

    A resort hotel is considering starting a basic skills program for its housekeeping, food service and maintenance staff, many of whom are immigrants who speak limited English and have an average educational level of about 9 years. The employees need to be able to communicate orally with customers, to be able to read job instructions and safety information and to be able to write simple notes and memos to customers and management. They also need to be able to do simple arithmetic, such as calculating the number of amenities to place in each room and totaling mini-bar tabs.

    Write out a list of the terminal and enabling objectives for a basic skills training program. Which skills would be prerequisite, if any? What would be the performance and results objectives of this training?

# Chapter Ten :
# Training Deliverables and Instructional Strategies

While objectives guide the instructional designer, the client who sponsors and pays for the work is typically more interested in deliverables. This chapter will describe the kinds of deliverables that designers typically create, including: lessons, modules, courses, programs, curricula, self-study, performance support and structured on-the-job training (OJT). It will also introduce all the myriad ways in which training is being delivered to learners and the important considerations when working with electronic or other technological delivery systems. Finally, we will consider the range of instructional methods available to trainers and how these can be translated into deliverables.

### What is a Training Deliverable?

A training deliverable may be defined as any end-product of an instructional design process. The deliverable is what the client is paying for and what the learner receives. Deliverables may take many forms. In the broadest sense, a course, workshop or seminar is a typical training deliverable. These are often further sub-divided into components, such as workbooks, manuals, lesson plans, overheads, audio-visuals, tests, etc.

Defining the deliverables is one of the first steps in designing a new training program, and often involves negotiations between the designer and the client. With the advent of technology-based learning, the range of deliverables has increased greatly, resulting in a much more complicated set of choices than in the past.

### Examples of Training Deliverables

Years ago, training deliverables were invariably print-based: textbooks, workbooks, written exercises, tests, etc. Today, the range of deliverables has expanded to video, audio, overheads, computer-based training, multimedia, Internet, and virtual reality simulations. The array of choices can cause confusion for both designers and their clients. Quite often, a client will request training without a clear idea of how it might be delivered. It is up to the instructional designer to help the client sort through the many choices available, examine the trade-offs and select deliverables that are most likely to facilitate learning while accommodating the many restraining factors at work in most organizations.

As an example of the complexity of choices available today, let's consider a hypothetical example of a request for training to support a new customer service call center that a large financial institution is planning to open in a year. The client authorizes a needs assessment which discovers that the 200 newly-hired employees who will staff the call center will need extensive training in customer service, telephone techniques, conflict resolution, problem-solving, computer software, telephone system operations, product knowledge and the company's policies and procedures.

Given the large amount of training to be conducted and the fact that it all must be designed and delivered within a year, the instructional design team assigned to work on this project begins to consider the various deliver options available. First, they classify the training needs by type:

| | |
|---|---|
| **Communications Skills:** | **Business Skills:** |
| Customer Service | Policies and Procedures |
| Telephone Techniques | Product Knowledge |
| Conflict Resolution | **Technical Skills:** |
| **Analytical Skills:** | Computer Software |
| Problem Solving | Telephone Operations |

Next, they consider the various delivery options suited to each of these four skill areas. Communication skills, since they require human interaction, would be good candidates for classroom learning involving small groups of 10-20 to allow maximum interaction among learners. Instructional strategies for these skills would include role plays, case studies, and videos. Thus, the deliverables for communication skills training might include:

- A Participant Workbook
- Color Overheads
- An Instructor's Guide
- Role Plays
- A Case Study on Customer Service
- A Written Quiz (Final Exam)
- A Video on Conflict Resolution

Once these deliverables have been defined and approved by the client, the designer would then turn to defining the content for the training and estimating the time required to learn it. The time estimate would then help to determine how long the workbook needs to be and how many role plays, case studies, videos and overheads will be needed.

Let's turn now to the next skill area—analytical problem solving skills. Once again, problem solving is a skill involving human interaction, especially as practiced in a call center, so this skill lends itself best to classroom training. Like the communications training described above, the problem solving course would need a similar set of materials, with extensive use of case studies and role plays of typical customer problems that call center employees will be asked to resolve.

The business skills portion of the call center training covers industry knowledge of financial products and company knowledge of policies and procedures affecting customers. Since this kind of knowledge is contained primarily in reference manuals and books and it is largely used as background information, a self-study approach to learning these skills would work well. The designers could develop a self-study workbook to guide learners through the existing product and policy materials, and include exercises and quizzes to check for understanding and also ensure that participants complete the self-study course successfully.

An innovative approach to delivering the policies and procedures knowledge that makes particular sense in a call center environment would be the use of on-line reference materials. The company's relevant customer policies and procedures could be put in digital format, loaded onto the call center's server and made available to each employee at their desktop. This might be done in a simple Windows help file, searchable by key words and topics, or via a company Intranet and Web browser, where hypertext and other interactive features of the World Wide Web could be employed. If this kind of on-line reference were combined with an initial self-study course on the material, then employees would be able to learn the foundation concepts without having to memorize the details, since these would be available whenever needed.

Finally, call center employees would need to learn a variety of technical skills, including the computer software running on the call center's PCs, and the use of the center's interactive voice recognition telephone system. These technical skills would lend themselves ideally to computer-based training (CBT), since learners would be using PCs to learn these skills anyway. A well-designed tutorial could even be built into the call center's database software so that employees could learn at their desks at their own pace. For practice, a special training database, replicating the company's real customer database, could be provided to employees, who would then be able to simulate their work environment almost exactly. For employees who lack any PC skill, a brief classroom orientation should be enough to teach them some basic computer literacy. At that point, they would be ready to use the CBT at their desks.

Although the telephone systems could also be easily taught through CBT, the company might decide that what employees need to know to operate their telephones could be learned on-the-job. To ensure that this learning occurs in an efficient and effective manner, the instructional design team could create a structured on-the-job training course that supervisors or senior-level employees could easily deliver to small groups of employees or even one-on-one. The course would include a lesson plan, props, visuals, learner job aid and a learning evaluation.

Thus, in this example, we have seen how a single training project, involving the creation of a new call center, could productively employ a variety of delivery mechanisms and generate a equally diverse set of deliverables. Adding them all up, the instructional designers on this project would be responsible for the following deliverables:
1.  Two Participant Workbooks
2.  Two Instructor's Guides
3.  Role Plays
4.  Two Case Studies on Customer Service and Problem Solving
5.  A Video on Conflict Resolution
6.  A Video on Problem Solving

7. Color Overheads
8. Two Written Quizzes (Final Exams)
9. A Self-Study Workbook
10. A Computer-Based Training Program
11. An On-line Reference Program
12. A Structured On-the-Job Training Course

### *Estimating Training Deliverables*

Once you have defined the deliverables for a project, the client will naturally want to know how long it will take to design and develop these and how much it will all cost. Although the next chapter deals with budgets and schedules in detail, the building blocks of an instructional design budget are the estimates for how many deliverables are needed and how long each of these will be. In this section, we will look at two common estimating techniques, one based on time to design and the other based on the amount to be designed.

### Time-Based Estimates

One of the most commonly used techniques requires estimating how long it will take to design and develop an hour of instruction. This is usually expressed as a ratio. For example, a common industry rule of thumb for print-based classroom training is 30 hours of design and development time for each hour of instruction, or a 30:1 ratio. If this ratio is applied to a one-day workshop, it would yield a design and development time estimate of 240 hours (or 30 days) of labor required to complete a one-day course.

The time ratio method is easy to use and makes sense to both designers and clients, but it is fraught with inaccuracy. A recent study published by the American Society for Training and Development's Benchmarking Forum reported average design to delivery ratios ranging from as little as 2:1 to as much as 100:1 for classroom training. With such a huge range, picking any one ratio as a fixed standard is impossible. Part of the problem with these reports is that people do not all include the same things in the estimates. Some people count only design time, some only development time while others include both design and development, plus needs assessment time. It is well-known that needs assessments can take as long as the design and development phase combined for a large, complex project. Because of the tremendous variability in needs assessment time requirements, I believe it is better to leave that phase out of the design and development estimate. In many years of practice, I have observed that design and development time typically runs in the range of 10-30 hours per hour of classroom instruction.

For computer-based, video-based or other media-based training designs, the time estimates escalate dramatically to cover the amount of time required to shoot and edit video, create and scan graphics, create storyboards, add music and sound effects, voice-over narration and assemble all these elements into an interactive learning program. Even though the advent of advanced computer-based training authoring software now allows non-programmers to create CBT and multimedia, the time required to master these complex programs, and debug quirky computer glitches can be daunting. The ASTD Benchmarking Forum reported a very wide range of design and development time estimates for CBT and multimedia, ranging from a low of about 50:1 to as high as 500:1. Like print media, a great deal of this variance is explained by the different ways that people calculate design time and what they include in their estimates, but the medium itself is also a key variable, as well as the goals of the training.

Below are a few of the most common time variables for CBT/Multimedia:

- the more interaction designed into the program, the longer it will take
- the more multimedia elements designed into the program, the longer it will take
- the more original content that has to be created, as opposed to reusing libraries of existing content, the longer it will take
- the larger the project and the more specialists that need to be involved, the longer it will take
- the more expensive and difficult the hardware and software platforms are, the longer it will take
- the more extensive the training recordkeeping and reporting requirements are, the longer it will take
- the more individualized the program is, the longer it will take

The best estimating technique is to rely on past experience as a guideline. If you have previously designed and developed one-day management workshops in 25 days or 10-hour multimedia programs in 90 days, then chances are good you can do it again in that time, unless special circumstances intervene. Among the special circumstances to watch out for are the following:

- brand new or highly complex content will take longer to design
- technical content generally takes longer than non-technical, all other things being equal
- lack of subject matter experts or difficulty contacting them will add time
- elaborate desktop publishing or multimedia requirements, like color manuals, full-motion video or original graphics, adds time
- for trainer-led instruction, inexperienced trainers need more direction than experienced ones, resulting in a more detailed leader's guide
- a highly diverse audience requires more design time than a more homogenous one, and novices always require more time to design for than experts
- experienced designers require less time than inexperienced ones, and those with past experience that closely resembles the present design project will be the fastest, all other things being equal

Of course, if you don't have relevant experience, you still have to come up with an estimate. So the table below presents some general rules of thumb regarding time-based estimates.

*Table 10-1:   Rule of Thumb Guidelines for Estimating Design and Development Time*

| Design Element | Content Type | Design Time Ratio |
|---|---|---|
| Participant Manual | familiar, non-technical | 3:1 |
| Participant Manual | unfamiliar, technical | 5:1 |
| Leader's Guide | familiar, non-technical | 2:1 |
| Leader's Guide | unfamiliar, technical | 4:1 |
| Visuals/ overheads | simple, text-based | 1:1 |
| Visuals/ overheads | complex, graphic-based | 5:1 |
| Videos | simple, voice-over, 1 location | 50:1 |
| Videos | complex, live audio, many scenes/locations | 150:1 |
| CBT | simple, text-based | 50:1 |
| CBT | complex, graphic-based | 300:1 |
| Multimedia | simple, graphic-based | 150:1 |
| Multimedia | complex, video-based | 600:1 |

## Training Deliverables and Instructional Strategies

You saw earlier in this chapter that a great variety of deliverables are used these days in implementing training. Although the choices can be bewildering at times, they should be based on a systematic approach to instruction. In order to match instructional strategies with effective deliverables, it is important to understand the types of strategies available and the best delivery channels for each strategy.

To begin with, it is important to understand how learning occurs in a classroom or other formal setting. Many researchers have pointed out that people learn differently in a formal setting than they do when left to their own devices (Schank, 1990). Left on our own, most of us engage in a process of trial and error, in which we begin to experience the thing we want to learn about directly, review the errors we make and then revise and try again until we get it right. This is the way people learn to play sports like golf or tennis, to sew, to repair houses, to use PCs and many other everyday things.

When in a classroom, however, the learning process changes, due primarily to the presence of an instructor, who is responsible for facilitating the learning of others and to whom learners cede some control over the learning process. The environment in which classroom learning takes place is another key difference, since it is generally a place separate from the real world in which learning will be applied. Finally, centuries of educational tradition weigh heavily on classrooms and influence people's behavior in them.

At its core, formal learning environments have four key elements at work, as the illustration below shows:

*Figure 10-2:*

## *Interaction of Four Key Training Elements*

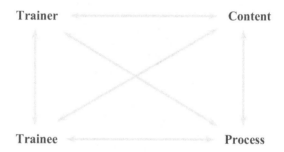

As the graphic shows, the four elements—trainer, learner, content and process—create 12 distinct interactions, each of which is occurring simultaneously as the training proceeds. No wonder good trainers are in demand. It is no simple thing, outward appearances notwithstanding, to successfully manage so many interactions at once, especially while standing before an audience.

Of the four elements, the one that is closest to instructional strategy is the process of learning, for it is with this process that instructional theory is primarily concerned. But the process cannot be isolated from the content or the learners and trainer either. This is why educators have never been able to come up with a single 'best' instructional method that works in all cases. Instead, the process of instruction must be adapted to the other elements to produce the most ideal learning outcome possible under the conditions of learning presented to the designer.

### *Instructional Methods*

In examining process more closely, it helps to place instructional strategies on a continuum from active learning to passive, as the graphic below illustrates.

On the left side of the continuum are active learning strategies like trial and error and on-the-job learning that closely approximate the way most people learn naturally.  On the right side, are passive learning strategies like listening to lectures or reading books that were the hallmark *Figure 10-3:*

# The Learning Process

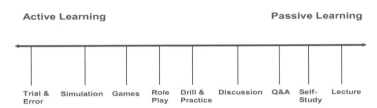

**Active Learning**                                    **Passive Learning**

Trial &   Simulation   Games   Role   Drill &   Discussion   Q&A   Self-   Lecture
Error                            Play   Practice                             Study

of traditional educational institutions (and still are the norm in far too many schools).  Along the continuum are a variety of other instructional methods that are commonly employed, including more passive methods like: lecture, self-study, and question and answer, and more active methods like: discussion, drill and practice, role play, games and simulations.

Two issues regarding instructional methods concern the designer. One is choosing the appropriate method to fit the objective of the training. The second is ensuring a variety of methods are employed throughout training to maintain learner interest and appeal to various learning styles. Regarding the first issue, it is critical to match methods appropriately to the learning objective in order to ensure learning occurs.  To understand this issue better, we should first consider the nature of most formal learning. This is summarized in the model below.

This model shows five major parts to any training lesson.  The first part is the orientation.  This is led by the instructor and typically covers the following topics:
1.   Introductions of class and instructor
2.   Learning objectives
3.   Orientation and overview of subject matter
4.   Reasons for learning the content
5.   Logistics of the training session

Other than class introductions, most of this material is best delivered by the instructor using lecture, since the instructor is typically the only person in the class who knows this information.  The lecture is often followed by a question and answer period to allow learners to clarify any of the information they have heard or to ask about things they haven't heard yet. Some of the topics, such as reasons for learning the content, may be addressed through discussion or small group activity.  In this case, the instructor facilitates a class discussion of these topics.

*Figure 10-4:*

## Formal Learning Model

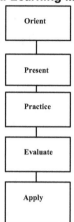

After the introduction comes the main body of the lesson, which is further sub-divided into three parts: presentation, practice and evaluation. Each of these parts will likely have its own instructional method. Presentation typically involves the instructor demonstrating how to perform the skills being taught, or using a video tape or other visual aid to demonstrate the skills. It also requires the instructor to explain how the skill is performed, including tips and techniques to make it easier for learners to master the skills. The practice step requires learners to try the skill themselves in some controlled practice setting, so they can begin to build competency and fluency in performing the skill. Finally, the evaluation step involves the instructor posing questions to learners to determine if they understand presentation and practice they have just experienced. These questions may be posed orally or in writing. Feedback on the practice session should concentrate on reinforcing what learners did well and correcting mistakes with constructive suggestions for improvement.

The table below gives some suggested instructional methods that may be used with each step of the body of a lesson.

The conclusion of a training lesson generally consists of a summary of what was presented, a transition to the next topic or course, and advice on how to apply what was learned on-the-job. Much of this is delivered by the instructor using lecture, like the introduction, but games and drill and practice can be used to get learners to summarize a lesson, while discussion or written exercises are often used to help learners identify how they will apply training on the job. Of course, the creative training designer often invents new instructional methods or variations of old ones to suit the unique needs of a particular training program. So, the suggestions presented here are simply a starting point for good instructional design.

*Table 10-5:*

| Lesson Step | Suggested Instructional Methods |
|---|---|
| Orientation | Small/large group icebreaker, lecture, reading Q&A, game, discussion |
| Presentation | Lecture, Video, Visual Aid, Case Study |
| Practice | Role Play, Drill and Practice (written/hands on), Game, Simulation, Discussion, Case Study, Test |
| Evaluation | Question and Answer, Small Group Activity, Drill and Practice (oral), Game |
| Application | Action planning, learning contract, follow-up survey, job aid, electronic performance support |

*Table 10-5: Lesson Steps and Instructional Methods*

### Summary

In this chapter, we have considered the issue of training deliverables and the related issue of choosing instructional methods that support various kinds of deliverables. We have also examined the range of deliverables that trainers create and some ways to estimate the amount of deliverables and the time required to create them.

In the next chapter, we will delve into training design schedules and budgets in detail, as part of the broader planning process for instructional design.

# Discussion Questions and Exercises

1.  Compare and contrast the following instructional methods. Think of an example of a good application for each method from your personal experience.
    Lecture vs. Self-study
    Discussion vs. Role play
    Simulation vs. Game
    Trial and Error vs. Practice drills

2.  Develop a list of deliverables and an estimated design time for the following training program:
    Three-day Leading Change Management workshop for 100 mid-managers to be facilitated by a core of 5 instructors. The client expects a workbook, an online reference guide, PowerPoint, video case study and pre and post-assessments.

**Deliverables**                                    **Time Estimate**

# Chapter Eleven :
# Training Design Budgets and Schedules

Instructional designers use resources to create training programs. Thus, they must concern themselves with managing these resources effectively, especially money and time. Clients want to know what training will cost them and when they can expect to receive finished product. So, like other business managers, training designers need to have effective budgeting and scheduling skills. This chapter will provide the rudiments of budgeting and scheduling training design projects, including special techniques used by experts to estimate costs and track time. In creating a work plan, it is easier to move from schedule to budget, since the costs will be dependent on how long the project will take. Thus, we will start with schedules first and then cover budgets.

### Training Design Schedules

Budgets and schedules go hand in hand, as each depends upon the other. If training costing methods are imprecise, then scheduling and planning are even more subject to whim. Often, it is the client who dictates the schedule, with the designer in a mad rush to make impossible deadlines. When Training has control of the schedule, it frequently slips, since self-imposed deadlines can easily be postponed. The most common complaint about instructional design is that it takes too long. In this day and age, everyone wants instant results. They don't want to be told that the training they need now won't be ready for another six months.

So, scheduling is a critical skill, especially for designers who act as project managers. Without realistic, but aggressive schedules, instructional design projects do take too long. With good scheduling and the planning that stands behind it, design projects can be brought in within deadline, leaving everyone with a better feeling about the whole process. The key to scheduling is to accurately predict the time it will take to complete each task, and then execute within that time. If you can get that right, the rest is just formatting.

The basics of scheduling start with a complete list of all the phases of the project. Typical design phases include:

- needs assessment
- task analysis
- learner analysis
- context analysis
- design
- development
- implementation
- evaluation

Next, within each of these major phases, develop a complete list of the tasks to be performed on the project, arranged in chronological order. Then, the critical part comes—estimate how long it will take to complete each task. In the next section, you will learn more about how to estimate the length of various tasks. Be sure that you allow time for reviews, vacations, holidays, illness and delays. These things happen on virtually every project. Give an additional contingency of 5-20%, depending on the complexity of the project and the number of unknowns. If you know who will be assigned to perform each task, indicate that information next to each task. You may know that a particular designer is going to be faster on a particular task because of similar recent experience, or that an intern assigned to the project is going to be slower, due to lack of experience.

## Time Estimation Techniques

In order to successfully manage schedules and budgets, time estimates must be accurate. This is one of the biggest challenges facing designers and trainers, since we have no agreed-upon standards for estimating training design and delivery times. The techniques that have been described in previous sections require assumptions about how much content needs to be developed, either as measured by the number of hours or days of instruction, or the amount of material needed. Both of these techniques have severe restrictions, but they are the best estimation techniques currently available. In this section, I will describe how time estimation techniques have been applied to a number of different training design projects. This practical guidance should help increase the accuracy of time estimation, but ultimately, designers need to come up with an estimation system based on their own experience and the nature of the project they are working on.

## Estimates Based on Hours of Instruction

The most common method to estimate design time is to base it on the amount of time the instruction will last. As mentioned in the last chapter, a common industry rule of thumb is that it takes roughly 30 hours of design and development time to create one hour of classroom training, and about 300 hours of design and development time to create one hour of computer-based training. These estimates are based on the experiences of hundreds of companies and thousands of designers, but as an average, they have a very wide range. I have personally worked on design projects that were assembled in as little as two hours per hour of instruction and also worked on some that took as much as 60 hours to develop an hour of classroom instruction. For computer-based training, the range is even wider, from as little as 20 hours to develop an hour of simple, text-based CBT to as much as 600 hours to develop a single hour of highly complex, multimedia-based training, complete with full motion video, color graphics, and an elaborate student interface and management system programmed from scratch.

With such a huge range, what is the designer to do? I recommend starting out with the average design time for the particular medium to be used, and then considering factors that might increase or decrease the design time.  In the table below, the major factors that increase or decrease design time are listed, along with some thumbnail guidelines for estimating their impact on the design schedule.

From this table, it is possible to extrapolate a range of design times that covers various contingencies and idiosyncrasies of specific projects.  If all of the factors that increase design time happened to be present on a given project, it might increase in length three or four times.  So, a typical day of classroom training that might be designed in one month, could take as long as three or four months, if the design required an extensive participant reference manual, a detailed Leaders' Guide, a video and a formal evaluation and if the client couldn't easily decide what he wanted.  On the other hand, the same day of classroom training could be developed in as little as a week, if the designer is also presenting the course, if a participant workbook can be easily produced using existing word processing software, if audio-visual materials are not required and if the client could clearly state the outcomes she seeks.

Although such a wide range may appear unsettling at first, once you have some experience with various types of projects, you will begin to develop a set of guidelines based on your own experience that can help to refine time estimates.  No matter how carefully you plan, though, remember that each training design project is unique.  Like offspring, each has its own personality and characteristics that cannot be fully predicted at the outset.  By basing estimates on a good system and maintaining excellent client relations, any schedule changes can be handled as they emerge.

As an example, consider the participant materials to be created for the fictional instructional design workshop discussed earlier in this chapter.  At a rate of 20 pages/ training hour, a total of 160 pages would be created for an eight-hour workshop.  Based on the preliminary budget estimate, the designer would need to write 40 pages per day or about 5 pages per hour in order to complete the participant manual within the allotted time.  This represents a fairly rapid writing pace, but it assumes that the design blueprint has already identified the content to be taught in some detail.

Of course, a designer can, with a little practice, develop his/her own time estimates based on actual experience in designing training programs.  With these actual time frames, a more reliable estimate will result.

### Training Design Budgets

Budgeting training design projects is still more of an art than a science.  Too many variables affect a given project to predict precisely how much it will cost at the outset.  A number of tools and techniques are available to aid designers in coming up with reasonable estimates, though, and in tracking actual costs versus projections once the project begins.

_Table 11-1:_      **_Factors Affecting Training Design Time_**

| Factors that Increase Design Time | | Factors that Decrease Design Time | |
| --- | --- | --- | --- |
| _Factor_ | _Impact_ | _Factor_ | _Impact_ |
| Needs Assessment must be completed as part of design project | Add 30-50% to the baseline estimate | Needs Assessment Completed Prior to Design/ Development | Reduce total design time by 30-50% |
| Need a Job Task Analysis as part of design project | Add 2-3 days per job analyzed | Job Task Analysis already completed prior to design | Subtract 2-3 days per job analyzed |
| Client has difficulty specifying training content and objectives | Add 2-5 days for multiple meetings and design reviews | Client has clearly specified what needs to be trained | Subtract 2-5 days from design review process, assuming a single design review meeting |
| Content is new, unknown or complex | Add 25-35% to the baseline estimate | Content is familiar and straight forward | Subtract 25-35% from the baseline estimate |
| Instructors need a detailed Leaders' Guide | Add 5-10 hours per hour of instruction | Instructors can teach from a lesson plan/ content outline | Subtract 5-10 hours per hour of instruction |
| Participants require a detailed reference manual (not just a workbook) | Add 5-10 hours per hour of instruction | Participants only need a workbook with major content points and class exercises | Subtract 5-10 hours per hour of instruction |
| Content requires a custom video | Add 50-100 hours per hour of video | No custom visuals or video is required | Subtract 5 hours per hour of instruction for no visuals and use baseline estimate for no video |
| Materials require extensive desktop publishing | Add 3-5 hours per hour of instruction | Materials can be produced with ordinary word processor | Use baseline estimate |
| Multiple instructors require a Train the Trainer course | Add 3-5 hours per hour of instruction | No formal Train the Trainer is needed | Use baseline estimate |
| Content must be substantially revised after pilot test | Add 3-5 hours per hour of instruction | Content does not require substantial revision | Use baseline estimate |
| Course requires testing | Add 5-10 hours per test | Course does not require any formal testing | Use baseline estimate |
| Course requires a formal evaluation | Add 10-15% to the baseline for evaluation | Course does not require a formal evaluation | Use baseline estimate |
| Computer-based training will run on new platform or use new authoring software | Add 25-35% to the baseline estimate, 35-50% if both are new | Computer-based training uses existing platform and authoring software | Reduce baseline estimate by 10-20% |

We need to consider two kinds of training budgets. The first is a preliminary budget that is usually prepared at the outset along with a proposal to provide training services. The second is a more detailed operating budget once a project has been approved and work has commenced. The purpose of the first budget is to give the client a general sense of what the project will cost and in some cases to require the designer to state a maximum cost for the project that will not be exceeded without renegotiating the contract between client and designer. The second budget is meant to guide the training design project and give the project manager a tool to monitor costs and project progress. We will consider each type of budget in the following section.

Table 11-2:     **Material Estimation Standards**

| Training Deliverable | Average Quantity Used in Typical Training Session |
|---|---|
| Participant Reading Materials | 20 pages/hour |
| Lesson Plans/Lecture Notes | 15 pages/hour |
| Overheads/Flip Charts | 10/hour |
| Audio Script | 1.5 pages text/minute of audio |
| Video Script | 2 pages text/minute of video |
| Graphics/Artwork | 10/hour |

### Preliminary Proposal Budgets

A proposal to design training invariably requires an estimated budget. This gives both the designer and the client information about the likely overall cost of the project and the major factors contributing to the cost. Except in fixed price competitive bidding situations, the preliminary budget is meant to be just that—a rough estimate of what the project will likely cost, but not a detailed budget plan.

To prepare a preliminary budget, several assumptions must be made about the proposed project. One key assumption is the amount of training that is likely to be required, usually stated in number of days or hours of training. This information should be based on the training needs assessment. If a preliminary budget is required prior to completion of the needs assessment, care must be taken to base it on very conservative assumptions, so as not to underestimate the possible costs. A second approach is to prepare a budget that has a range of costs, including a low, midpoint and high end, depending on various contingencies. For example, if a designer were asked to bid a training project for a custom workshop on stress management, one key assumption would be the length of the workshop. If the client and the designer are uncertain about the required length, the designer might prepare three cost estimates: one for a brief half-day workshop, one for a full day and one for a two-day workshop. In this way, the client can see the range of options available and the designer protects against the possibility of under or overestimating the job.

Once the length of the training has been estimated, the next step in creating a preliminary budget is to list the resources needed to complete the project and the estimated cost of these resources. Typical training design resources are listed below:

1. Labor Costs
   - Professional labor
   - Contract labor
   - Administrative labor
2. Non-labor Costs
   - Graphics/Overheads
   - Publishing and Printing
   - Video/Audio
   - Software
   - Travel and Shipping
   - Office Supplies
   - Overhead Expenses (telephone, fax, utilities, office space)

Once all the cost elements of a project have been identified, the next step is to estimate the rate and duration of each cost element. It helps at this point to break the project down into its component parts, such as:

- needs assessment
- task analysis
- design blueprint
- material development
- training delivery
- evaluation

Once the components have been identified, you are ready to calculate costs. For labor, use actual or projected hourly rates and multiply these times the likely duration of each component of the project. For example, if professional designers are paid an average of $50.00 per hour and their time will be required for approximately 50 hours of materials development, the estimated budget for professional labor on that component would be $2,500. Likewise, the estimated labor rates and duration for any contract labor and for administrative labor should be calculated. By summing up all the labor components, you will arrive at an overall labor budget.

For non-labor items like publishing, it may be possible to obtain quotes from printers based on estimates of material length. If such quotes are unavailable, a second approach is discussed below under cost estimation techniques. It is based on estimating the number of non-labor items needed and the approximate time required to create them.

After the labor and non-labor cost items have been identified and estimated, it is wise to build in a contingency fee of 10-20 percent to cover the unknowns. For a standard project where most assumptions can be verified,

*Table 11-3:* **Sample Preliminary Proposal Budget**

| Step | Deliverable | Time Estimate | Rate | Total |
|------|-------------|---------------|------|-------|
| 1 | interview subject matter expert and examine existing documents and articles to gain an understanding of the required content of the workshop | 2 days | $500/day | $1000 |
| 2 | design a workshop blueprint that includes: objectives, content outline, instructional strategies and learning activities. | 2 days | $500/day | $1000 |
| 3 | develop participant materials using Powerpoint based on a revised design blueprint | 6 days | $500/day | $3000 |
| 4 | develop overheads and a lesson plan based on the design document | 2 days | $500/day | $1000 |
| 5 | deliver the six-hour workshop up to 12 times per year at public sessions and conferences | 12 days | $500/day + travel expenses | $6000 |
| 6 | evaluate the workshop based on:<br>• participant reactions<br>• participant learning<br>• on-the-job usefulness<br>• business results | 2 days | $500/day | $1000 |
| | **GRAND TOTAL** | 26 days | | $13,000 |

a smaller contingency percentage is warranted. For large projects, or those with many unknown variables, a contingency of 20 percent is not unreasonable.

The budget above is an example of a budget proposal to design and deliver a one-day training program on instructional design.

This budget provides sufficient detail to let the client know how much the project will cost, while still allowing for flexibility. A 10 percent contingency fee is already calculated into the totals. If you don't care to share with the client your actual per diem rates, that column can be eliminated from the budget that is shared with the client. It is best to avoid simply giving an overall cost estimate, though, since this may not appear credible to the client who has no way of knowing what cost components it contains.

### Final Working Budget

Once a proposal has been accepted, a final project budget should be prepared to help track expenses throughout the life of the project. Although the final budget should be based on the preliminary one, it will be more detailed so as to help the project manager monitor expenses and ensure the project is completed within budget and schedule.

Some excellent software tools are available to help manage large-scale design projects. These typically allow the user to enter all the project tasks, estimate their length, calculate the labor costs based on hourly or daily rates and factor in other expenses as needed. If these tools are unavailable, a simple spreadsheet can accomplish the same purpose. The example below shows the kind of information to be included. It is based on step three of the preliminary budget presented above.

*Table 11-4:* **Final Working Budget**

| Task # | Task Name | Dura-tion | Start | Finish | Resource Name | Rate | Total Cost |
|---|---|---|---|---|---|---|---|
| 3.1 | Participant Manual - 1st draft | 4 days | 5/4 | 5/5 | Designer | 480 / day | $1920 |
| 3.2 | Participant Manual - edit draft | 1 day | 5/11 | 5/11 | Designer | 480 / day | $480 |
| 3.3 | Participant Manual- Desktop Publish | 1 day | 5/12 | 5/12 | Desktop Publisher | 320 / day | $320 |
| Total | | 6 days | | | | | $2720 |

Notice that this final budget includes actual costs based on the individual resources employed and also includes actual days worked, based on the project schedule. This budget can be used to track progress and determine if the project is staying on schedule and within budget. Additional columns for actual costs and time can be added to help track and monitor a project at even finer levels of detail.

### Accelerating Training Design

The next thing to consider is which tasks can be done concurrently. The more tasks you perform simultaneously, the shorter the schedule becomes. Concurrent design has been used successfully in engineering to cut design times by 200% or more. For training designs, the most frequent form of concurrent design is to assign two or more designers to develop materials concurrently, thus shortening development time, typically the longest in the instructional design cycle. If more than one medium is being used, having all media developed concurrently saves considerable time, too.

A riskier approach, but one that potentially speeds design time even more, is to begin development while the design phase is still being worked on. This is typically done through use of rapid prototyping, a technique involving the quick creation of a model of the training program that can be tried out with a few learners, and the evaluation feedback then used to make corrections and launch development. This approach is particularly valuable in computer-based training, where story boards and design templates can be used to sketch out the content of training rapidly. Once client feedback is obtained, initial development often commences while the design phase is still being wrapped up. A more radical approach is to begin design and development before the needs assessment is completed. In this case, partial data from the needs assessment is immediately moved to design, while waiting for additional data to be gathered and analyzed. This approach involves the greatest risk, because preliminary data may be proven completely wrong by later analysis.

An example of the latter approach is a training needs assessment of the basic skills needs of a company's hourly workforce. The initial needs assessment identified a significant percentage of the workforce that lacked the necessary basic skills to perform their jobs. Armed with this information, the company decided to move ahead with on-site English as a Second Language classes for its lowest-performing immigrant workers, even while a job task analysis was being completed on all of the affected jobs. This allowed the company to accelerate its plan to address the problem, while a more comprehensive custom-designed training program was being developed. Once it was ready, the workers who had attended ESL classes had developed enough foundation skills in English to be able to benefit from the workplace literacy curriculum that was eventually developed for all hourly workers.

None of the techniques for accelerating training design come without their perils. Any time designers break from the chronological order of things, they risk going off in the wrong direction and wasting effort. Those who have experience with concurrent design and rapid prototyping agree that three essential conditions should be present before trying these techniques. First, course strategies, formats and structure must be clearly specified and agreed upon by all working on the project, to avoid a Tower of Babel syndrome. Second, designers working in parallel must maintain close communications, particularly with regards to changes to the course structure, content or project direction. Teamwork is an essential ingredient of success. Finally, excellent project management is critical to ensure barriers are mitigated, resources are available when needed, schedules are monitored and team members are informed about the status of the project and the work of colleagues (Overfield, 1994).

Many good project management software packages now exist to assist the design project manager plan and schedule projects. With software, tasks can be linked to specific resources, schedules can be automatically generated, and costs can be tracked against the budget. They also produce beautiful Gantt charts, graphs, PERT charts and other useful tools to help manage projects. But don't be lulled into thinking the software can do the scheduling for you. It cannot. Project management software is only as good as the person using it. Make sure that the time assumptions you enter into the program are realistic and complete. And keep the data in the software up-to-date in order to monitor the project accurately.

*Summary*

In this chapter, we have looked at the elements of budgeting and scheduling design projects. In the budgeting area, we examined the various cost elements of training budgets, and described techniques to assemble a preliminary proposal budget and a final working budget. In the scheduling area, we discussed techniques for assembling a schedule, ways to cut design time and to use project management software to aid the process. We also presented advice on estimating time requirements for design projects, including the factors that increase and decrease design time.

In the next chapter, we will explore training design project management in greater detail.

# Discussion Questions and Exercises

1.  Describe your experience in estimating training schedules and budgets. Which techniques presented in this chapter would be most useful?

2.  What are the pitfalls and challenges of preparing preliminary budgets and schedules for clients? How can you minimize unpleasant surprises and develop feasible estimates?

### Case Study: Leading Change Management Workshop

Using the same case as Chapter 10, develop a preliminary schedule and budget for the following training design project: Three-day Leading Change Management workshop for 100 mid-managers to be facilitated by a core of 5 instructors. The client expects a workbook, an online reference guide, PowerPoint video case study and pre and post-assessments.

# Chapter Twelve :
# Training Project Management

Instructional designers work on projects of diverse scope, from one person efforts involving a single training lesson to massive design projects employing hundreds of people and thousands of hours of training design. Whenever projects become large, they require expert project management skills to keep them on budget and schedule and to meld the many people working on them into a coherent team. Designers acting as project managers must also work with clients to help them realize their business goals, with learners to ensure that instruction meets their needs and with a diverse range of professionals whose expertise may be needed to assist the instructional designer reach the clients' goals. This chapter gives the nuts and bolts of training project management, complete with examples of small and large-scale projects and a number of useful job aids to lead design projects.

### Basic Elements of Project Management

Although instructional design projects have special characteristics, the basics of project management do not differ significantly from other types of projects. Good project managers, regardless of their area of expertise, must manage three elements successfully to complete a project. These are known as the project management triangle, as illustrated below:

*Figure 12-1:*

## *Project Management Triangle*

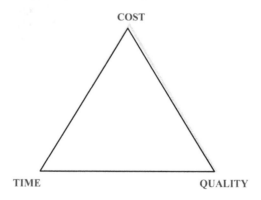

The triumvirate of time, cost and quality sometimes appear to be at odds. A common saying in design projects is that you can have any two of the three, but not all three at once. This may be too cynical a view, but it does reinforce the notion that project management is a matter of trade-offs. You typically can't simultaneously achieve the lowest possible cost, the shortest possible time and the highest possible quality in a single design project. Thus, it is critical to know which of these elements matters most to the client paying for the project, so that it may be emphasized.

### Role of the Project Manager

The Project Manager is crucial to the success of projects, since the main reason projects fail is poor management. Project Managers are typically responsible for five aspects of the project:

1. Planning
2. Organizing
3. Staffing
4. Directing
5. Controlling

Each of these elements will be described in this section.

Planning occupies the first phase of a project. As we saw in the last chapter, an important element of planning is estimating the budget and schedule for the project. Another key area of planning is matching the project's goals with the overall corporate or organizational goals that the design project has been asked to achieve. Finally, project plans must be communicated to various stakeholders, clients and project members so that they clearly understand the project's purpose, rationale and scope. Because of the limited time frame that most design projects exist, careful planning up front is essential to getting the project off to a fast start and keeping it on track.

Organizing a project refers to grouping and arranging resources needed by the project. Among the resources that all design projects use are:

- time
- money
- space
- people

Additionally, some design projects require material resources, equipment and other specialized items.

We have already discussed the issues involved in organizing the costs and schedules for projects. The personnel required for a project is another key resource to be considered. Most projects have dedicated personnel assigned to them, but some must get by with part-time staff who also continue to perform the other duties of their regular jobs. Space requirements of projects include work areas for staff, meeting rooms, storage space, and equipment space. If work is to be conducted in field locations, then travel and portable equipment expenses must be accounted for in the budget. Projects may also require their own equipment, such as computers, work samples, training props, communications equipment, etc.

To ensure that all aspects of the project are properly managed, it is important to set project objectives early on. The objectives should clearly state the goals of the project in measurable terms. For example, if a goal of a design project is to produce a three-day management seminar on teambuilding, then the objectives of the project might include:

- Design a content outline for the seminar within two weeks.
- Design a course blueprint for the seminar within one week.
- Develop a participant guide for the seminar within one month.
- Develop a leader's guide for the seminar within two weeks.
- Develop an evaluation plan for the seminar within one week.

Each of these objectives is associated with a major task of the project, and can be monitored against plan to determine if it has been achieved or not.

The next management function is staffing. This refers to hiring, training and utilizing human resources to achieve the work of the project. Two types of staffing organizations are used in design projects: task organization and matrix organization. A task organization assumes that the project exists separate from the normal functional organization and that people are dedicated to the project and assigned a specific set of tasks to achieve. In a matrix organization, the project members continue to perform their regular duties while working on the project. They are thus held accountable by both the project manager and their line manager. Although the matrix approach allows for dual utilization of resources and creates a balance between the project and the on-going functions of the organization, it can also lead to conflict between project and functional managers and a heavy burden on project staff's time.

The heart of project management is directing the day to day operation of the project once it begins. Directing includes monitoring schedules and budgets to ensure the project stays on track, making decisions and troubleshooting problems as they emerge. Though this work is similar to any management position, the project manager often lacks formal authority and must rely on expert or referent authority, as well as persuasion, to direct a project successfully.

Controlling refers to actions that ensure the project meets its goals. One key requirement for project control is to receive regular and accurate feedback about how the project is progressing. A second challenge is coordinating the work of various staff members so that the project stays on schedule and members know what others are doing on the project. When something goes amiss, the project manager must quickly intervene and take corrective action to get the project back on track.

### Results-Based Project Management

Since the purpose of design projects is to create training that gets business results, it is important to keep the results of the project in mind at all times and to monitor the project against its objectives regularly. One useful tool for doing this is the Integrated Project Planning and Management Cycle, a project management system developed by the East-West Center in Hawaii to manage international education and human resource projects (Goodman & Love, 1980). As the chart on the next page shows, the Project Cycle consists of four phases:
1. Planning
2. Activation
3. Operation
4. Evaluation

*Figure 12-2:*

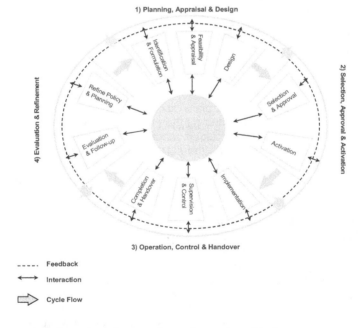

## Integrated Project Planning & Management Cycle

The planning phase has three major tasks assigned to it:
1. Identification and Formulation
2. Feasibility Analysis and Appraisal
3. Design

The identification and formulation task involves the assessment of training needs, and the development of a project proposal to meet those needs. The feasibility and appraisal task includes determining if it is possible and desirable to create a project to address the training needs. It also covers an examination of whether the project can meet its goals, and the various strategies available to address the identified need. The design phase includes a complete project design blueprint, with budget, schedule, training objectives, training deliverables, and project objectives.

Once the planning phase is complete, the project moves to the activation phase, during which work commences on the project. The activation phase has two primary tasks: selection and approval and activation. The first task includes gaining final approval of the project design from the client, including selection of the best alternative, if a competitive bid process is employed. Once approval has been given, the activation task includes the following activities which give the project life:

- funding a budget for the project
- establishing work schedules
- recruiting and assigning staff
- creating a project organization
- creating policies and procedures for the project

Once all of the above are in place, the project moves to the operation phase. This includes three primary tasks:

1. Implementation
2. Supervision and Control
3. Completion and Handover

During the implementation task, design and development work begins in earnest, following the plans approved earlier. The supervision and control task is one performed by the project manager throughout this phase. The main purpose of project management controls is to ensure that activities occur in conformity with the plan and schedule, and that prompt corrective action is taken if the project deviates from plans. The final task is project completion. As the project winds down, project resources are released or reassigned to other work, and project deliverables are handed over to whoever will be implementing the training. Sometimes a formal handover to another department, agency or organization is required; sometimes training designers are responsible for the entire project, through delivery and final evaluation. If a handover will occur, it must be planned carefully to ensure a smooth transition.

Since the operation phase is typically the longest of the four phases, it requires the greatest effort and attention of the project manager. To manage this phase, a number of techniques and tools may be used. One of the most popular is the Gantt Chart, which displays project tasks and the time allotted to complete them in graphical form using horizontal bars. The example below is a Gantt Chart for a typical training design project.

To prepare a Gantt Chart, first develop a list of all the project tasks. Then, sequence the tasks in the order they will occur and estimate the time required to complete each one. For each task, a bar should extend from the starting date to the ending date. Completion of important tasks should be listed as project milestones.

*Figure 12-3:*

# Sample Gantt Chart

| Task | Jan | | | | Feb | | | | Mar | | | |
|------|---|---|---|---|---|---|---|---|---|---|---|---|
| | 1 | 2 | 3 | 4 | 1 | 2 | 3 | 4 | 1 | 2 | 3 | 4 |
| Needs Analysis | ██ | ██ | ██ | | | | | | | | | |
| Training Design | | | | | ██ | ██ | ██ | | | | | |
| Registration/ Logistics | | | | | | | | | | | | ██ |
| Design Blueprint | | | | | ██ | ██ | ██ | | | | | |
| Materials Development | | | | | | | | | ██ | ██ | ██ | |
| Client Approval | | | | | | | | | ██ | ██ | ██ | |
| Train the Trainer | | | | | | | | | | | | ██ |

As we learned in the last chapter, some tasks may occur concurrently. In that case, the two tasks will have overlapping bars. On the other hand, many tasks will be directly dependent on other earlier tasks. In that case, linking the two tasks ensures that the dependent task cannot begin until its predecessor has been completed.

Although the Gantt Chart is a widely used and helpful tool, other methods allow even greater precision in controlling projects. One of the most commonly used is the Critical Path Method (CPM) Chart, a project scheduling tool that shows the interrelationships among project tasks and the project's critical path, or minimum required time to completion.

To construct a CPM Chart, you would first identify all the activities and tasks associated with the project and arrange them in sequential order, much like you would prepare a Gantt chart. The next step is to prepare an arrow diagram, a chart which shows how the tasks of the project are connected or interrelated. Then, you would estimate the duration of each task, and calculate the total schedule time, including any float time (time that is not productively used by the project, such as waiting for approvals). Finally, you would establish and calculate the project's critical path by measuring the total time it will take to move through the tasks along the project's most direct, or critical path. The example below shows a CPM Chart for an instructional design project.

For projects that require a handover to another department, agency or company, it is important to plan for a smooth transition to minimize disruption and ensure the project will continue after handover.  To plan a smooth handover, follow these four steps:
1.  Prepare a completion and handover schedule
2.  Reassign project resources or develop a plan to sell/dispose of them
     *Figure 12-4:*

## CPM Chart for Train the Trainer Course

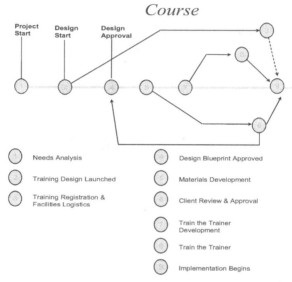

Project Start
Design Start
Design Approval

Needs Analysis
Training Design Launched
Training Registration & Facilities Logistics

Design Blueprint Approved
Materials Development
Client Review & Approval
Train the Trainer Development
Train the Trainer
Implementation Begins

3.  Develop a detailed plan to handover the project in conjunction with those who will be taking over the project
4.  Write a completion report which details the history and accomplishments of the project to date
     The final phase of the Integrated Project Planning and Management Cycle is Evaluation.  It covers two steps:
1.  Evaluation and Follow-Up
2.  Refinement of Policy & Process
     The evaluation of the project should actually be on-going.  This allows for formative evaluation as the project unfolds so that corrective action may be taken when needed.  The evaluation referred to in this section is the summative evaluation of the project's impact and results. The purposes of this evaluation are to determine whether the project met its objectives and to identify the business results it produced.
     To develop a summative evaluation of a training design project, it is useful to follow these steps:
1.  Review any previous formative evaluations of the project to date
2.  Establish the criteria for evaluating the project, including:

- Effectiveness—objectives achieved, business results obtained
- Efficiency—project costs and schedule versus plan, return on investment
- Significance—project's contribution to organization's strategic goals

3. Choose an appropriate evaluation design and methodology to conduct the evaluation
4. Prepare an evaluation report which discloses the results of the project, its strengths, weaknesses and shortcomings and deliver the report to key stakeholders

More information on evaluating training design projects can be found in Chapter 21 on evaluation later in this book.

Once the evaluation has been completed, the refinement step commences. During this step, the project should be examined again in light of its results and shortcomings to determine what refinements to the process and structure of the project would help participants manage future projects better. It is useful to look beyond the project itself to recommend any improvements that should be made to corporate policy and procedure to better support future design projects. If the project is to be handed over to another group, they should receive the evaluation report along with suggestions on how to refine the project based on the evaluation results.

## Summary

In this chapter, we have examined a model for managing training projects called the Integrated Project Planning and Management Cycle. We have discussed the four phases of project management in detail and given tips and examples regarding how to use the model to plan instructional design projects. Among the useful tools introduced in this chapter are project management software, Gantt and CPT charts, and budget and scheduling tools. In the next chapter, we will explore the role of design blueprints and prototypes in instructional design projects.

# Discussion Questions and Exercises

1. How would you work with a client to define priorities on a training design project using the project management triangle?
2. Which of the project management steps do you find the most difficult? Why?
3. Compare and contrast the Gantt chart and the CPM chart. What are the advantages and disadvantages of each?

### Case Study: Leading Change Management Workshop

Using the same case as Chapter 10, develop a preliminary Gantt chart and CPM chart of the following training design project:

Three-day Leading Change Management workshop for 100 mid-managers.

# Chapter Thirteen :
# Design Blueprints and Prototypes

The culmination of the design phase of the Instructional Systems Design model is the creation of a design blueprint, a detailed document that includes the objectives, the budget, the schedule, the project team, the proposed content, at least in skeleton form, and often a prototype of what the finished training program will look like. The concept of rapid prototyping, borrowed from engineering, allows instructional designers to get a tangible product in the hands of clients much faster than could be accomplished previously, and allows them to examine the product, clarify objectives and make changes prior to investing heavily in the development phase, where most of the resources are consumed. This chapter describes the elements of a good design blueprint and prototype, using examples to illustrate its utility.

### The Design Blueprint

The design phase of training is similar to the architectural phase of building. In both phases, the concepts and ideas that drive the project are given their first concrete form. In the case of building, the architect prepares a detailed drawing that will guide the contractor as he constructs the building. In the case of training, an analogous blueprint guides the development and implementation of the training vision originally defined by the needs analysis. The training blueprint, unlike its architectural namesake, is not a drawing or sketch of the final product, but rather a detailed set of specifications to guide development. It is an expanded course outline which gives the client and designers a clear picture of the overall course structure and content.

The critical elements of the training blueprint include the following:

- Summary of Needs Assessment Findings
- Course Objectives
- Prerequisites, if any
- Content Outline
- Presentation/Demonstration Methods
- Practice Activities
- Training Deliverables
- Assessment/Test Description
- Evaluation Plan

We have already discussed most of these elements in the preceding chapters. At this point, we simply assemble these elements in a package to be shared with clients, subject matter experts and other interested stakeholders. This gives them the opportunity to modify the structure and content before materials are developed. If the course content or structure must be changed to meet training needs, it is much easier and cheaper to do so with a blueprint than after the materials have already been drafted. Once materials have been drafted, they may still be edited and modified, but the cost of doing so escalates dramatically.

### Training Blueprint Examples

To see how the blueprint is constructed and used, we will examine examples of blueprint elements, taken from a fictional train the trainer course. The first part of the blueprint is a summary of the needs assessment findings, especially those related to job/task analysis, context analysis and learner analysis.

If a job/task analysis was conducted as part of the needs assessment, a summary of the findings helps to document where the content of the training is coming from and what knowledge and skill is necessary to perform the jobs and tasks under investigation. The Task Analysis Report below is an example of how the task analysis data can be summarized and presented as part of the blueprint.

---

*Figure 13-1:* **TASK ANALYSIS SUMMARY REPORT**

**JOB/COURSE:** Train the Trainer **FUNCTION/SECTION:** Trainer

**TASK/LESSON:** Training Design, Implementation and Evaluation

**PREREQUISITES:** Basic Presentation Skills

**EQUIPMENT AND MATERIALS:** Flip chart, overhead projector, Participant Manual, Leader's Guide

**REASONS:** New trainers need to know how to design and deliver effective training programs

**STANDARDS:** Participants must demonstrate mastery of the course by passing a knowledge test and presenting a mini-lesson. A passing score of at least 80 percent must be obtained on both written and performance tests.

**INITIATING EVENT:** Whenever a new trainer is hired or promoted into a training role, they must first successfully complete the Train the Trainer course before teaching on their own.

**TASK STEPS**
1. Determine need for training by conducting needs analysis and needs assessment.
2. Determine training content by conducting job/task analysis, learner analysis, and context analysis.
3. Write learning objectives.
4. Write design blueprint.
5. Gain client approval.
6. Develop learning materials.
7. Deliver training program.

---

8. Evaluate training program.

| Concepts/Principles: | Examples: |
|---|---|
| **Adult Learning Theory** | **Adults are self-directed learners** |
| **Instructional Systems Design Model** | **Analyze-Design-Develop-Implement-** |
| **Instructional Methods** | **Evaluate** |
| **Evaluation Methods** | **Leading discussions** |
| | **Measuring learning** |

As the example above shows, the task analysis provides the content and structure of the course. This information is valuable to include both in the design blueprint.

The remaining needs assessment data may be briefly summarized in the design blueprint. The Performance Analysis findings should be restated, especially those that indicate why training is needed. The Context Analysis information that is useful to include covers how the course will be implemented, including where it will be held, who will be presenting, and what equipment and materials will be used. The Learner Analysis information should cover how many people will be trained, their job titles, existing knowledge and skill and preferred learning styles. This background information will help clients see the rationale for the proposed training program.

Once the preliminary information has been summarized, the blueprint should then move into a detailed description of the course, starting with the proposed objectives. The following sample blueprint for a train the trainer course provides examples of the blueprint's major elements.

*Figure 13-2:* **Train the Trainer Design Blueprint**

| *Training Objectives Module (4 hours)* |
|---|
| **Objectives:** |
| 1. To describe the four components of a training objective. |
| 2. To write learning objectives for training programs. |
| |
| **Prerequisites:** |
| Complete Training Needs Assessment module. |
| |
| **Content:** |
| *Instructional Strategy:* |
| Present concept of a learning objective using lecture and demonstration. |
| Present principle of how to write an effective learning objective. |
| Analyze examples of effective and ineffective learning objectives. |
| Present principles for sequencing multiple learning objectives. |

*Key Points:*
The four components of a learning objective are: target behavior, content, conditions, standards. Learning objectives should be written from learners' point of view, and should use action verbs for behaviors and specific nouns for content. Conditions and standards are optional. An effective objective should clearly communicate what the learner will be able to do after instruction and should be measurable, so there is a way to know if learners have mastered them. Multiple objectives may be sequenced by classifying and ordering them as prerequisite, enabling or terminal objectives.

## Presentation:
*Deliver Method:*
Concepts and principles will be taught using interactive lecture and demonstration. Participants will read along in their manual and will be asked to analyze various examples of objectives to identify their components and determine whether they are effective or not.
*Media:*
Concepts and principles will be summarized on overheads. Examples will be presented in the student manual and presented on a flip chart/white board for class discussion.

## Practice:
*Classroom Exercises:*
Students will write sample objectives. Students will also identify problems with sample objectives and edit them to improve them.

## Tests:
Students will be asked to prepare the objectives for a training program they teach and turn these in for grading. They will also be required to take a final examination in the course, including questions about objectives. They must pass this test with 80% or better.

## Deliverables:
This module includes a participant manual, a leader's guide, and overheads. These three items will be developed, published and delivered prior to the start of instruction.

## Evaluation:
Students will be evaluated based on classroom participation, a homework assignment and their performance on the final exam. Those who successfully complete all the modules will receive a certificate. Those who do not will be allowed to retake the modules they need and try the exam again.

### Formative Evaluation and Gaining Client Approval

Once the design blueprint has been written and reviewed by the training team and/or designer, it should be presented to the client for review and approval. Two key issues emerge during blueprint reviews. The first is whether the proposed training will meet the needs of the client and the organization as specified in the needs assessment and original training proposal. If work has proceeded properly, with client input along the way, the training blueprint should address the training needs identified earlier. Sometimes things change, however, or the designers really didn't fully understand what the client wanted. This is a chance to review the fundamental purpose of the training and what it is likely to accomplish before investing heavily in development and implementation. Even if wholesale changes are needed, it is cheaper and easier to do them at the design stage rather than later on.

The second key issue is whether the proposed training is relevant to participants' jobs and will enable them to perform better. Here the focus is on questions like the following:

- Is the content accurate?
- Is the content in the right sequence?
- Is the content at the appropriate difficulty level?
- Are the examples realistic?
- Are the exercises and activities reflective of the participant's jobs and helpful in learning the skills?
- Are the objectives appropriate for the audience?

Answers to these questions will likely provide refinements to the training blueprint, but probably not necessitate radical changes. This type of detailed review is best left to subject matter experts who are in a position to judge the accuracy of the content and the congruence with the requirements of participants' jobs. Sponsoring managers will probably want to review the design document too, but their focus will be more on issues of overall relevance in addressing the business need they identified in the first place.

Thus, many design blueprint reviews require two audiences: the managers who are paying for the training and the subject matter experts who are able to judge the accuracy and relevance of the training content. Getting both parties to agree to the blueprint ensures that the design is ready to move forward into full-scale development.

If major changes are needed, then a second review round may be needed before final go ahead can be granted. In rare cases where the client will not approve a blueprint, despite efforts to address their criticisms, the training program typically gets canceled. Although that may seem to be a waste of resources and a great frustration to designers, it is far better to realize that a proposed training program is not going to reach its goals at this point, when something less than half, or even a third, of the total project resources have been spent, rather than find this out only after employees have been trained.

The process of fine-tuning a design until it is at its best is part of formative evaluation. This looks at ways to improve training processes and to apply principles of continuous improvement. Although formative evaluation is largely qualitative, three common techniques are used to gather formative evaluation at the blueprint stage:

1. Peer review (internal review by peers and others to provide constructive feedback)
2. Expert review (internal/external review of experts in the subject matter who provide constructive feedback)
3. Pilot test (try out of designs in their prototype stage, as described below)

## *Rapid Prototyping*

A technique that is increasingly popular, especially for multimedia and other costly training designs, is rapid prototyping. This means preparing rough drafts of training content quickly for the purpose of client reviews and learner input so as to accelerate development. Typically, content is formatted using a template, a shell or a storyboard so that the client can get a sense of what the training will look like without all the expense of adding graphics, color, management systems, leader's guides and the like. For print-based courses, the use of word processing templates allows content to be quickly written in a format similar to what the final product will be. Often, the prototype will consist of a single lesson as an example, with the design blueprint serving as the source for other module content. For computer-based training, the prototype may be a paper-based storyboard of the proposed computer screens with content sketched out, but other graphic, audio, video and interactive elements left out. An alternative approach is to create a prototype using existing computer-based training templates.

These prototypes can be reviewed along with the design blueprint and can actually be tried out with one or two learners to get a sense of whether they will work for the audience. Feedback can be quickly incorporated into the final design and help guide development. The use of rapid prototyping in design engineering has resulted in the reduction of design time by a large amount, on the order of 100-200 percent or even more. In instructional design projects, rapid prototyping saves time mainly on large-scale projects or those involving multimedia, where the development and production costs are very high.

The key to using rapid prototyping is to prepare materials only to the point where they can be tried out, but are still easily modified if changes are needed. Clients also need to understand that they are not viewing a finished product, but rather a work in progress, so that they have the right expectations about what they are reviewing.

### *Conclusion of Section Two: Grounding Training Design in Results*

To conclude this section of the book, let's look back at the results-based training model introduced at the beginning and see how the design phase can be grounded in business results. Recall that training results are of four basic types:

- learning
- performance
- financial health
- strategic growth

Of these, learning has been the traditional concern of trainers and certainly the driving concern behind the design phase. While it is crucial to ensure that the training design will facilitate participant learning of the knowledge and skills they need, this result alone no longer suffices.

Performance is the new mantra of training professionals. In the design phase, attention to job performance should be given in the design blueprint and any prototypes that are designed. If new job skills are being learned, it is important to show how the design will enhance acquisition of these skills, and how the training will simulate the job environment. If existing job skills are being enhanced, broadened, or improved, it is important to demonstrate how the new skills will be applied in the workplace and what performance results these will achieve or problems these will solve. Attention to transfer of skills to the job in the design phase helps to keep the training program targeted on performance and will help both participants and their managers see how the skills should be applied and reinforced to improve performance.

Financial results will not be known for certain at the design phase, but the designers should have a clear idea of which type of financial result they are aiming for: cost avoidance, cost reduction, revenue increase, or capital utilization. This information should be discovered during the needs analysis and summarized in the design blueprint to help clients remember why the training is being designed. For some training, it may be possible to identify at this point the baseline measurements that will be used to evaluate the financial impact of training. It may even be important to collect some of this information at this time so that comparisons can be made after the training has been implemented.

Finally, if a training program is planning to impact the strategic results of an organization, in terms of creating new products or services, improving customer service, opening new markets or streamlining operations, these proposed results should be identified in the design blueprint with a clear plan to evaluate them once the training has been implemented.

Once clients have had an opportunity to review the design blueprint, including the results to be achieved, they can make modifications or ask for clarifications that will enhance the likelihood of success. Even if the client simply endorses the blueprint as is, it provides a clear agreement to move forward with the training and builds anticipation for the proposed results.

# Discussion Questions and Exercises

1. What elements of a needs assessment should be included in the design blueprint?

2. Which design blueprint elements might be most difficult to obtain client approval for? Why?

3. How can you use formative evaluation techniques to improve design blueprints?

**Case Study: Design Blueprint**
Using a training topic you are working on (or using this chapter as a topic), develop a high-level design blueprint. Use Design tool eight in appendix two as a guideline.

# Section Three:
# Development

Though the training development phase is often lumped together with design, in fact it represents a distinct phase of the training design process with its own unique tasks and characteristics. Furthermore, it is quite common to have entirely different people working on the design and the development phase. For these reasons, it is treated as a separate section in this book. The development section will consist of four chapters: Drafting Materials, Developing Tests/Assessments, Quality Control and Full-scale Production.

### Materials Development Process

The development phase of training design is the time to roll up one's sleeves and begin to produce training materials in volume. It has all the hallmarks of a production environment—large volumes of material, intensive effort by many people, tight deadlines, and all too often, lots of stress for everyone involved. To get through this phase unscathed, it is essential to have a good plan of attack. This should start with a clear notion about the key components of the development phase. These are presented in the development model below.

*Figure 14-1:*

*Development Process Model*

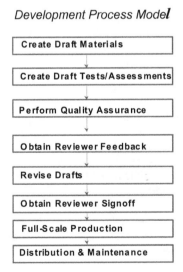

# Chapter Fourteen :
# Drafting Training Materials

Once the design blueprint and prototype have been reviewed and accepted, the development phase can begin. This is when training materials are created, along with any needed software, videos, props, audio-visual aids or supporting materials. Most development efforts begin with draft materials, which are then reviewed by subject matter experts and clients before moving on to full-scale production. It is particularly important for multimedia training designs to employ prototypes and draft materials because of the high cost of having to redo work that does not meet the clients' or learners' needs. This chapter will discuss the process of creating training materials of all types, and will present various scenarios for having this work done, including using instructional designers, subject matter experts, trainers or non-training professionals such as computer programmers and filmmakers.

### Creating Draft Materials

Drafting training materials is typically the longest, most labor-intensive phase of training design. To make the process more efficient, it is helpful to have a clear set of specifications, contained in the design blueprint, and a detailed task analysis or course outline. These guidelines will indicate what content is to be included and the learning process that will be employed during training.

The purpose of draft materials is to create a first-cut of what the final training product will look like. This can then be reviewed internally by the design team and the project manager for consistency with the blueprint, and by external clients and subject matter experts for content accuracy and job relevance. It is important that the draft materials contain all the content that will eventually appear in the training, including participant notes, exercises, activities, evaluations, audio-visuals, etc. Visuals may still be rough, but should clearly indicate what the final product will look like, so reviewers have the opportunity to judge the final product. Drafts do not have to go through extensive desktop publishing or other final production, since any changes that are required will only necessitate repeating this step again. Thus, draft materials should possess three characteristics:

- Easily and quickly produced
- Easily and quickly revised
- Same level of detail as the final product

Below we will consider some special issues regarding different types of media used in training.

### Print-Based Development

Since most training materials are still print-based, and writing is an act that takes considerable time, a number of techniques have been developed to speed the writing process. The most common is the use of templates, or pre-determined formats, for various kinds of material, most commonly participant guides and leader's guides. The widespread use of word processing software to produce training materials has led to the use of templates. These specify exactly how the finished product should look, from such key instructional decisions as what sections should be included and in what sequence, to the nitty-gritty details of what fonts, headings, headers, footers, page layouts and paper size should be used. The template should be developed by someone with expertise in the software to be used and then discussed with the design project team to ensure that all needed formats have been covered.

It is also helpful to provide a brief orientation to the use of the template, especially if a large number of designers will be using it. It is amazing how many different interpretations one can get from the same template. To be sure everyone is on the same page, provide a tutorial on the use of the template, complete with sample pages. This will ensure a more consistent final product. Once designers have begun working with a new template, ask them to submit a few pages and review them to see that everyone is using the template the same way. If not, you can make modifications without having to redo much of the effort. You may also discover that some changes are needed in the template itself to accommodate the needs of the training course and content. Although many different types of templates are available, the sample in Appendix Two, p. 288, is a good example of a template that can be used both for participants and instructors.

### Video/Multimedia Development

If the training program will use video or multimedia, it is particularly important to use organizing tools to plan development carefully and avoid wasted effort. For video, the standard development process is to first write a treatment that describes the settings, plot, characters and structure of the proposed video. A general treatment should be generated at the design blueprint stage, but a more detailed treatment should be written at the outset of the development phase. Once this has been approved and reviewed, scriptwriters can then begin writing the script while cinematographers develop a storyboard of the video. These can then be reviewed and approved before moving into video production, where the costs of video really begin to mount.

Once video production has begun, it is helpful to examine rough cuts of the video as they are shot. These may simply be outtakes of the day's shoot or may be edited the way they will appear in the final video, minus titles, graphics, music tracks and any special effects. If rough cuts are to be shared with clients or SMEs, it is important to alert them that what they will be seeing is far from the final product, otherwise they may think the quality does not live up to their expectations.

For multimedia, Internet or other technology-based training, the first key decision is made at the design stage with the choice of media. This should be based on two considerations:

1. which technology platform offers the best medium at the best value for the learning need?
2. what is the primary purpose of the learning technology?

The first question should be answered based on the company's existing technology capabilities and the options available to develop and deploy learning. If the company has an extensive network of PCs in place, then using PC-based training delivery is a logical choice. If the company already has an Intranet, then delivering training using it is a viable option. If the company employs a central mainframe, then using this platform may make sense. The second question should be answered based on the training needs identified in the needs assessment. Technology-based learning systems are typically aimed at one of three types of training programs:

1. Knowledge-building
   Learners acquire information and concepts that make them more knowledgeable, such as learning OSHA Hazardous Materials standards, or new product information.
2. Skill-building
   Learners acquire new job skills that they can immediately apply on the job, such as how to use a new computerized order entry form or how to troubleshoot and repair a piece of machinery.
3. Performance Support
   The learner accesses information to help them complete job tasks in real-time as needed, such as an on-line help system for telephone customer service representatives or an Intranet-based library of engineering specifications and standards for product design engineers.

Once the purpose of the training has been clearly determined, it is imperative to use storyboards or flowcharts to create the structure of the program before committing expensive resources to final production. The storyboard is a key tool, since it can be quickly assembled and gives the client a good indication of what the final product will look like. For many multimedia courses produced using authoring software, it is possible and desirable to create a flowchart of the lesson's structure first before programming detailed content. The flowchart will indicate the screens that users will see and the sequence of the instruction. It should also indicate branches in the program and the various support tools and reference materials that may be included. The flowchart is a vital tool for the design team, especially the programmers, since it indicates clearly how the content will flow throughout the program and how various screens are connected. It may not be the most useful tool to present to clients, however, since it is often very complex and confusing to an outsider. Some developers simply create an outline of the course using a word processor and present this to the client to show how content will be mapped and sequenced.

Another useful tool for multimedia development is the use of screen templates and libraries of previous courses, images, graphics, video and audio that can be reused on the current project. As part of the storyboard development, many multimedia designers also create a template to guide development of the final product. The template will include screen layout, colors, fonts, location of navigational tools, help files, and other screen details. When the template is shown with the storyboards, it provides a very clear picture of what the final product will look like without the expense involved in actually creating the entire program.

After the preliminary design has been reviewed and approved, designers can then move ahead with development confident that their work is on target. Once development is underway, it may proceed in many different directions, depending on the complexity of the project and the number of specialists involved. If graphics, audio or video need to be included, production of these elements typically proceeds concurrently with software programming and development. Although most multimedia and Internet training programs are developed linearly, much like print-based materials, they do not have to follow this approach, and it may be advantageous not to.

One technique that has been used with success is to develop the program in layers. This involves producing all the content needed for the program at a high-level first, working from storyboards, and then gradually adding more and more layers of detail, including interactivity, animation, video, audio, complex navigation and finally putting the log on, installation and student management sections together at the end. The advantage of a layered approach is that it allows the developer to more quickly produce content that can then be reviewed by the client and revised before most of the development resources have been spent.

The discussion above assumes that the content of the program is fairly stable. That may not in fact be the case, especially when developing training for a new piece of software or other emerging technology. In cases where the content is still shifting during development, it is better to concentrate resources early on to creating the program's structure, architecture, levels of interactivity, management system and other software environmental factors. Then, once the content has been finalized, it can quickly be added to the existing elements of the program.

The basic process of designing and developing technology-based learning is not radically different from print-based, but it requires much greater planning and much more detail due to the complex nature of the media, hardware and software involved. For technology-based learning, the devil is truly in the details. This can be seen from the flowchart below for designing and developing multimedia training which has been adapted from the approach used by Accenture Consulting (Howell and Silvey, 1996).

*Figure 14-2:*

**E-learning Training Design and Development Process**

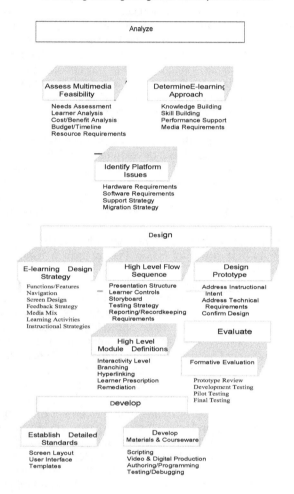

## Working with Materials Developers

In today's multimedia environment, instructional designers may work with a host of experts when developing materials. To be successful, it is necessary to understand something about the world in which these experts work and the kind of guidance and support they will need to be effective. This section discusses strategies for working with various types of material developers, including writers, video producers, software programmers, graphic artists and subject matter experts.

Instructional designers most frequently work with writers in developing materials, since nearly all training, even multimedia, begins with the written word. If these writers have a training background, they may need little guidance beyond the specifications in the design blueprint and the materials template. Those who lack a formal training background will need some help in interpreting the design blueprint and implementing it they way the designer intended. Of particular importance is specifying the objectives to be achieved, the instructional strategies to be used and the learning activities that will allow learners to practice key skills and demonstrate mastery of the content. Writers unfamiliar with any of these key elements of the design will need some coaching in order to turn out a product that is compliant with the original design concept.

A second area of concern with writers is the tone and style of writing for a particular audience. Though the design blueprint ought to include information from the learner analysis, writers often need assistance in translating this information to a writing style compatible with the audience. This is particularly a challenge when the writer has little personal experience with the organization or the target audience. A good template can help to give writers a sense of what is required, but choosing the proper writing style is a complex artistic and technical process of translating content into concepts and principles that can be readily grasped by the learner. Some of the key choices that writers make in creating content include the following:

- Determining what terms are already known to the audience and which ones require a definition
- Making assumptions about prerequisite audience knowledge, such as industry background or foundational understanding
- Choosing a writing voice and tone that is appropriate for the subject matter and the audience
- Avoiding loaded language or terms that might be inappropriate for a given audience or organizational culture
- Maintaining respect for the audience, and not insulting them with either too much or too little information

Though experienced writers are used to adjusting their style to their audience, it is up to the instructional designer and the project manager to educate material developers about the audience they are trying to reach.

A second type of materials developer frequently used to write training materials is the subject matter expert (SME). This individual has expert knowledge of the training content and so probably won't need a great deal of direction with regard to the technical content of the course beyond the guidance presented in the design blueprint. What the SME will need help with is choosing an appropriate writing style for the audience and translating the instructional strategy and learning activities into useful training content. As materials developers, SMEs can be highly effective if they have good writing skills to start with and have been trained on how to translate instructional design intentions into usable learning materials.

However, many SMEs turn out to be poor materials developers. Among the things to watch out for when working with SMEs as developers are the following:

- Poor writing skills
- Poor understanding of instructional design strategies
- Writing at the wrong knowledge level for the audience (typically writing at too high a level for novices)
- Failure to conform to design specifications and writing standards
- Slow speed due to lack of experience or lack of time available to concentrate on writing

When working with new SMEs, it is best to have them attend a Train the Trainer workshop before beginning a development project. Once they have some of the basics down, a thorough orientation to the project at hand can help identify problems before they get out of hand and give SMEs the skill they need to be effective materials developers.

Increasingly, instructional designers find themselves working with professionals in other disciplines, including video producers, computer programmers, graphic artists and the like to produce multimedia or other high technology training. When working with these professionals, it is crucial to clearly define expectations and training goals and standards up front to avoid confusion and disappointment later on. It thus behooves instructional designers to learn something about the work of professionals in other media so as to better understand how they can translate instructional intent into quality training materials and the limitations that they face in this work. Of course, this doesn't mean that the instructional designer must be a jack of all trades; these days no one can be expected to know everything. The trick is to know enough about how other professionals work to make maximum use of their contribution while allowing them to do what they do best, namely practicing their specialized task in the most creative way possible. Below are some specific tips for working with various types of content experts.

Video and film people should have expert knowledge of their craft, including script writing, storyboarding, locations and sets, casting and directing actors, cinematography, pre and post-production, etc. When working on training projects, these professionals typically need direction from the instructional designer about the goals and objectives of the training, the specific content and objectives of the video, the organizational culture and learning styles of participants, and the role of the video in teaching the content. These things should be communicated clearly up front, either in meetings or more formal training sessions for video people.

Additionally, video producers need guidance about the budget and logistics of the video production, including deadlines, cost constraints, special client requests, and distribution medium so that they can use this knowledge to produce video that meets the needs of the client within budget and time constraints. It is useful to review these items with video producers up front so that you don't get surprised by the final product.

Monitoring progress, especially in the early phases of production, can help ensure the video remains on target. Many designers attend some of the early shoots, for example, to get a sense of how the video is being made, and review outtakes or rough cuts of video footage before it goes into post-production. This allows for revisions and edits that can be done cost effectively while maximizing the video's impact. Designers may also need to help facilitate client review of videos in production to allow their input early on in the video development phase.

Working with graphic artists presents a similar set of challenges as working with video producers. Graphic artists, like video people, need a firm grounding in the instructional specifications of the project and the role that graphics will play in the final training program. They may also require specific instructions on how to prepare graphics for publication, including size, color, format, fonts, digital protocols, computer platforms and the like. One technique that works well is to create a set of specifications for graphics that spell out the following key information:

- number of graphics required
- electronic format and protocols to be used
- quality standards for color, image resolution, size, callouts, numbering
- samples of graphics to be used in the proper format if possible

Armed with this information, graphic artists are much more likely to create images that fit the need of the training program, and therefore will not need to edit or revise nearly as much of the content as they might otherwise.

Working with computer programmers on multimedia, WBT or CBT projects presents a set of challenges unique to these media. Typically, computer programmers lack expert knowledge about instructional design, so they will need to be trained in the use of design blueprints and specifications. Instructional designers, in turn, need to understand something about how programmers do their work and the limitations and problems they confront when building training content to be delivered by computer. The most difficult challenge is usually getting computer experts to recognize the learning objectives and instructional strategies to be employed in the program. Until they fully understand exactly what the designer is trying to accomplish, they are unlikely to be able to support the project with relevant computer code and content. Thus, it helps to involve computer people early on in the design phase, both to learn about the purposes and objectives of the training and the limitations of the computer platforms to be used to deliver the training.

Once everyone has a firm grasp of the project's goals and constraints, it is imperative to decide what hardware and software tools will be used and how training content is to be developed. If the instructional designer and programmer plan to collaborate on a project, both must be clear about their respective roles and responsibilities. For example, the instructional designer may be responsible for creating all the content in a previously chosen authoring software, and the programmer is only responsible for creating a series of program patches to existing computer networks or mainframes, or creating a student management system in computer code. For this collaboration to go well, both parties must clearly understand what the other party is doing at all times and coordinate their efforts so as to avoid duplication or dreaded incompatibilities.

If a computer programmer is hired to convert an entire text-based training program to on-line or multimedia format, he/she should work under the direction of the instructional designer who originally developed the course or at least someone intimately familiar with the content and instructional strategies of the course. This will help the computer expert decide how to translate the content to the new medium without compromising key instructional goals or content quality. A key competence for designers is knowing the computer system well enough to be able to give meaningful guidance to programmers or other specialists. If this knowledge does not reside in the training department, it may be necessary to acquire it from outside, or from within the information technology department.

### *Summary*

In this chapter, you have examined the issue of creating draft materials based on design blueprints. You have learned about why draft materials are important, what they usually entail and how to work with various types of materials developers to produce draft materials. Although much of this discussion assumes that you are working with various experts in a large instructional design project team, the same rules and techniques apply when designers are asked to produce materials themselves. In the latter case, the task at hand may be more difficult for one person to accomplish, but this difficulty is offset by the relative ease with which a single person or small project team communicates information about the project and actualizes the designer's original intent.

# Discussion Questions and Exercises

1. What do you think are the major challenges of working with materials developers, especially those who are not trainers?
2. What are some techniques instructional designers can use when working with print or multimedia developers?
3. How does e-learning design differ from classroom training design?

**Case Study: The E-learning Initiative**

A high tech software company wants to convert its entire classroom training curriculum to e-learning, using a newly purchased Learning Management System (LMS) and the company's extensive intranet. The curriculum includes technical training, management training and sales training. Using the e-learning design model (Figure 14-2), develop a high-level plan for this project.

# Chapter Fifteen :
# Developing Tests/Assessments

Although many training programs do not contain formal tests, the trend today is to build in assessments of learning to ensure that trainees are mastering the skills being taught and to provide evidence to clients of the effectiveness of training. This chapter will describe the role of testing and assessment in training and provide guidance in how to create reliable and valid tests, including both traditional paper and pencil exams and performance assessments. The chapter will also briefly describe the legal issues involved in using testing to make training decisions. Examples of tests and procedures to validate them will be presented.

## The Role of Testing and Assessment

Testing has been a feature of training programs for many decades. Today, testing and its companion, assessment, have taken on new roles as trainers search for ways to obtain measurable results. The traditional purpose of testing was to assess individual trainee learning and determine whether individuals were qualified to perform skilled jobs, especially those that involved some element of risk, either to the performer, the product or the customer.

Although individual assessment continues to be an important purpose of testing, it has assumed at least three other important roles:
1. Selection– tests are increasingly used to select candidates for hire or promotion.
2. Program Evaluation– tests can help determine the quality of learning and the eventual impact of this learning on work performance and business results.
3. Instructional Improvement– tests can assist in pinpointing weaknesses in instruction so that continual improvements can be made to the training process.

Let's look at an example of how testing can be used for all four purposes mentioned above. Assume that a large biomedical company has decided to open a new high tech manufacturing facility to produce a new drug. In designing the training for manufacturing associates, a series of tests are created that measure the objectives of the training. The test is first used as a selection device to screen potential new hires and transfers to determine which applicants have the most knowledge already. Those who score the highest on this selection exam are then recruited to work in the new facility. Before they begin work, they are sent to a two week training course to teach them the skills they'll need. They take a test after completing the course and must score 80 percent or higher to be considered qualified to perform. Those who fall below this score must repeat the course and retake the test. To evaluate the training program, learners' scores on the selection exam and the course final exam are compared to see how much better trainees do after completing the course. For example, if the average applicant scored 60 percent on the selection exam, while the average trainee scored 90 percent on the training final exam, and it could be demonstrated that both exams measure the same objectives, then the 50 percent increase in test scores could be attributed to the training course, thus demonstrating its contribution to a qualified work force. Finally, the individual test items could be analyzed to determine which ones learners scored higher on and which ones they scored lower on as a way of assessing how effective various portions of the training were. If it were discovered that learners did very well on health and safety topics, but very poorly on the use of equipment and machinery, then designers could use this information to redesign the portion of the training devoted to equipment and machinery to ensure a higher level of learning.

In this example, testing is used to select applicants, measure their individual progress through training, determine the overall impact of the training and make improvements to the instructional process.

## Types of Tests

Because tests are used for so many different purposes and the consequences of their use can be potentially risky, different types of tests have emerged over time for these differing purposes. The two most commonly used tests are norm-referenced and criterion-referenced tests. Each has its unique characteristics and uses. Norm-referenced tests are used to determine the relative status of individuals with regards to a particular body of knowledge. These tests sample a wide range of knowledge and then spread out the individuals taking them, so that the performance of the best and the worst can be easily identified. Such tests are mainly used for selection of candidates or ranking of performers. In these cases, the intent is to compare all the test-takers against each other and identify those who are at the top. Norm-referenced tests are mainly used in business for applicant screening and promotions, but they are widely used in education for things like measuring public school pupil performance, selecting candidates for special education programs, like gifted or remedial education, and college admissions.

Norm-referenced tests have been around for nearly 100 years and have the benefit of an extensive history of statistical validation. Some of the most famous tests, such as IQ, SAT, GRE, etc. are norm-referenced.

Over the past 40 years, a different sort of test has emerged as a useful tool for training –the criterion-referenced test. Unlike norm-referenced tests, criterion-referenced tests determine the absolute status of individuals with regard to the criterion being measured. The measurement focuses on whether an individual has mastered a certain performance or skill level, regardless of his relative performance against other test takers. Criterion-referenced tests are most useful for the kinds of measurement that trainers are typically interested in, such as whether individuals have mastered certain necessary skills, whether instruction is effective and whether learning has occurred in training programs. For all these purposes, criterion-referenced tests work best because they establish a clear standard against which trainees are judged to be competent, a standard that can be directly linked to the content of training.

When trainers have tried to use norm-referenced tests for this purpose, they find that problems occur. One common problem is that an individual's score on a norm-referenced test is difficult to interpret, since it is a comparison of how that person did on the test against the performance of all other test-takers. It doesn't indicate how well the person can perform the specific skills needed in a job, only whether a given individual is likely to do better or worse than others who took the same test. Because of the nature of how norm-referenced tests are constructed and validated, they tend to draw test items from a very broad knowledge base, typically much broader than that taught in a given training course. This broad knowledge pool is essential to gain a spread among test-takers, since it is unlikely that anyone would know all the answers to all the questions. Thus, a typical norm-referenced test might yield scores ranging from a low of 25 percent to a high of 99 percent, with individuals bunched up in the middle at about 75 percent, but spread out across the entire range of scores. To get this kind of spread, it turns out the best questions are those that approximately 50 percent of test-takers get wrong. Items that everyone gets right or gets wrong don't differentiate among test-takers and so are usually dropped from the test in favor of those that about half get right. Now this may be great if you are looking to select the top 10 percent of test takers for admission to a college or hiring the top 5 percent of test takers for an entry-level job, but for measuring learning, the norm-referenced test has proven to be a poor benchmark. If after taking a training course, only 50 percent of the trainees could correctly answer questions about the content of the training, this would not be seen as a successful outcome. Rather, in a well-conducted training session, 90-95 percent of trainees should be able to answer questions about the content correctly, while only a handful will get items wrong. This expected result of good instruction wrecks havoc with norm-referenced tests, since the assumptions on which they are built require that half the test takers get items wrong on average. When nearly everyone gets items correct instead, it creates what testing experts call a skewed distribution, meaning all the scores are bunched up at the top, instead of in the middle. This then causes problems in validating such tests, which rely on statistical techniques drawn from the field of probability, based on the famous bell curve phenomena of scores bunching in the middle and being dispersed at both the high and low end of the range.

In fact, it was just such problems with norm-referenced tests that caused psychometricians (experts who design tests) to develop criterion-referenced tests in the first place (Popham, 1978). They had observed that in highly successful educational settings, test scores tend to be skewed toward the top of the range, rather than distributed in a classic bell-shaped curve pattern, and that this resulted in problems interpreting the test results. They also observed that many norm-referenced tests regularly used to measure student progress were not very sensitive to measuring what students actually learned in class, thus creating problems in interpreting the scores. After all, if a norm-referenced test being used to measure a school's success at educating its students does not actually measure what students are learning, but instead measures a much broader construct like 'intelligence', then the results of the test and especially the conclusions drawn from it are invalid. It is common these days to blame schools for doing a poor job of educating kids. If this claim is based on norm-referenced test results that do not actually measure what students are learning, then this represents a misuse of the test. It is akin to teaching someone how to swim and testing them on whether they can play golf instead. The poor results on the golfing exam simply tell us that test takers are bad golfers, but it tells us nothing about their ability to swim, which is what they are being taught how to do.

### Creating Reliable, Valid Tests

Because of the host of problems that trainers and educators have confronted with norm-referenced tests, they have fallen out of favor for instructional purposes. So, in the remainder of this chapter, the focus will be on how to construct and use criterion-referenced tests, since these have been found to be a more reliable and valid measure of learning and job performance.

First, before going into the details of test construction, it is important to understand how the quality of a test is determined. Any test, either criterion or norm-referenced, must possess two qualities to be useful: reliability and validity. Reliability refers to the consistency of measurement. This is often referred to as the stability of the test over time. That is, if someone takes a test today and scores 80 percent, then we would expect that if they retook the test a week later and nothing had happened in the interim to change their knowledge, they should score 80 percent again. If a person's score on repeated retests varied significantly, then we would question the reliability of the test, and therefore have little confidence in its results.

Think of a thermometer. Like a test, it is a measuring tool. If a thermometer says the temperature is 70 degrees one day and only 50 degrees the next, when we know in fact that the temperature on both days is really the same, we would stop using that thermometer and get a new one. To be reliable, the thermometer must register the correct temperature day after day, not just once. Analogously, tests should measure the correct results time after time.

Of course, it is not always feasible or desirable to retest people over and over just to prove a test is reliable, so other methods have been developed to determine test reliability. One that is used quite often is equivalency. This technique involves creating two equivalent forms of a test and comparing trainees' performance on both forms of the test. If trainees score approximately the same on both forms, the test is considered to be reliable.

A third method used for large scale testing or professionally published tests is to consider the internal consistency of the test by taking the items and splitting them in half to form two equivalent internal forms or by using a mathematical formula known as the Kuder-Richardson correlation (K-R 21) that compares performance on each test item to the performance on the mean average of the entire test. These statistical methods have certain limitations, such as assuming that scores are distributed in a bell curve, but can provide some recognized measure of reliability. For both of these techniques, reliability scores of at least .70 are considered to be signs of a reliable test, although this figure is very much influenced by the number of items in the test, with longer tests typically achieving higher scores than those with fewer items.

Though these statistics and others can be obtained from a good testing software package, the formula for the split half correlation is given below so that you can see what is being measured.

### Split Half Reliability Formula

$$r = \frac{2r^1}{1+r^1}$$

r = correlation between the 2 halves of the test
$r^1$ = correlation of the split half of the test

In this case, **r** may range from a high of 1.0, signifying perfect correlation between the two halves, to a low of 0.0, signifying no correlation between the two halves. Again, scores above .70 are typically considered to be evidence of a good correlation, and a reliable test.

Reliability is recognized as a necessary condition for a good test, but it is not sufficient to guarantee the test is well-constructed. Instead, a test must also possess validity. This is defined as the extent to which conclusions and interpretations of test results are accurate for the purpose at hand. In other words, does the test really measure what it purports to measure? Validity is the ultimate quality of a good test, but it assumes that the test is reliable too. Going back to the thermometer analogy, let's assume that we have evidence of the reliability of the thermometer, in that its temperature agrees with the U.S. Weather Bureau's official temperature reading for the same location. Next, we would ask ourselves if the thermometer is a valid measuring device. To answer this question, we would have to know for what purpose we plan to use the results, in this case the outside temperature. There is really only one valid purpose of a thermometer, and that is to tell us the current temperature. For that purpose, our thermometer is a valid measuring device. If we chose instead to try and use the thermometer to tell us when to purchase a stock, we would be using the thermometer for an invalid purpose and therefore the thermometer would lack validity for that purpose. Of course no one would use a thermometer to pick stocks (I hope), but people do very often use tests for purposes that are unsuitable to their design and therefore reach invalid conclusions.

One example that caused great controversy years ago was the use of IQ tests to measure educational progress in school. It was found that IQ test results do not change very much over time, due to the broad nature of the construct they measure and the fact that they are norm-referenced tests. Thus, trying to use IQ tests to measure learning turned out to be an invalid use of these tests, since test results did not change much regardless of whether students were learning or not. A more recent example of the invalid use of a test is the statewide testing of student achievement in California, where every student, including those who were illiterate in English, had to take the test and scores were reported and used to draw conclusions about the quality of education. As many educators pointed out, the low test results for non-English speaking students were hardly a surprise, and certainly not a fair measure of how well schools were doing. After all, if any of us were asked to take an examination in a foreign language we did not know, we would certainly score poorly. The only valid conclusion in this case is that we do not know that language. Conclusions about our ability to learn, our performance in other subjects like math, social studies and science, or the schools' effectiveness in teaching are not valid uses of the test.

So, if validity is so important and yet so difficult to establish, how does one go about ensuring that tests are valid? Over the years, experts in testing have developed three different types of validity that have been accepted by those using tests as well as by the legal community who are often asked to rule on validity questions when someone sues over the use of testing in education or employment. The three validity methods are:
1. Content Validity— the relationship between the content of a test and the domain of knowledge, skill and performance that it purports to measure.
2. Criterion Validity— the relationship between a test's results and some other relevant recognized criterion, such as a person's job performance, or another reliable, valid test measuring the same content.
3. Construct Validity— the extent to which a test measures the underlying psychometric constructs it was designed to assess.

Each of these types of validity requires different methodologies and includes trade-offs of cost, time and accuracy. Although a full treatment of these issues is beyond the scope of this text, a number of excellent sources on test validity and reliability can be consulted for a more complete explanation (Popham, 1978; Coscarelli and Shrock, 1989).

Regardless of the type of validity that one attempts to establish, the best place to start constructing a valid test is with the learning objectives of the training. These are statements of changes in behavior that training is designed to bring about. The objectives should be based on a thorough assessment of training needs and the performance requirements of the job.

When solidly grounded in job performance, learning objectives are a clear link between test items and work-related knowledge and skill. It is important to establish this link in order to show that a test is valid for use in training. Without such a link, someone might legitimately question the validity of the test results, or even challenge the entire test in a court of law.

Once the objectives have been developed, test items may be written to assess each objective. Taken together, all the objectives of a training program may be considered the performance domain. A valid test needs to establish a clear link between the performance domain and the items on the test.

The first type of validity, content validity, establishes this link by asking a group of experts to judge whether the test items appear to be measuring the objectives in the targeted performance domain. If a majority of the experts agree that the items are a good sample of the domain, then the test is considered to be content valid. Items which do not, in the opinion of the judges, measure the performance domain are rewritten or dropped from the test. In addition to establishing content validity, subject matter experts can also help to establish passing scores for tests by estimating what percentage of the current work force would likely get individual items correct. These individual ratings are then averaged for all test items to arrive at an expected passing test score. For example, if a panel of four experts came up with the following difficulty ratings for a five item test, these would then be averaged to establish a minimum passing score for the test.

*Figure 15-1:* **Sample Passing Scores for a Training Test**

| Test Items | Expert 1 | Expert 2 | Expert 3 | Expert 4 | Average |
|---|---|---|---|---|---|
| 1 | 85% | 90% | 95% | 85% | 89% |
| 2 | 75% | 80% | 85% | 80% | 80% |
| 3 | 65% | 70% | 65% | 75% | 69% |
| 4 | 50% | 60% | 55% | 65% | 58% |
| 5 | 70% | 75% | 70% | 80% | 74% |
| Overall Average | | | | | 74% |

In this case, the passing score for the exam would be set at 74 percent. Once trainees began to take the test and sufficient data had been accumulated, actual test performance could be examined to determine how many trainees passed at this score. Based on this information and the performance of trainees on the job, the passing score might be adjusted upward or downward.

The second approach to establishing test validity is criterion validity, which is the relationship between a test's results and some other relevant criterion. For training tests, the most relevant criterion is job performance. Two types of criterion validity may be relevant: concurrent validity and predictive validity. The first refers to correlation with present job performance, while the latter looks at correlation to future job performance.

Let's examine concurrent criterion validity first, since it is easier to establish. Assume that a group of employees are about to be trained on a new manufacturing assembly technique using computer-controlled machinery. To certify these individuals as qualified to perform this work, it has been established by a panel of experts that trainees need to obtain a minimum passing score of 80 percent. Trainees attend a week-long class and take a final exam. Their scores are then compared to their current performance appraisal rating, measured on a scale from 1 to 5. The average correlation between their test scores and their current appraisal ratings is .75. This is evidence of criterion validity because of the relatively high correlation between test results and job performance as measured by supervisors' performance ratings. For predictive validity, the same procedure would be employed, except that future performance appraisal ratings would be used instead of current ones. This technique is well-suited to validity studies of new hires who do not have a current work history. Besides performance appraisals, other ratings of performance can be used, such as: self-ratings, peer ratings, expert observation, or objective measures of work productivity and output.

The third type of validity– construct validity– is less often studied because of its complexity, but construct validity is arguably the most powerful form, because it establishes a direct link between test items and the underlying constructs, knowledge and skills it was designed to measure. The reason construct validity studies are more rare is the difficulty and expense it requires conducting them. Two of the most common methods of establishing construct validity require an extensive research study involving groups of trainees and other employees. One of these is called differential population studies, in which the performance of two distinct populations are measured on a test and compared to see if the groups do in fact perform significantly different. For example, a training test designed to qualify senior lab techs could be given to a group of 20 current senior lab techs and a group of 20 junior-level techs who are slated to attend the training. Because of their different skill levels, one would predict that the senior techs would perform better than the junior ones. If the average score for the senior techs turned out to be 90%, while the junior techs only average 70%, this would be evidence that the test is measuring the skills needed by senior techs, because it properly distinguishes between two differently skilled groups of employees.

A second common technique used to establish construct validity is known as intervention studies. In this case, one attempts to establish that trainees perform significantly different on a test before and after they have taken training that covers the content of the test. For example, if a training program designed to train new hires how to underwrite insurance policies has a certification exam requiring a passing score of 75%, one could establish construct validity by giving a sample group of new hires the test before they attend training, and then retesting them immediately afterwards and comparing their scores. We would predict that trainees should perform significantly better on the test after attending training than before hand. If the average score on the pre-test were 50%, while the average score after training were 85%, we would conclude that the test demonstrates the ability to measure learning that occurred in the underwriting training class and therefore possesses construct validity.

### Legal Issues Regarding Training Tests/Assessments

All this discussion of test reliability and validity may seem a bit academic, but it is anything but in today's litigious workplace. Tests used for hiring and training have become a fertile ground for lawsuits challenging a company's right to test applicants and employees, especially when such tests adversely affect minorities or women. Although the courts have found that testing is legal in the workplace, they have established guidelines to prevent discrimination and abuse, and protect employee rights.

Recent court cases have established three key principles for testing in the workplace. These are:
1. Tests must be directly job related.
2. Tests must be objective and unbiased.
3. Tests that adversely impact minorities or women must be examined and records kept of the adverse impact.

The first requirement is really the crux of the matter. Any test used in the workplace must have demonstrated a direct link between the content of the test and the required knowledge and skill needed to perform the job being tested. To establish this link, a validity study must be conducted. The best way to establish the link between a test and a job is to conduct a job task analysis of the position, identify key skills required to perform the job, write these skills as learning objectives and then base the test items on the objectives. In this way, the link between the job and the test is direct and unequivocal. A test that has been validated in this way is likely to withstand legal challenge, even if it adversely impacts certain groups of employees. Courts have long recognized that an employer has the right to hire, retain and promote the best qualified individual for a given job, regardless of the impact that this may have on other employees. Recent rollbacks of affirmative action programs have given even greater weight to company's arguments that they have an absolute right to hire and fire based on an individual's qualifications and job performance.

The second legal requirement for workplace tests is that they be objective and unbiased. This is a qualitative standard, since test objectivity is a judgment call. Certain areas of bias have been identified and should be avoided in testing. Bias typically falls into one of three areas:
1. Test item bias.
2. Test administration bias.
3. Test interpretation bias.

Test items may be found to be biased if any of the following problems occur in any of the test items:
1. Offensive language– use of racial or gender slurs, stereotypes, expletives or other language that might be considered offensive. The

courts are likely to strike down any test that can be shown to contain offensive language.

2. Excessive stimulation– tests that contain provocative or controversial content, such as references to sex, religion, politics, racial minorities or cultures are considered biased because the provocative content may prevent a test taker from concentrating on finding the correct answer.

3. Multiple connotations– test items that may be interpreted several ways due to the connotations of the language used should be avoided to reduce the possibility that different groups of people may interpret the question differently, thus threatening the item's validity. An example would be the use of slang in a test item, such as the word 'cool', which carries the connotation of being popular and fun and also lacking heat.

4. Wordiness or obtuse language– test items containing wordy, jargon-filled or confusing language may be biased against those who lack an understanding of the vocabulary, even though they may know the content of the test item. Where possible, use simple, straight-forward language rather than jargon or difficult vocabulary.

5. Job relevancy– test items should be based on job-related content, not specialized knowledge unrelated to the job. For example, a test item on an electrician's exam that refers to a football metaphor may be considered biased against women, since they are less likely to be familiar with football terminology and such vocabulary is clearly not related to an electrician's job.

Test administration bias may occur if test takers do not enjoy the same environment, facilities, and time. Administration bias may also occur if those administering and proctoring the exam do not act consistently from one test administration to the next. For example, giving oral directions to one group while failing to give the same directions to another group would constitute test administration bias. Likewise, giving one group an hour to complete a test while limiting another group to 30 minutes would introduce bias against the group given less time.

Finally, bias in test interpretation occurs when some groups of people consistently perform better or worse on a test than others. The courts have created a standard for test interpretation bias known as the 4/5ths rule. This rule states that if the passing rate for any group is less than 80% (4/5ths) of the passing rate of the highest scoring group, the test is held to have an adverse impact on the lower scoring group. For example, consider a selection test for police officers. The table below gives fictional average mean scores for White males, Black males, Hispanic males, Asian males and females. In this case, Asian males have the highest passing rate, on average, of 85 percent. Compared with them, the other four groups had average passing rates as follows below.

*Figure 15-2*: **Sample Mean Passing Rates on Police Selection Exam**

| White Males | Black Males | Hispanic Males | Asian Males | Females |
|---|---|---|---|---|
| 80% | 60% | 55% | 85% | 70% |

In this case, two of the groups had average passing rates below 80 percent of the highest group: Black males and Hispanic males. Since these two groups passed at the lower rate, the test would be considered to adversely impact Black and Hispanic males. Despite the adverse impact, the test would not automatically be considered biased. However, the finding of adverse impact would create an onus on the employer to demonstrate that the test was directly job related and unbiased, and furthermore the police department would need to keep records of the adverse impact and periodically review these against its affirmative action and equal employment opportunity goals to see if the test was preventing them from achieving their employment goals. If challenged in court, the police department would need to show that the lower average score achieved by Blacks and Hispanics is due to their lack of job-related skills and not due to systematic test bias.

*Figure 15-3:* **Average Passing Rates as a Percentage of Asian Males**

| White Males | Black Males | Hispanic Males | Females |
|---|---|---|---|
| 94% | 71% | 65% | 82% |

### Test Construction Principles

The best way to avoid test bias is to construct tests according to the principles of good test development. These principles have guided test developers over many years and have been proven to help eliminate bias and other validity problems in test items. Remember that a test is only as good as the sum of its individual items. Therefore, paying attention to the construction of individual items is very important.

One thing that can help eliminate problems with test items is to develop a set of test specifications, such as those found in Appendix Two, p. 290. The purpose of test specifications is to clearly state what test items are supposed to measure and how they are to be constructed. This is particularly useful when more than one person is going to be writing test items, so that a consistent approach is taken that will increase the chances of producing a reliable and valid test.

Test specifications should contain at a minimum the information in Figure 15-4 below. Armed with the test specifications, test developers can then write test items that are reliable and valid measures of the learning objectives for the test.

Besides a good set of test specifications, a number of other test construction principles help test writers to develop good items. These guidelines are summarized in the table below, which may be used as a job aid for test developers.

### Analyzing and Reporting Test Results

Testing has many advantages, among the most important of which is the ability to analyze test results using established scientific principles.

*Figure 15-4:* **Test Specification Requirements**

**Test Title**
The title of the test should be a clear description of its content.
**General Description**
A one paragraph statement of what the test measures and what test takers must do.
**Test Objectives**
A list of the learning objectives that the test is designed to measure.
**Sample Item**
An example of the items contained in the test. The sample should not be taken from the actual test. The sample may be used during test administration to help test takers understand what they are required to do.
**Stimulus Attributes**
A complete description of the questions that will be asked on the test, including the types of questions, the origins of question content, length of questions, difficulty level, etc.
**Response Attributes**
A complete description of the answer choices, if provided. This should also include criteria for the correct answer and criteria for distracters (incorrect answers) that may be included in the test.
**Scoring Guidelines**
A complete description of how the test is to be scored, including the number of points awarded for each correct answer, procedures for awarding partial credit, if applicable, and the suggested passing score for the test.

*Figure 15-5:* **Test Construction Job Aid**

The following guidelines can help test developers write reliable, valid test items that will be objective and unbiased.
- Clear Test Directions
- Guess Factor of No More Than 33 Percent (multiple choice with at least 3 choices per item)
- All Questions in Each Section of a Test are of the Same Type
- Only One Correct Answer per Item
- Unambiguous, Clear, Straight-forward Items
- No Unintended Clues Given
- Test Items Measure Test Objectives
- Test Items Do Not Contain Cultural Bias

Because testing is a relatively objective way of measuring learning, test results may be analyzed using a number of statistical techniques. Among these, the two most popular are descriptive statistics and inferential statistics.

Descriptive statistics refer to ways of describing test results so that they may be readily understood. Of course, the most common descriptive statistic is simply a list of scores arranged in rank order, from top to bottom. This information is used to report scores to test takers and to determine the relative rank of those who took the test. A second technique is to construct a frequency table, which lists the rank order of scores by the number of testees achieving each score. The table below gives an example of a frequency table for a job certification exam.

The frequency table can easily be converted into a histogram, or a graphic representation of frequencies, as the figure below illustrates for the data in the frequency table.

*Figure 15-6:* **Sample Frequency Table**

| Raw Score | Frequency | Percentage of Testees |
|-----------|-----------|-----------------------|
| 50 | 1 | 5% |
| 49 | 2 | 10% |
| 47 | 2 | 10% |
| 45 | 3 | 15% |
| 44 | 4 | 20% |
| 43 | 2 | 10% |
| 41 | 2 | 10% |
| 40 | 1 | 5% |
| 38 | 1 | 5% |

*Figure 15-7:*

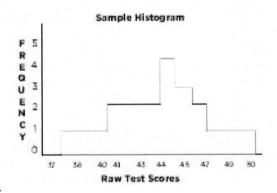

*Figure 15-8:*

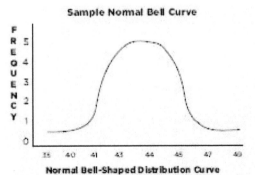

Finally, another common descriptive graphic is a distribution graph, which shows the frequency of scores with a smoothed curve line instead of the jagged stair steps of a frequency table. An example of a distribution graph known as a bell curve is shown below. A fourth type of descriptive statistic that is frequently reported is central tendency, or in layman's terms, the average score. Strictly speaking, there are three averages, not one. The first is the mean or arithmetic average. This is the one we are all most familiar with. It is calculated by adding up the sum of all the scores on a test and then dividing by the number of testees.

For example, if 10 people took a test and achieved the following scores (in percent), the mean would be the total divided by 10.

**Test Scores**

90
80
95
75
60
80
100
55
70
<u>85</u>

Total = 790  (Mean = 790 ÷ 10 = 79%)

A second type of average is the median, or the mid-point of all scores. This is arrived at by arranging the scores from low to high, or vice-versa, and selecting the mid-point, as the list below illustrates. These are the same set of scores used earlier, only arranged in rank order from top to bottom.

**Test Scores**

100
95
90
85
<u>80</u>
80
75
70
60
55

In this example, the median is 80%, since it is the fifth score of the 10 in the list.

Finally, the last average is the mode, which is the most frequently occurring score in a list. In the example above, the mode would also be 80%, since it is the only number that occurs twice. If no number occurred twice, the list would not have a mode.

Of the three averages, the mean is the most accurate and most useful central tendency. The other two averages, median and mode, have more specialized uses, primarily with very large data sets. One additional phenomenon worth noting is that in perfectly distributed sets of data, or those that comprise a true bell curve, the mean, median and mode are all identical, since the three averages would all coalesce around the same mid-point if scores were evenly distributed on both sides of the average. Thus, one quick way to check whether a set of scores represents a normal, or bell curve, distribution is to see if the mean, median and mode are all the same, or at least close. In the example above, the distribution of scores is very close to being normal, since the mean is 79 and the median and mode are both 80.

This leads to one final concept regarding descriptive statistics –the variability of scores. This is measured two ways: the range and the standard deviation. The range is simply the difference between the highest and the lowest score on a given test. The range is a quick way to determine how spread out the scores are. Narrow ranges indicate that testees were all fairly closely bunched, while wide ranges indicate that testees were spread out in a large range. In the example test above, the range of scores was from 100 to 55, or a total of 45 points. That represents a fairly wide range of scores on a test. If the lowest score had only been 80 with a high of 100, the range would have been from 100 to 80 or 20 points, a fairly narrow range for a test.

A more precise measure of variability is called the standard deviation, which is often assigned the symbol $s$. The standard deviation is a fairly complex calculation that measures the average variability of all the scores on a test by calculating the sum of all the individual score's deviation from the mean. A small $s$ indicates a narrow range, while a larger $s$ indicates a wide range of scores. This can also be illustrated by the spread of the curve on a normal distribution chart, as the examples below illustrate.

Although the standard deviation has a number of useful functions in statistics, the best way to think about it is in terms of how spread out test scores are, and what that means about the people taking the test. For selection and promotional tests, it is common to see a fairly large standard deviation, since the purpose of these tests, as with all norm-referenced tests, is to spread out test-takers so that the very best ones can be readily identified. On certification exams and tests taken after a training course, the standard deviation ought to be smaller, since most of the people taking the exam should have learned the necessary skills in class.

In fact, highly successful training programs often produce a restricted range of scores, since virtually everyone passes the test. For example, if 20 people attended a certification training course in x-ray technology, the range of scores on the final might be 75 to 95%, or only 20 points. That is, the lowest score was a 75, while the highest score was a 95. If the passing score is set at 80 percent, then the vast majority of testees would pass the exam. The distribution of scores would not appear normal, but would be skewed toward the right, as the figure below illustrates.

*Figure 15-9:*

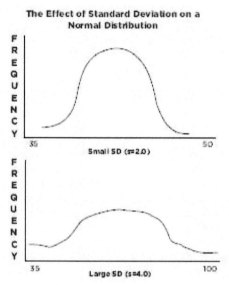

The Effect of Standard Deviation on a
Normal Distribution

F
R
E
Q
U
E
N
C
Y

35                                              50

Small SD (s=2.0)

F
R
E
Q
U
E
N
C
Y

35                                              100

Large SD (s=4.0)

Before leaving this chapter, a word should be mentioned about another branch of statistics that can be useful in analyzing test scores. Known as inferential statistics, this represents conclusions that can be reasonably drawn based on a test's results. Although a complete treatise on inferential statistics is beyond the scope of this book, two of the most commonly used techniques for test data are worth mentioning, since they are frequently cited in the literature and in published test specifications.

The first of these concepts is the correlation coefficient, already alluded to earlier in the discussion of test reliability. A correlation is simply the statistical relationship between two or more numbers. The coefficient is usually symbolized by a small letter $r$, and ranges from +1.0 to -1.0. The easiest way to see the correlation of two numbers is to plot it on a graph, as the examples below show. Besides positive and negative correlation, it is possible to get no correlation. This is represented by $r=0.0$. On a chart, the scores would be scattered about with no apparent pattern. The proper interpretation of a 0.0 correlation is that the two numbers or variables are completely independent of each other, much like the size of a person's thumb and the size of their net worth have nothing in common.

A second class of inferential statistics looks at differences among scores to determine if the difference is merely due to random chance or if it represents a difference so large that it is considered "statistically significant." By this somewhat nebulous term is meant any difference that is larger than what one would expect from the normal distribution of scores as shown in a distribution or frequency chart. One of the great mathematical insights about statistics is that numbers which fall in

## Normal Bell Curve and Standard Deviation

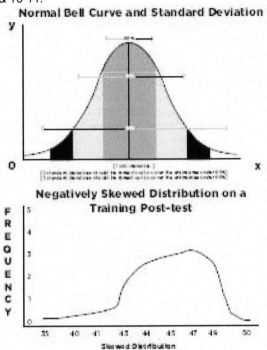

## Negatively Skewed Distribution on a Training Post-test

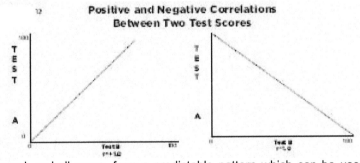

*Figure 15-12:*

## Positive and Negative Correlations Between Two Test Scores

a normal, or bell curve, form a predictable pattern which can be used to infer whether a given score fits within the normal distribution or represents a significant departure from the norm. If we assume that scores on a test should fit a normal distribution curve, we can use the inherent statistical properties of the curve to determine if a given score fits the norm or represents something out of the ordinary. If a given score is sufficiently different to be outside the normal distribution, then we can conclude that something caused this difference. That something might be a training program that was recently completed or a mentoring program on the job, or a recent pay raise or any number of other variables that intervened in the normal course of things to cause a statistical difference. This, in a nutshell, is what statistical significance is all about.

Although many different statistical tests are available, the one most often used with test data is the *t test*, represented by the letter *t*. This is a comparison of two test scores to determine whether any differences between the two are due to random chance or some statistically significant intervention like training. For example, assume that we would like to compare trainees' scores on a pre-test to their scores on a post-test. We'd like to hope that trainees do better on the post-test, but we're not sure how much better they would need to do before we could declare our training program a success. The *t test* allows us to measure the difference between the pre and post-test scores for a group of test-takers and compare this to the mean and standard deviation of the test scores to determine if any difference is greater than one would expect based on the normal distribution of the scores. To help determine the level of significance, the value of *t* is set at some level of probability to rule out the possibility of the difference being due to random chance. Probability for a *t test* is usually set at $p<.05$, which means that the *t* score must be large enough so that the probability of this occurring randomly is less that five times out of a 100 (or .05). If the *t* score is greater than its random probability, then we can conclude that the difference between the pre and post-test is due to something other than chance, something like the training program we are evaluating. If the *t* score is less than what we would expect from random chance, then we would conclude that there is no significant difference between the pre and post-test scores and therefore our training program apparently produced no significant change in learners.

The *t test* and other more powerful inferential statistics like multiple regression and Analysis of Variance (ANOVA) enable training and test designers to measure changes in learning, performance and other key variables with a degree of precision that can add credibility to claims of training success. Furthermore, these techniques can help to establish causal links between training and the learning of new skills, knowledge and attitudes.

### Performance Tests

Another category of tests that is frequently employed to measure learning outcomes is the performance or hands-on, test. This is defined as any test that requires the actual performance of job skills under observation. It is most often used with psychomotor skills like typing or repairing equipment. The observer may be an instructor, supervisor, experienced worker or outside expert. After observing the trainee perform, the performance is rated against the standards set for the task. Those who meet or exceed the standards pass the test, while those who fall short must retake the exam or the training.

To assure that performance tests are reliable and valid, they must be carefully designed so that the task to be performed is clear and the scoring is unbiased and accurate. One technique which helps is to create performance test specifications and scoring checklists like the ones in Appendix two, p. 293. The observation checklist assists observes to evaluate individual performers and to ensure reliable, objective scoring of all test takers. The best way is to break the task into smaller steps, so that each one is observed and recorded separately. Points are awarded for each step properly performed and the total score is compared to the passing score set for the test.

Although performance tests are ideal for measuring many skills, they are time consuming to administer and score. The labor-intensiveness of these tests limits their use, but they should be considered when a high-stakes decision is required. One example of a performance test is a flight simulator for pilots. By demonstrating that they can handle an airplane in a simulator, they ensure the flying public is safe.

Summary

In this chapter, you have learned about the role of testing in training design. You have been introduced to two different types of tests: norm-referenced and criterion-referenced and examined their role in training and selection. You have also learned about two powerful concepts for determining the quality of tests– reliability and validity, and ways to ensure a test possesses both. You also examined how to construct good tests and ways of analyzing the results using both descriptive and inferential statistics.

# Discussion Questions and Exercises

1. Compare and contrast norm-referenced and criterion-referenced tests. Give an example of when you might use each type.
2. What are some ways to demonstrate the reliability and validity of a test?
3. How can we use descriptive and inferential statistics to analyze test data?

**Case Study: Trainer Certification**
A professional organization wants to offer a trainer certification program to its members. Learners will complete a five-day training course and then be assessed to determine if they meet the minimum competency standards defined for the profession.
*How would you develop a testing and assessment plan for this certification program?*

# Chapter Sixteen :
# Quality Control and Formative Evaluation

One of the key issues during the development phase is to ensure the quality of training materials. Although quality concerns are present throughout the design process and are addressed in part by effective needs analysis and design work, training developers must be particularly attentive to doing the right things and also doing things right, the twin hallmarks of effective quality control. This chapter describes the quality control techniques that expert designers use to ensure consistently effective training design and development.

### What is Quality Control?

Quality control is a system for maintaining desired standards that is based in part on establishing processes that result in the right things being done right the first time and in part on inspecting samples of the product after the fact to determine if they meet the defined standards. The control of quality is based on the notion that it is possible to define the standards and specifications that yield quality and to create systems that will ensure these standards are met.

To establish quality standards, it is helpful to separate quality into two types: internal and external. Internal quality is primarily an engineering problem. It consists of defining what are the right things to do and ensuring that those things are done correctly the first time. For instructional designers, internal quality is a function of applying the instructional systems design, results-based design and performance improvement approaches to training problems in a systematic and creative way. Much of the internal quality of a training design project is built in at the design phase, when key decisions about content, media and methods are made. But the quest for internal quality does not end with the design phase. As training projects enter the development phase, a constant monitoring of internal quality is necessary to assure that the final product is a reflection of the design blueprint and the original analysis that identified the need for training.

External quality is defined by the customer and is a reflection of their needs, requirements and constraints. The key to external quality is understanding the needs of customers and translating these into training solutions that work within the constraints of time and money. Typically, external quality is measured by such things as:

- budget
- schedule
- training suitability

- training reliability
- training accuracy
- training results

Effective quality control must take into consideration both internal and external quality standards and meld these into a system that delivers value to customers time after time. Although each training project is unique, an effective quality control system should result in a repeatable design process that gets good results each time.

### Training Quality Assurance

The responsibility for quality is shared among three distinct constituents. The first of these is the customer for the training, especially the client who is paying for it, but also the individuals who will receive the training. It is the customer's responsibility to clearly articulate their training needs, to cooperate fully in investigating and verifying the needs and in providing sufficient resources to address the magnitude of the needs. They should also stand in final judgment of the outcomes of training, since they have the largest stake in those outcomes.

The second major constituent of quality is the instructional designer or team of designers who are responsible for designing and developing the training. Designers are responsible for properly identifying the training need, translating it into a workable training solution and developing the content and methods that will result in the most efficient learning for trainees. Designers practice quality control by following established design processes and checking their own work against design specifications.

Finally, the last constituent of quality is the project manager or training manager who is ultimately responsible for the success of the design project. This individual must orchestrate the entire design effort and build in quality control checks along the way to catch any deviations from agreed-upon standards. The project manager must arrange timely reviews of the work as it progresses to ensure the work is being done according to plan and to take prompt corrective action when needed to get a project back on track. Although good project managers delegate much of the authority for quality control to the team of people working on the project, they are always ultimately responsible for the project's results.

### Ways to Build In Quality

The best quality control system is embedded so deeply in the production process that it becomes an integral function of the process, not something added on later as an after-thought. Thus, the best quality control system for training design is simply to follow time-tested methods to analyze, design, develop, implement and evaluate training such as those promulgated in this book. By following a systematic process, the chance that errors may enter in and derail the project is lessened while the chance of achieving a successful outcome is enhanced.

*Table 16-1:* **Assigning Quality Control Responsibilities for Design Projects**

| Design Activity | Quality Control Technique | Responsibility |
|---|---|---|
| Conduct needs assessment | 1. Create a reliable, valid assessment design<br>2. Ensure reliable data collection and analysis | Instructional Designer / Project Manager |
| Design Training Blueprint | 1. Ensure a creative training solution that solves the identified need.<br>2. Ensure that proposed training solution is feasible. | Instructional Designer / Project Manager<br><br>Customer |
| Develop draft training materials | 1. Orient developers to the needs of the customer and the blueprint specifications.<br>2. Use a template to standardize training presentation.<br>3. Develop a prototype and review it for accuracy and fit.<br>4. Provide timely feedback about the quality of work. | Project Manager<br><br>Editor/ Desktop Publisher<br>Instructional Designer<br>Project Manager/ Customer |
| Produce Final Training Materials | 1. Review work for consistency, accuracy and quality.<br>2. Ensure that needed changes are completed. | Instructional Designer /<br>Customer<br>Instructional Designer / Editor |
| Pilot Test Training | 1. Conduct a formal evaluation of the pilot.<br>2. Ensure that any needed changes are completed. | Instructional Designer<br>Instructional Designer / Editor |
| Implement Training | 1. Conduct Train-the-Trainer.<br>2. Transition materials and course maintenance to Implementers. | Instructional Designer<br>Project Manager |
| Evaluate Training | 1. Conduct formal evaluation of reactions, learning, skill transfer and business results.<br>2. Use evaluation results to refine the training design process and to improve the quality of training. | Instructional Designer / Customer<br>Instructional Designer/ Project Manager |

For large training projects involving many people's efforts, it is helpful to arrange orientation training for everyone working on the project so that they understand the customer requirements and the proposed process to be followed. The use of design templates and checklists also helps to ensure uniformity, especially for large-scale projects involving many designers. Once everyone has been oriented to the needs and requirements of the project, periodic review meetings help to keep the project on track and to deal quickly with issues and problems as they emerge.

Another quality control technique gaining favor is the use of prototyping. This entails asking designers to create a sample of the final training program on a small-scale at the outset of the project, and then subjecting the prototype to team and client critique to determine if it will meet the identified need. Although this process can be painful at times, it allows everyone associated with a project to clearly define in concrete terms what their vision of the final product and outcome will be. The inevitable fine-tuning that occurs after a prototype review is well worth the effort since it will head off more expensive changes downstream.

Since the responsibility for quality control is shared on design projects, it is helpful to spell out some of the major duties and name a specific person responsible. Although the nature of project personnel varies, the following guidelines should help to assign specific quality control responsibilities on a typical design project.

A checklist of quality control techniques is included in Appendix Two, p. 295.

### Taking Corrective Action

Whenever problems occur in a design project that threaten the quality of the outcome, prompt corrective action is necessary. This usually falls on the shoulders of the project manager, but the instructional designer may need to take action, if working alone on a small project. Effective corrective action should not be done in a moment of panic, even though the problem may indeed inspire panic among designers and clients. Instead, it is imperative to investigate the problem thoroughly, discover the root cause and come up with a solution that effectively deals with the cause of the problem, and prevents such problems from reoccurring in the future.

To do this effectively, the following corrective action process should be followed:

Figure 16-2:     **Training Design Corrective Action Process**

| |
|---|
| **Identify the Problem** |
| **Identify the Root Cause of the Problem** |
| **Develop a Solution to the Problem** |
| **Implement the Solution** |
| **Monitor the Situation** |

Let's examine each of these steps in detail, using examples to illustrate the process. The first step, identifying the problem, seems obvious. Typically, the problem surfaces in the form of a complaint from somewhere, but it may also be identified by regular monitoring of the project as it proceeds. Let's assume a fairly routine problem has occurred on a large-scale design project. The three designers working on the project have all come up with very different prototype modules that will lead to inconsistent material development, difficulty for trainers and learners and a dissatisfied client. At first glance, the problem is straight-forward – the three designers did not all follow the template given to them. Further investigation by the project manager reveals that the problem was not that simple after all. When discussing the situation with the three designers, the manager discovered that all three believed they were following the template to the letter, and yet they came up with radically different results. This led to the realization that the template itself had some problems that needed fixing, and that the overall training design blueprint had not been specific enough in creating the standards for designers to follow.

The second step in the process is to identify the root cause of the problem. In this case, a lengthy discussion among the design team revealed that the root cause was a lack of understanding among the designers about how to realize the design blueprint. One designer had taken a very detailed, process-oriented approach that resulted in a very thick set of materials for the prototype; another took just the opposite approach of providing a quick overview with virtually no step-by-step instructions, while the third designer had taken a middle-of-the-road approach. Furthermore, a second root cause of the problem was the template itself, which could be used in several different ways, and which lacked some formats for procedures and learning activities. This lack of specificity had led the three designers to modify the template in different ways, resulting in very different-looking prototypes.

The third step is to identify solutions to the root causes identified. In our example, this was accomplished by having the designers sit down together with the project manager and the client's representatives and rehash the design blueprint to determine once and for all just how much procedural and process detail the training audience required. This discussion resulted in a decision to limit the training course to a conceptual understanding of the process and procedures and to refer learners to technical reference manuals for the specific keystrokes and instructions they needed to perform job procedures.

The second root cause was the template. The designers met with the desktop publishing group who had designed the template and discussed how it should be used, in the wake of the decision to concentrate on conceptual learning. The meeting resulted in greater clarity about how to use each of the existing styles and also a decision to add several more styles that were lacking and would make it easier for the designers to format procedures and learning activities.

The next step is to implement the solutions. In the first case, the designers were asked to revise their prototypes based on the clarification of the design blueprint and to resubmit them. The second iteration resulted in a much greater harmony among the three designers with only a few minor issues to iron out. Regarding the template, the desktop publisher revised the template according to the decisions reached with the designers and reissued it. The designers used the revised template to redo their prototypes, and this was also reviewed by the project manager, the designers and the client. The second iteration was much closer to the design blueprint and the client's vision. This then allowed the project to move forward with the rest of the courses.

The final step is to monitor the situation to ensure that the problem does not recur. The project manager and the desktop publisher reviewed each module as it was developed, looking for compliance with the design blueprint and the template. If any changes were needed, these were communicated back to the designer quickly so that they could be incorporated into future modules as well. Gradually, as the project went on, the number of revisions fell to near zero. The corrective action had worked and the client was extremely pleased with the end result.

Of course in this example, everything works out well in the end. Some problems are not so easily solved, especially those involving philosophical differences about how a course should be developed and presented. In these more intractable cases, it is imperative to have a thorough discussion of the issues, to verify the needs of the client and the audience and to reach a consensus about how best to proceed. If a consensus cannot be reached, the needs of the client should be paramount and these should drive the final solution. In the worst cases, designers may need to be replaced in order to ensure that the original training vision is realized.

It may also be necessary to provide further coaching and training to designers who do not have the necessary skill to achieve the design vision. This should be handled delicately, maintaining their self-esteem and positioning this as an opportunity to strengthen knowledge and skill rather than a form of punishment. Some of the best learning for instructional designers occurs in the heat of battle when they are confronted with a problem or challenge that taxes their abilities. Like all learners, it is important to give designers a chance to succeed and to provide the support and training they need to do so.

### Formative Evaluation Techniques

Formative evaluation is intended to strengthen and improve the program being evaluated. To be most effective, it should be carried out throughout a training design project. Among the techniques that have worked well for trainers are the following:

- **Needs assessment evaluation:**
  Collect data about who needs the training, how great is the need, what is causing the problem and what potential solutions might meet the need.
- **Evaluability assessment:**
  Determine what type of evaluation is feasible for training projects and who should be involved in the evaluation.

- **Design assessment:**
  Review the design blueprint that defines the training, using input from key stakeholders such as the client, the target audience, key decision-makers, training experts and subject matter experts.
- **Implementation evaluation:**
  Collect data from key stakeholders about whether the training is being implemented, how satisfied trainers are with the process and what changes to the process should be considered for future projects.

*Summary*

This chapter has briefly described the quality control function of training design projects, with a focus on preventing problems by using effective control techniques, including the use of a systematic instructional design process. Responsibilities for quality control were described and suggestions on how to manage design projects for quality were presented. When problems do arrive, advice on how to quickly take effective corrective action has focused on the use of a Training Design Corrective Action process.

Once the quality of the training design process and products has been assured, training design can move into full-scale production with confidence, knowing that the right things have been done right the first time.

# Discussion Questions and Exercises

1. Who do you think should be held responsible for the quality of training designs? Why?

2. How would you apply the Corrective Action process to address quality problems on an instructional design project?

3. Why is formative evaluation necessary for good instructional design?

## Case Study: The Client from Hell

A client for an e-learning design project refuses to approve the final design blueprint, despite several revisions and many conversations. She insists that the design is still missing the mark, but cannot say with precision what exactly is wrong. Instead, she keeps telling the designers to go back to the storyboards and make the design more "interesting and engaging."

*How would you address this client's concerns and get the project back on track?*

# Chapter Seventeen :
# Full-scale Production

Depending on the scope of the training design project, production may entail little more than creating final versions of materials or it may become nearly a separate project of its own, involving hundreds of people working simultaneously to produce the final product. The media being used has a great impact on the production phase as well. The more that multimedia elements are introduced into the training design, the more elaborate the production step can become. This chapter covers the entire range of production issues, from one person efforts to large multidisciplinary teams.

## *From Development to Production*

The boundary between development and full-scale production is not a fixed one. For some smaller-scale projects, full-scale production may mean little more than printing the final masters on a laser printer and then photocopying them and assembling into a three-ring binder. For larger-scale efforts involving audio-visual materials, the production phase is much more complicated, involving a myriad of professionals from video, audio, computer science, graphic arts, printing, etc. In either case, however, we can define the point at which projects move into full-scale production as the moment when the client has approved draft materials and given the go-ahead to produce the final training materials. Depending on the nature of the project, the training designer may simply be responsible for producing one high-quality set of master materials, from which all other copies will be made, or may also need to oversee the reproduction of all materials to be used by trainers and learners, including books, audio or video tapes, computer disks, Web pages, Podcasts, MP3 files, etc.

In this chapter, we will discuss both production and reproduction issues, since one grows directly out of the other. Although designers are not always responsible for reproduction, it is helpful to understand how the process works. We will also consider all forms of media, not just print, since so many design projects these days incorporate multimedia elements.

## *Working with Producers and Publishers*

One of the things that makes full-scale production and reproduction unique is the involvement of production professionals who are not instructional designers. Whether they are printers, video producers, graphic artists or computer programmers, these individuals are among the first, besides the client, to work with an instructional design after its formulation by the designer. Furthermore, production professionals often join an instructional design project after it has started, and do not have the benefit of the project's history to help them understand its objectives and instructional intent. Producers are motivated by the desire to create the highest quality masters that the project can afford. But sometimes they place greater value on the look of materials than on their functionality. The risk is that the production may veer towards slick and pretty at the peril of losing some of its instructional integrity.

To maintain the proper balance between instructional integrity and production values, the design team must assert leadership over the production process and maintain editorial control. It must also find ways of communicating to producers what is needed so that they share the same vision and can thus achieve a harmonious balance between the instructional intent and the final production.

One of the most successful ways to ensure a good fit with production is to hold a formal orientation for producers when they are brought on board the project. The orientation should present the design strategy and goals of the project in terms that producers can readily understand. It should paint the big picture and show how all the design elements fit to form a whole. Beyond the big picture, the orientation should also cover the following topics:

- Client production guidelines and standards
- Copies of draft materials
- Samples of produced materials that are similar to what the client wants
- Schedule and deadline requirements
- Budget and cost requirements
- Production requirements and creative license
- Production methods and processes

Production people need to obtain a clear picture of what the training materials are supposed to look like, how they will be used and the schedule and budget constraints affecting the project. It also helps for them to know about any client-imposed standards and requirements, such as needing all print materials to have the look and feel of existing courses, or requiring computer-based materials to be able to run on existing platforms and servers. To the extent that samples exist to guide producers, these should be provided with clear instructions on how to obtain the same result on the current project. Depending on the complexity of the project, the orientation may take several meetings to conclude. For larger-scale projects, it is helpful to appoint someone to coordinate full-scale production efforts with various producers. For example, you may wish to appoint an editor for all print materials whose job is to work with desktop publishers, graphic artists and printers to produce the final product. For audio-visual materials, a production coordinator can help to coordinate the work of scriptwriters, directors, actors, post-production people, computer programmers, etc., freeing the project manager to focus on bigger issues.

Once the production team has been oriented and the schedule has been finalized, it is important to monitor production closely to ensure that it stays on track. This can be accomplished by reviewing samples of work as they are produced, attending important production sessions to witness the process first-hand and evaluating production masters along with the client to assure that they will meet customer requirements. Samples should be reviewed in a timely manner to catch problems before they get too expensive to fix. Once a project is in full-scale production, any change becomes costly, but expenses really begin to mount if changes are needed after masters have been produced. To avoid this problem, insist on seeing samples at each step along the development and production path. For print materials, the following are key points at which to review progress:

*Table 17-1:*          **Print Production Sample Checkpoints**

| | |
|---|---|
| Final drafts completed | _____ |
| Copy-edited draft materials completed | _____ |
| Sample page layouts completed | _____ |
| Print masters completed | _____ |
| Final, revised masters ready for reproduction | _____ |

For e-learning production, whether video, audio, or computer-based, the following table summarizes key production checkpoints.

*Table 17-2:*          **Multimedia Production Sample Checkpoints**

| | |
|---|---|
| Necessary equipment, facilities and people are available | _____ |
| Storyboard, treatments and concepts are completed and approved | _____ |
| Sets, casts, music and aesthetics approved by client and designer | _____ |
| Rehearsals completed and approved | _____ |
| Shooting and recording sessions approved | _____ |
| 'Rough cut' and unedited media approved | _____ |
| Visual and sound editing sessions observed | _____ |
| Computer programming and authoring have been tested and approved | _____ |
| Masters approved by client | _____ |
| Final, revised masters approved for reproduction | _____ |

Reviewing production at each step of the process may seem tedious and unnecessary, but unless you have justified faith in the producers you are working with, the time spent in review will pay for itself quickly by assuring that the production stays true to the original design and that mistakes are caught quickly when they can be fixed without incurring great costs. If this seems like a lot of trouble, imagine the trouble you would encounter if a video you had commissioned needed to be totally reshot because the producer thought he was supposed to be telling your CEO's life history, not providing an orientation to your company's products and strategic vision for new hires. Just such a snafu cost one company over $50,000 to reshoot a fifteen-minute video.

To assist in reviewing masters, a comprehensive evaluation checklist has been provided in Appendix Two, p. 297 for both print and multimedia production.

### Reproduction Issues

Once the final masters have been produced and approved, the project moves into a phase that often signals the beginning of the end of the instructional designer's involvement. This is when hand-offs to reprographics, implementers and clients occur and when the risk of a fumble is extremely high. To minimize problems, designers need to stay involved with the project until all hand-offs have taken place and the distribution and reproduction systems are established and running smoothly.

It makes sense to involve reproduction people in the orientation and discussions you hold with producers. This way, they will know what the project's goals are, and will anticipate the support that they will be asked to provide for the project. Once oriented, the next issues to tackle are the method, schedule and budget for reproduction. For print materials, common reproduction methods include photocopy and offset printing. Binding methods include: three-hole punch and three-ring notebook, comb-bind, velo-bind, staple, saddle stitch, etc. Other print material issues include use of tabs and dividers, assembly of student and trainer materials, overheads or flip charts, single versus double-sided reproduction, print and paper colors, covers, collation, and packaging. For audio-visual and multimedia materials, reproduction methods include: tape duplication, color photocopies, digital copy, CD-ROM, and DVD reproduction. Other issues to be considered are: packaging, labels, storage requirements, installation requirements, equipment and platform requirements and technical support.

Once these issues have been discussed and a workable solution has been agreed upon, those responsible for reproduction will be able to quote a cost and develop a schedule to meet the requirements. The schedule and budget will need to be carefully reviewed by the project manager and the client to determine if it fits within the needs and parameters of the project.

### Distribution Systems

Once the reproduction system has been identified and finalized, the next issue to handle is the distribution system for materials, including storage, shipping, and scheduling additional reproduction when needed. These logistic issues are often thorny, since they typically involve more than one department or vendor to accomplish, and the possibility for error is high. Furthermore, the best training program in the world is useless if it is unavailable at the proper location on the day and time it is needed.

For storage systems, the key issues are: space, quantity, security, and convenience. Space is often at a premium in organizations, so finding a location to store materials, especially voluminous print materials, is a challenge. This is compounded by quantity requirements. Obviously, the more quantities of materials that need to be stored, the larger the storage area. Quantity is sometimes driven by reproduction costs. Substantial savings can be achieved by printing larger quantities than smaller, since the set up and labor costs are substantially the same whether printing a few dozen copies or thousands of copies. By printing more at once, the cost per copy can be reduced significantly. Unfortunately, that means finding larger space to store all those copies. It can also be wasteful if the program requires changes that make the copies in storage obsolete. One of the dirty little secrets lurking in training department closets across the country is the plethora of obsolete training materials still sitting on the shelf, never to be used. This inventory represents a significant waste of money for many training operations.

The best advice on storage systems is to store only as much as you will realistically use over a 3-6 month period and to reorder when supplies run low. This will cut down on storage space needs and reduce the quantity of obsolete materials that ultimately will need to be scrapped or recycled, even though it may raise reproduction costs somewhat.

Another key storage issue is security. Although training materials are not typically the object of theft (if only our work were considered that valuable!), unauthorized access to training materials can cause problems, and some shrinkage may indeed occur for popular programs or those using multimedia. At the same time, security should not be so tight as to prevent legitimate access to materials by instructors and others who require them. Ideally, material storage should be close enough to the training site so that materials can be obtained quickly and easily. If this is impractical, such as when using off-site training facilities, it is crucial to have materials shipped in advance by a reliable source so that everything is ready when needed.

One of the best ways to ensure a good storage system is to flow chart the storage and distribution process ahead of time, paying special attention to identifying responsibilities for reproduction, storage, shipping and distribution, and identifying trigger points for activating the various components in the system. For example, if a management training program is scheduled to be offered four times per year, sufficient quantities of materials for at least two sessions should probably be stored close to the training site. Responsibilities for reordering, shipping and distribution must be clearly specified. This flowchart can then be referred to as a job aid whenever someone needs to access the storage system.

Like storage, the distribution system should be clearly spelled out so that everyone involved understands their responsibilities and the process flows smoothly. Distribution systems typically benefit from formal procedures that describe the following tasks:
- how to obtain additional materials
- when additional materials need to be ordered
- who is authorized to request additional materials
- who is responsible for reproducing and shipping materials
- what shipping method is to be used
- how much advance notice is required to ship materials
- do multimedia materials require special handling, installation, scheduling or reproduction, and who will be responsible for these tasks

Those in charge of distribution must have clear procedures for all these issues to avoid problems. They should also have specific contacts for each of the training programs in storage and distribution so that any problems that crop up can be dealt with expeditiously. It is helpful to have both storage and distribution systems reporting to the same people to assure better coordination. If this is not possible, then ongoing communication among trainers, reproduction, storage and distribution people is essential.

Another quality assurance technique that can help is conducting an inspection of the proposed storage location and distribution system. During the inspection, look for any potential problems or deviations from specifications so that these can be corrected before they cause disruption to the training system. It may be beneficial to bring the client along too, so that they can see how the storage and distribution systems work and can provide final approval for the arrangements that have been made or suggest any needed changes.

### Maintenance Systems

An ancillary issue that must be addressed along with distribution is the maintenance system for training materials that are anticipated to have a long shelf-life. Maintenance issues refer not simply to the storage of existing materials, but to the plan for updating materials as needed and maintaining the instructional integrity of the training program, including on-going train the trainer sessions for new instructors, conversion of multimedia materials to new platforms and updated software systems, and the incorporation of new training programs in the company's curriculum.

Maintenance issues can become a whole separate function of the instructional design department, especially for programs with volatile content. For example, one large multinational company had two staff positions solely dedicated to keeping a library of customer service and customer information system self-study materials constantly updated and maintained. This is an extreme case, since the software upon which the training program was based underwent revision every year, but it illustrates the attention that material maintenance deserves.

Among the maintenance issues that training designers must handle are the following:

- how often will materials be updated?
- who will be responsible for updating?
- who will pay for updating?
- who will assure that masters and original electronic copies are stored and retrieved when needed?
- what process will be used to restock materials and to dispose of obsolete materials?

Many instructional design groups prefer to have the client take responsibility for maintenance, and this makes a lot of sense, since the client has the greatest vested interest in maintaining the training program for future use. The problem with this approach, however, is that many client organizations are ill-equipped to handle this function and are likely to let the maintenance system atrophy without intervention from the training or instructional design department. If training agrees to take on maintenance of courses, it must have the resources to perform this task adequately, or else the system is likely to break down, resulting in future antagonism with the client.

The best advice is to negotiate maintenance issues as part of the overall agreement on full-scale production. This way, maintenance does not simply become a victim of neglect, or subject to haphazard demands. Instead, like the rest of the instructional design process, course maintenance should be driven by a systematic plan that makes sense to both clients and instructional designers.

### Summary

In this chapter, you have learned about the key issues involved in full-scale reproduction of materials, including moving from development to full-scale production, working with production experts, creating a viable reproduction, storage and distribution system and deciding how to handle long-term course maintenance.

# Discussion Questions and Exercises

1. What are some key issues to attend to during full-scale production?
2. How can instructional designers work effectively with developers and clients to accelerate production?

**Case Study: Production Evaluation Checklist**

Using Tool 12 in Appendix 2, evaluate the production of training materials for a Leadership program that includes the following deliverables:

- Participant Workbook
- PowerPoint Overheads
- Online Reference Manual
- Leader's Guide
- Video Case Study
- Online 360 Assessment Tool

# Section Four:
# Implementation

The implementation phase of training design, also known as the delivery phase, is when learning occurs. It is the culmination of the three phases that have gone before it. In years past, implementation invariably meant delivering a training program in a classroom setting with a trainer or facilitator standing in the front lecturing to groups of trainees. Today, with the advent of learning technologies, implementation may mean a diversity of things, including trainees sitting in front of a computer taking a self-paced tutorial, watching a video or satellite television broadcast, logging on to a company Intranet, reading a book or self-study manual, meeting in small discussion groups to work on actual business problems, being coached one-on-one by a supervisor or mentor, or any combination of these activities. This section will broadly address all of these types of training implementations in three chapters: Train the Trainer, Classroom Delivery, and Non-classroom Delivery. The intention of this section is to provide general implementation guidelines rather than specific presentation skills and techniques. For readers who wish to study the presentation of training as a separate set of skills, they will be referred to a multitude of books that already exist.

The model for implementation is presented below. The chapters in this section will explain how this model works in detail.

*Figure 18-1:*

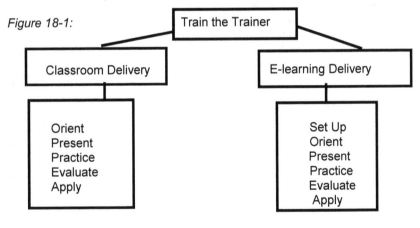

# Chapter Eighteen :
# Train the Trainer

The implementation phase often begins with a handoff, from designer to instructor/facilitator. Of course, if they are one and the same person, then train the trainer is unnecessary. But if someone other than the designer will implement the program, then they will need training in both the content of the training design and in the intended methodology for delivering it. The extent of this training is a function of the facilitator's current skill and knowledge level with regards to both the subject matter and the delivery method. At one extreme, train the trainer may be as informal as a brief meeting in which the designer walks the facilitator(s) through the design and materials, and answers any questions they may have. At the other extreme, formal train the trainer certification programs may need to be created and delivered to prepare novice instructors to deliver new subject matter effectively. In the latter case, this step in the process almost becomes its own mini-instructional design project. The entire range of train the trainer programs will be presented in this chapter.

### Assessing the Need for Train the Trainer

Like any other training program, train the trainer sessions should be based on an assessment of the needs of the learners, in this case the trainers or facilitators who will be delivering the program. The needs assessment should focus on two key questions:
1.   What do trainers need to know and be able to do in order to effectively deliver the proposed training program?
2.   What is the gap between trainers' current knowledge and skill and the requirements of the proposed training program?

Armed with this information, the training designer can then structure a train the trainer session that will meet the needs of the trainers and ensure a successful program delivery. As indicated above, train the trainer sessions broadly fall into two categories: foundation programs meant to prepare new trainers to be successful across a variety of programs, and specific programs meant to prepare experienced trainers to deliver a new content program.

The key to this distinction is the experience level of the proposed trainers. When dealing with novice trainers or those without a formal background in training and development, it is best to have them attend a foundation train the trainer program that covers the basics of training and development. These programs often include the topics in Table 18-2.

Foundational Train the Trainer programs are widely available these days through colleges and universities, private vendors and professional organizations. It is probably not necessary to develop such courses oneself, unless an organization has a large number of people to train or wishes to pursue an internal certification program for quality or other reasons.

*Table 18-2:* **Typical Foundational Train the Trainer Curriculum**

| |
|---|
| **Introduction to Training and Development** |
| • **Overview of the Field** |
| • **Training's Impact on Organizational Performance** |
| **Fundamentals of Instructional Design** |
| • **Training Objectives** |
| • **Course Design** |
| • **Lesson Plans** |
| • **Materials Development** |
| **Fundamentals of Training Delivery** |
| • **Presenting Technical Training** |
| • **Facilitating Management and 'Soft Skills' Training** |
| **Fundamentals of Training Evaluation** |
| • **Evaluating Learning** |
| • **Evaluating Skill Transfer** |
| *Optional Topics:* |
| • **Training Needs Assessment** |
| • **Human Performance Technology** |
| • **Testing and Assessment** |
| • **Training Project Management** |
| • **Learning Technology** |
| • **Evaluating Business Results** |

Once an individual possesses the basic foundation knowledge and skill, additional train the trainer programs can concentrate on the specific content and methods to be employed in a particular training program. For these types of specific train the trainer sessions, the goal is not so much instructing trainers how to teach as to orienting them to the specific content and instructional strategies of the course that they will deliver. A typical agenda for such a Train the Trainer course is presented in the table below.

*Table 18-3:* ***Specific Train the Trainer Sample Agenda***

| |
|---|
| 1. History and schedule of the program |
| 2. Overview of the course objectives and purpose |
| 3. Overview of the training materials |
| 4. Course logistics and administration |
| 5. Demonstration of how to teach the course |
| 6. Practice mini-teaching a module |
| 7. Question and answer/ problem resolution |

To be most effective, a separately-designed train the trainer program should be created, especially when training large numbers of instructors, since larger numbers can result in significant inconsistency in delivery. For one or two people, a simplified version of Train the Trainer often entails one or more of the following strategies:

- audit the training program
- stage a dry run walk-through of the training
- conduct a one-on-one tutorial session
- create a self-study train the trainer using the instructor guide
- arrange a pilot or microteach session to practice
- co-teach a session with an experienced trainer

Any of these methods may be sufficient by themselves for highly experienced trainers, but for those who do not possess experience a formalized train the trainer program is well worth the investment required to run it. After all, it is the trainer who will have the greatest single impact on the quality of the training once it leaves the instructional designer's hands. If the quality of the people delivering the program is poor, the quality of the program itself can be no better, despite whatever instructional integrity the program may possess.

### Instructional Strategies for Train the Trainer

The Train the Trainer session should be conducted by an experienced trainer who is also very familiar with the training content. An instructional designer with training facilitation background is an ideal choice for this assignment. If no one is available to instruct, it may be necessary for the course instructional designer to prepare someone to conduct the Train the Trainer session. The strategy of train the trainer is really two-fold. First, prepare trainers to deliver the content, and second, prepare trainers to facilitate learning using the instructional methods and learning activities developed for the course.

The first objective is best met by familiarizing trainers with the program's background and the specific content to be taught. This may be done by employing any of the following instructional strategies:

- mini-lectures on the content
- pre-read the student and/or instructor guide
- show a video on the content
- get expert job performers to discuss the content
- teach some or all of the content for trainers
- discuss the content in small groups

Most train the trainer programs include several of these methods, but a bare minimum would be to at least have trainers read through the materials for the course to familiarize themselves with the content.

To achieve the second objective of preparing trainers to facilitate learning, the train the trainer session should provide both a background and rationale for the instructional strategies and learning activities chosen and hands-on practice in facilitating the course. The background and rationale can be delivered using the same methods as those for objective one listed above. The hands-on facilitation can be accomplished through one or more of the following strategies:

- have trainers conduct a mini-lesson for other trainers
- videotape trainers conducting a mini-lesson and critique it
- select a few of the learning activities and have trainers experience them first hand
- have trainers conduct learning activities in small groups
- demonstrate how to conduct key portions of the course

If an instructor's guide has been prepared for the course, it should be used extensively throughout the Train the Trainer so that prospective trainers become very familiar with the content, layout and use of the guide. This will serve as their reference and job aid as they begin to teach the course, especially the first few times.

If the instructional design does not include an Instructor's Guide, then it is helpful to prepare a lesson plan for prospective trainers. The lesson plan should include the following essentials to help new trainers facilitate learning:

- Lesson Name
- Learning Objectives
- Materials and Equipment Needed
- Time Estimates for the Lesson
- Key Content Outline Points
- Instructional Strategies (what the trainer does)
- Learning Activities (what the learner does)
- Evaluation Activities

Lesson plans may take any form that is helpful in summarizing the course and guiding trainers. One format that has worked well for both new and experienced trainers is included in Appendix Two, p. A301.

## Summary

This chapter has discussed how to prepare trainers to deliver training programs effectively. Both foundational and content-specific Train the Trainer programs have been described, and specific instructional strategies for conducting Train the Trainer sessions have been provided. Finally, information on using Instructor Guides and lesson plans has been presented.

Now it is time for the moment of truth – the implementation of a newly-designed training program. This will be considered in the next two chapters.

# Discussion Questions
# and Exercises

1.  What are the key differences between foundational Train the Trainer programs and course-specific ones?

2.  What are some instructional strategies to employ for an effective Train the Trainer class?

**Case Study: Line Managers as Trainers**

A health care company has designed a new Basics of HR course for the managers to help them comply with many new federal and state personnel laws.  The client wants the training cascaded from top management to first-line supervisors and believes it will be best receive d if line managers deliver the training.

*Prepare a Train the Trainer plan for this project, using the techniques discussed in this chapter.*

# Chapter Nineteen :
# Classroom Delivery of Training

Approximately 67 percent of all training is delivered in a traditional classroom. The methods used today are anything but traditional, however. Trainers have departed from the academic lecture method and embraced more interactive teaching methods such as: discussion, role play, case study, small group work, etc. To effectively deliver well-designed training programs, classroom instructors need to possess a range of presentation and facilitation skills. This chapter will introduce the skills needed to deliver classroom training and suggest ways to develop these skills.

### A Model for Classroom Training

Although classroom trainers utilize a wide variety of teaching methods these days, most are based on an underlying model of how adults learn. This model is based on many years of research, although to my knowledge, it has not appeared in this precise form before. The model is presented below.

### Orienting Learners

The first phase of training delivery is typically referred to as the introduction, but I prefer the term orientation because it is a more accurate description of the purpose of this phase. Adult learning psychologists tell us that adults learn best when they are ready to learn (Knowles, 1984 b). Readiness is a function of need. That is, adults learn best when they sense they need to, in order to make a change in their lives, to improve themselves, to prepare for new challenges, etc. Thus, the key component of any training introduction should be creating a need to learn in the mind of the learner.

This can be accomplished several ways, but all rely to some extent on motivating the learner. Adults are motivated by both extrinsic and intrinsic rewards. Extrinsic rewards include the following:

- promotion
- pay raise/ money
- recognition
- peer approval
- honors
- gifts and other tangible items

Of course, trainers rarely have the option of bestowing significant extrinsic motivators on learners, aside from a few symbolic rewards like gifts from a grab bag, but learners are often sent to training because they have been newly promoted or are preparing for a higher-paying job. Good trainers help learners see the explicit connections between classroom learning and job performance rewards. This can be a very powerful motivator to learn.

*Figure 19-1:*  **Classroom Delivery Model**

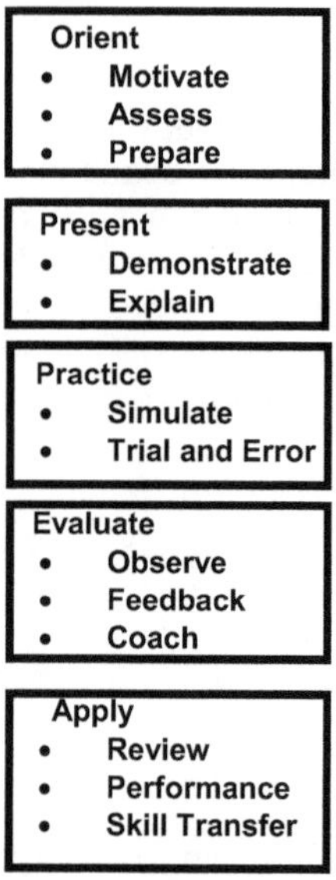

```
┌─────────────────────────┐
│ Orient                  │
│   •  Motivate           │
│   •  Assess             │
│   •  Prepare            │
└─────────────────────────┘
┌─────────────────────────┐
│ Present                 │
│   •  Demonstrate        │
│   •  Explain            │
└─────────────────────────┘
┌─────────────────────────┐
│ Practice                │
│   •  Simulate           │
│   •  Trial and Error    │
└─────────────────────────┘
┌─────────────────────────┐
│ Evaluate                │
│   •  Observe            │
│   •  Feedback           │
│   •  Coach              │
└─────────────────────────┘
┌─────────────────────────┐
│ Apply                   │
│   •  Review             │
│   •  Performance        │
│   •  Skill Transfer     │
└─────────────────────────┘
```

Intrinsic motivation refers to the internal satisfaction that people derive from their efforts. Most learners derive a sense of satisfaction from a successful learning experience. They enjoy a sense of achievement, of overcoming a challenge and of adding new knowledge and skills to their repertoire of abilities. For some adults, intrinsic motivation is a more powerful motivator than extrinsic, since their self-esteem depends on their sense of self-worth and self-confidence. Adults who are highly motivated by intrinsic rewards are typically high performing learners who have done well in classroom settings most of their lives and who look forward to learning new things.

It is important for trainers to understand what motivates adults to learn, since they must tap into the sources of motivation if they expect to see learning results in their classes. One of the findings of cognitive psychology that helps to explain human learning is that adults (and children for that matter) are typically far more motivated when they see value in what they are learning. This value prompts them to engage in the learning process. Value is really a combination of extrinsic and intrinsic factors, which taken together, create a powerful incentive for someone to make the effort necessary to learn something new. To help learners see value, trainers can typically appeal to two things:

1. why the skills being learned need to be performed in the workplace.

2.  what the impact of performance will be on other events and people of value to learners.

Let's consider an example of value, taken from a Train the Trainer course for new instructors. At the first session of the course, the instructor makes the following value statement about the course:

*As a new instructor, I'm sure many of you are wondering about how you are going to be successful in the classroom. This Train the Trainer course is going to help you succeed by giving you the knowledge and skills you need to present training in a dynamic, effective way that helps your students learn faster. Our company needs to speed up the learning process so that we can stay ahead of our competitors, who are also trying to figure out how to learn new skills more quickly. When you help employees learn, they will be able to return to their jobs, apply what they have learned and help the company succeed in the marketplace. That will benefit all employees, including you.*

Notice that the trainer appeals to both extrinsic and intrinsic motivation. The extrinsic rewards include the success of the company and the success of the learner on the job, which is implied to mean a better career for the trainer. The intrinsic rewards include doing a good job and being respected by one's students. This kind of motivational speech at the beginning of a training session helps to set the stage for successful learning.

The second major task of the orientation phase is to assess the current knowledge and skills of learners. Now, assessment may actually occur prior to the beginning of class, during the needs assessment phase, but a good classroom trainer knows that the individuals in a given class and the experiences they bring into the room with them create a unique dynamic. It is useful to discover what learners already know about the content of the training and how they feel about it in order to fine-tune the learning to meet the individual needs of learners.

Assessment can take many forms, from formal tests or other assessment instruments, including self-rating surveys, to more informal means, like asking everyone to introduce themselves and describe their previous experience with the content about to be presented. The choice of an assessment strategy is based on how much previous learner analysis has been done, how diverse the learning population is, and how much time is available for this activity. It is essential that some type of assessment take place, unless the trainer is already very familiar with the learners' backgrounds. I have even seen assessment take place in very large lecture settings simply by asking for a show of hands of how many people have taken a class like this before, and how many have experience with the content to be presented.

Once learners have been motivated to learn and the instructor has a sense of their current knowledge of the content, the last task of orientation is to prepare the learners to begin learning. This preparation typically takes two forms:
1.  Tell learners the objectives of the class.

2.  Show learners an outline of the class.

The objectives which have guided the design and development of the training should be shared with learners so that they can gauge the difficulty of the content and estimate how much effort they will need to expend to learn. Objectives also help to activate the learners' existing knowledge and get them thinking about how much they already know about the subject. A third reason to share objectives with learners is so that they clearly understand the standards by which their classroom performance will be judged.

For example, if an instructor in our fictional Train the Trainer course shared the following objective at the outset, learners would then be able to mentally prepare themselves for this activity, which will be evaluated to determine if they have mastered the content of the class:

1.  To present a 15-minute mini-lesson of a training program that you have designed.

This objective tells learners what they must do, and sets their expectations about the amount of effort it will take on their part to achieve the objective. If they have never presented a lesson before, this objective tells them that they are going to have to learn this new skill from scratch and had better be prepared to make a substantial effort. If, on the other hand, they have had considerable experience making presentations and teaching others, they may view this as a welcome opportunity to fine-tune their existing skills and gain additional practice. A few might even conclude that they aren't likely to learn anything new.

The second technique to prepare learners to begin learning is to share an outline of the content. This may be done in several forms, including a written list of topics, a table of contents of the student manual, or even a visual representation of the content in flowchart or graphical form. The outline, in whatever form it is presented, also helps learners estimate the difficulty of the class by helping them see in some detail the topics to be covered and allowing them to compare this to their own experience and knowledge. It also helps them make connections to previously-learned knowledge and skill and to ready their minds to receive new information about the topics to be presented. A visual model or flowchart can also serve as a job aid and reference for learners, much the way this chapter has begun by presenting a visual model of the classroom delivery process in order to help you see all the skills you will need to be an effective classroom trainer.

### Presenting New Information

The heart and soul of training is presenting new information to learners. In fact, years ago, trainers thought that this was all there was to training. If you could stand and deliver, you were considered to be an effective trainer. It was called 'platform skills', as in standing on a platform in front of large numbers of people and expostulating intelligently on your subject matter. Today, we know that presentation is only one part of effective training, but it is still clearly a very crucial part that must be done well in order for learners to succeed.

Presentation is typically made up of two distinct skills: demonstrating and explaining.  Each has a role and one may be more important depending on the subject matter.  For technical skills like computers and working with machinery and tools, demonstration is paramount.  The instructor must model the correct techniques and procedures so that learners can observe first-hand the right way to perform the task.  For soft skills like management and interpersonal communications, explanation often takes the lead role, since learners need to understand why they should behave in a certain way, and how their behavior is likely to influence others.  Of course, role models are also important for these subjects, but the learning cannot depend upon demonstration alone.

The demonstration portion of presentation may be accomplished several ways.  The most common is to have the instructor model the correct method while the class watches.  In a computer software class, the instructor may have his computer connected to a large overhead display so the entire class can watch as he demonstrates the proper keystrokes and menu choices to accomplish something like formatting a spreadsheet or sending an e-mail message.  A second method of demonstration is to have the proper procedures listed in a student manual in the order they are performed and containing sufficient detail so that the learner can follow the demonstration on the page.  A third method of demonstration increasingly used today is to employ videos or other audio-visual aids to demonstrate the skill for learners.  In a management training class on performance appraisals, the demonstration may be presented with a professionally-produced videotape showing a manager delivering a performance appraisal to an employee.  The video should demonstrate the ideal way to do this, thus creating a role model for learners to follow.  For technical topics, computer simulations can now demonstrate exactly how to perform a task and can show the actual outcomes of the performance.

Once the skill has been demonstrated for learners, the trainer must explain the skill to learners.  Explanation typically centers on one or more of the following:

- definitions of key concepts
- definitions of key principles
- examples of the skill in practice
- explication of procedures to be followed
- explication of policies governing the skill
- checking to see if learners understand the demonstration
- answering questions that learners have about the content

Let's take a closer look at each of these aspects of a presentation, using the example of a performance appraisal seminar for new supervisors. To begin the presentation, the trainer might give some definitions of key concepts like: job performance, appraisal, employee motivation, etc.  The purpose of these definitions is to help learners identify these key concepts and form a common understanding of what they mean on the job. Next, the trainer might give some definitions of key principles like maintaining employee self-esteem during the appraisal process. A principle definition explains how to do something or the cause and effect relationship between two or more things. In this case, the principle definition for maintaining self-esteem would be:

*During performance appraisal discussions, always focus on the behavior of the employee, not their personality, and always provide constructive feedback that can help the employee improve.*

This principle says that when we treat employees with respect and provide constructive feedback, we maintain their self-esteem and make it easier for them to hear our feedback and act upon it.

The third element of this presentation might be some examples of successful managers conducting performance appraisals. This could be done by showing a video tape, or by having learners read some case studies of performance appraisals. These examples would illustrate for learners the proper way to conduct an appraisal and would provide a role model for them to follow. The fourth element might be the presentation of a process model for conducting performance appraisals similar to the one listed below:

1. Ask the employee to assess their own performance.
2. Let the employee know what they have done well.
3. Focus on a few key areas for improvement.
4. Provide constructive feedback on how to improve.
5. Develop a performance plan for the coming year.
6. Close the discussion by summarizing key points and expressing confidence in the employee.

This simple process model forms the procedural basis for managers to follow in conducting appraisals. Each of the steps would be explained in some detail, with examples and tips on how to conduct each step in the process. This procedure, if widely adopted throughout the organization, would provide a uniform approach to appraisals that would help the company establish consistent performance management standards.

The fifth element would be a description of the company's policies regarding performance appraisals. These policies form the standard against which managers will be measured. The standards should include the following:

- how often appraisals must be conducted
- deadlines for submitting appraisals
- paperwork that must be completed to document the appraisal
- procedures for resolving complaints about appraisals
- how appraisals affect an employee's pay, promotional opportunities and employment

The sixth and seventh elements of the presentation are evaluative in nature. Once the trainer has clearly demonstrated the skill and explained how to do it, he/she should check to see that learners have understood the presentation before moving on. One way to check for understanding is to ask learners questions about the presentation, either orally or in writing. Some of the key questions that the trainer might pose to check learners' understanding of performance appraisals include:

1. What is an appraisal? (concept)
2. How do you maintain employee self-esteem during an appraisal? (principle)
3. Can you think of what you would say to an employee who becomes defensive about their performance? (example)
4. What is the company's six-step performance appraisal model? (procedure)
5. When must performance appraisals be conducted? (policy)

By posing questions like this, the trainer can tell whether learners understand the content of the presentation. When learners are unable to answer a question accurately, this is a clue to the trainer that further explanation of that point is required.

A second approach to checking for understanding that works with an active group of learners is to open the floor for questions. In this way, learners can probe for clarification or additional information on any of the topics of interest to them. The question and answer session tends to put learners in charge of the content, since they may ask any question they like. It requires the trainer to be more knowledgeable, though, since he/she cannot know in advance what kind of questions are going to be asked and therefore cannot prepare all the answers. It also depends on the active participation of learners. If a group sits silent when invited to ask questions, then this technique will not suffice to check for understanding. Sometimes, trainers use a combination of question-answer and posing questions to determine if learners understand the presentation before moving on to the next phase of the lesson –practice.

### The Role of Practice

One thing we know for sure about learning is that practice plays the key role in developing proficiency in a new skill. Thus, practice should occupy the majority of classroom time. Unfortunately, time pressures tend to intervene and reduce the amount of time devoted to guided classroom practice. In some cases, practice is skipped altogether, leaving it up to learners to practice on the job. This is a risky strategy, since research indicates that few learners are willing or able to practice new skills on the job without first having mastered them in a training setting. Thus, practice is crucial to ensure that newly learned skills transfer to the job and become part of the employee's job performance.

Aside from its role in transferring skills to the job, practice is also a key method the trainer can use to determine how well learners are doing in mastering new skills. If the trainer never sees learners perform new skills, he/she has no way of knowing if they have learned these skills. Moreover, when learners practice in class, the trainer can provide feedback to learners on their practice and help solve learning and motivation problems on the spot before they become impediments to learning new skills.

Since practice is so important and yet the time devoted to it is being reduced, it is critical to choose the right things to practice and also to ensure that trainees get the most from their practice. We used to think that the old adage, "practice makes perfect" was the ultimate learning principle. Nowadays, educational psychologists know the adage should be "perfect practice makes perfect." The difference is not mere semantics. Rather, it is the type of practice that trainees engage in that matters most in developing skills. If trainees practice the wrong things, or do so in the wrong ways, they may actually learn the wrong skills or learn nothing at all of use. So trainers and designers need to pay close attention to the types of practice they provide to ensure successful learning.

The best practice should simulate the actual performance of a skill on the job. The closer that the practice exercise comes to the real world, the better the learning that will result and the more likely it will be applied to the job. So the first principle of practice is to simulate the job as much as possible. The second principle is to choose to practice those skills that are most crucial to job success. These are usually the procedures and policies governing a skill, rather than definitions or examples. For the performance appraisal example above, the most critical skill to practice is the six-step procedure for conducting an appraisal. If learners don't get this right, then they are not going to be able to conduct a successful appraisal. Thus, the practice exercise for this seminar ought to involve having learners use the six-step process to conduct practice performance appraisals. This could be done by breaking the learners into small groups of 2-3 and having them role play an appraisal, with one person playing the manager and the other the employee and possible having a third person observe and give feedback on the role play.

Besides simulating the job, 'perfect' practice also allows learners to experiment and to learn from their mistakes. Thus, practice should have a trial and error component in which learners are encouraged to try out new skills, to make some mistakes and to learn from them. The performance appraisal role plays could meet this condition of practice by simulating some difficult performance appraisal situations, such as an employee who has had a recent drop-off in performance, an employee with whom the supervisor has had conflict or an employee who is demanding a raise or a promotion. These real-world scenarios give learners the opportunity to apply their new knowledge and skill to a challenging situation while still providing a safe environment in which to do so, since the other person playing the role of the employee is really a fellow manager who is also learning new skills. If the manager makes a blunder during the role play, no real damage is done (except perhaps to his ego), and he can reflect upon the mistake and see how to correct it the next time.

The role play exercise thus meets two of the conditions for perfect practice:

- it simulates on-the-job performance
- it allows for trial and error

There is one additional requirement for perfect practice and that is the next phase in the learning process –obtaining feedback on one's learning. Feedback is a critical component of any system, since it helps to regulate the system and keep it in equilibrium. For learning systems, feedback plays the important role of letting learners know how they are doing and helping them adjust their practice until they can perform new skills perfectly every time. Good feedback requires three things:

1. Observe the skill being used.
2. Provide feedback on what the learner did well and what needs to be improved.
3. Coach the learner on how to revise their practice so that they obtain the right results.

Most learning feedback focuses on the skill being learned, but attention should also be given to the learner's motivation, if this appears to be a source of problems. Motivation to learn, as indicated earlier, is tied to the learner's level of engagement in the subject matter, which in turn regulates the amount of effort the learner is willing to expend. During practice sessions, some learners may encounter difficulty that tends to discourage them. This reduces their effort, or in the worst cases, may prompt them to stop trying altogether. If they believe they may lose face with their peers, they may also stop trying rather than risk failure. If it appears that learners are struggling due to a lack of motivation, then coaching must focus on building up their confidence level. This can be done by pointing out shortcuts and tips that make it easier to perform the skill, or by breaking the skill down into smaller components that can more easily be mastered. Once the learner has regained confidence, then coaching should focus on fine-tuning the performance until it reaches acceptable levels.

Occasionally, trainers also encounter learners who are overconfident in their ability to learn and who therefore make little effort, thinking that the skill is a 'piece of cake.' If their perception of the skill's difficulty is inaccurate, they may also be poor performers because of lack of effort, even though they are perfectly capable of performing the skill well. In these cases, it is necessary to adjust their motivation to better match the task at hand. This may require pointing out that the skill is actually more difficult than the overconfident learner anticipated, and that the results they are achieving are not up to the standard. This may serve to convince an overconfident learner to make greater effort to practice the skill, which will eventually result in mastery.

This discussion shows that observing practice sessions is a crucial part of training, and knowing how to differentiate between skill and motivation problems is an important trainer skill. Unless the trainer properly diagnoses the cause of skill problems, he/she will be unable to recommend a proper remedy.

The final phase of classroom training is to apply newly learned skills on the job. Although this phase actually occurs after students leave the classroom, it is important to begin the transfer while learners are still in class and to continue to support learners as they try out new skills on the job. To help the transfer process begin, trainers should do three things at the end of lessons:

1. Review the content of the lesson.
2. Present job performance standards for the skills that have been learned.
3. Support the transfer of skills to the job with job aids, reference materials and line management coaching and rewards.

A review and summary of the lesson serves as a means of integrating all the discrete skills that have been learned and helping learners focus on the bigger picture, including how the skills will make them and the organization more effective. Presenting the performance standards expected on the job helps learners evaluate how well they are doing and how much additional effort they will need to make to reach the expected standards. Of course, trainers need to be cautious in setting standards for trainees. Typically, trainees will need several months of on the job practice before they are able to consistently reach the standards of journeymen employees, so make sure learners do not become discouraged by high standards that they are unable to meet right away. Point out that their skills will continue to improve with practice until eventually they reach the expected standard.

The final step of the conclusion is to give the learners tools to assist them in transferring skills to the job. The most common tool for this purpose is the job aid, a quick reference that helps to lower the perceived difficulty of the task and reduces the requirement to memorize new knowledge and skill. Job aids may be as simple as a summary sheet of the skills and procedures, or as complex as an electronic performance support system (EPSS), which is embedded in the computer software that the learner uses on the job. These more complex systems may actually be capable of adjusting the level of support depending on the actions of the learner and provide exactly the right amount of support at the right time.

For example, a utility developed an EPSS for its telephone customer service representatives that provided contextual help on demand. If they were trying to sign up a new customer for electric service, the EPSS would be able to provide specific help on filling out each computer screen as the representative navigated through the customer information system. The most sophisticated EPSS would also contain video clips of experienced representatives solving complex problems or handling difficult procedures, a library of all the forms the representative might need in electronic format, a complete set of policy and procedure manuals, searchable by key words, the latest product and policy information and an on-line tutorial for refresher training.   We will look at computer-mediated support systems in more detail in the next chapter.

Besides job aids, the other key component of skill transfer is the support of the learner's manager in applying the new skills.  This requires that the manager be knowledgeable about the skills and be prepared to serve as a coach and mentor to the learner.  Trainers can help managers with these roles by providing an orientation for managers that highlights the skills being learned and gives advice on how to support and coach learners on the job.   Trainers can also offer to go into the workplace and assist managers in coaching employees.  Furthermore, trainers can help learners support each other by creating learning communities outside of class who meet regularly to compare their experiences and deepen the learning process through on-the-job practice and innovation.  Finally, trainers can help companies set up apprenticeship systems in which new employees are paired up with experienced ones so as to accelerate the learning process.  Although skill transfer takes trainers outside their normal confines in the classroom, it also promises to boost the application of newly learned skills and therefore enhance the value of training.

### Using Demonstrations to Develop Skills

The general teaching model presented above works for virtually any kind of subject and with all kinds of learners.   When focusing on specific types of skills, some modifications of the model can help the learning process.  One of the most common types of training is technical or skill-based training that focuses on how to perform technical jobs like manufacturing, engineering, information technology, accounting, and the like.  Technical skills can be sub-divided into three basic types:
1.  Psychomotor skills
2.  Procedural skills
3.  Troubleshooting skills

Psychomotor skills are basic physical skills such as handwriting, typing, eye-hand coordination, etc. that form the basis for more advanced technical skills.  Most psychomotor skills are learned in school or acquired through on-the-job training, but a few of these may need to be taught in formal training.  One that comes to mind is typing skills for computer users.

Most job skills are procedural in nature, such as learning to change a tire, assemble a widget, solder a printed circuit board, balance an account, or design a circuit.  These are really a series of psychomotor skills linked together to perform a higher-order task.  The best way to learn procedural skills is by demonstrating the procedure step by step and practicing it in smaller chunks until the learner is able to perform the entire procedure from start to finish.

Finally, the most complex technical skills involve troubleshooting or diagnosing problems.  These skills are complex because they require both a complete knowledge of the procedure along with knowledge of all the various things that can go wrong with the procedure or the equipment involved. Troubleshooting skills such as repairing an engine, fixing a broken piece of equipment or discovering the cause of a computer malfunction are best taught in stages. First, the learner must thoroughly master the psychomotor and procedural skills inherent in the job and then they can learn troubleshooting strategies such as isolating the cause of the problem, and determining possible solutions to fix it.

For technical skills, the presentation phase of the lesson should rely heavily on demonstration, since this is the best method to learn complex procedures. By observing an expert perform, the novice can connect abstract theory to practical application and judge for themselves how much effort they will need to expend learning the new skill. The demonstration must be a genuine example of the performance as done on the job, complete with the proper tools and equipment, materials and simulated work environment. The closer the demonstration comes to reality, the easier it is for learners to master the skill and apply it on the job.

The other key component of skill learning is guided practice. The practice should also simulate the job as much as possible, including use of any tools, equipment, materials or supplies used on the job. An additional component of technical skills practice is the use of flow charts or other job aids to help guide learners through complex procedural and troubleshooting skills. Practice may need to continue for some time before true proficiency is achieved. The practice may begin in the classroom and then be continued for some time on the job under the tutelage of an experienced worker or manager. Gradually over time, as the skill is used more frequently, the learning moves from a conscious, deliberate level to an unconscious, automatic level of proficiency that marks true expertise.

Cognitive psychologists describe these two levels of knowledge as declarative and procedural. Declarative knowledge is the conscious, deliberate form that is typical of novice learners. When learning a new task, learners are self-conscious about their performance and much slower, since they must stop to think about each step in the process. Over time, they develop procedural knowledge that becomes automatic and faster, since they are able to perform without having to consciously think of each step before doing it. The fluency associated with procedural knowledge is rarely mastered in a classroom setting, since it takes many repetitions of the task to fully reach this level. Instead, most training programs strive to achieve a good declarative level of skill and then rely on job experience to develop fluency and expertise. Job aids can help this transition, too, by providing levels of support for new learners that can gradually be withdrawn as proficiency develops.

### Using Lectures and Discussions to Develop Knowledge

Not all training programs are skill-based. Many aim to teach knowledge instead, including theory, concepts, principles and competencies that are not easily learned through rote practice. When the training topic is knowledge-based, trainers must rely on different methods to teach than when the topic is strictly technical in nature. Among the techniques that work best for knowledge development is lecture followed by discussion, either in large or small groups.

The lecture portion of the lesson should focus on presenting key concepts and principles required to master and apply new knowledge on the job. For example, if a training program is teaching managers how to coach their employees, the lecture should concentrate on defining coaching, motivating learners to use it, describing the conditions under which coaching should be used and providing specific coaching skills and techniques for different situations. Once the lecture is over, the instructor should then move to a discussion mode in which he/she poses open-ended questions to stimulate thought among learners and help them see how they can apply the knowledge to their own situation. Discussions also encourage learners to share experiences among themselves and deepen their understanding by allowing for questions that did not get answered during the lecture. Because they require active participation, discussions are favored by most learners and are particularly helpful in developing communication, social skills and critical thinking.

A good discussion appears to be a spontaneous event that propels itself, but such is rarely the case. In fact, discussions require careful pre-planning and skillful facilitation to be successful. Before going into the specific skills of discussion facilitators, let's look at three different types of discussions and determine when they should be used. Discussions can be broken into the following types:
1. Content focus
2. Strategy focus
3. Brainstorming

The content discussion is most commonly used in training situations. The discussion centers on a topic which is introduced by the facilitator. The discussion is controlled to keep it focused on the topic. Tangential comments are deferred or excluded from the discussion so as to keep it on track. An example of a content discussion would be how to handle an employee disciplinary problem in a performance management class, using a five-step model introduced by the trainer.

The strategy discussion is focused more on the process than on the content. The trainer may introduce a topic, but allows a much freer discussion of the issue with little attempt to control the discussion. An example of a strategy discussion would be a strategic planning meeting in which participants chart the organization's course over a long period of time, say five to ten years. The facilitator introduces the topic and sets some general ground rules, but allows for a more wide-ranging discussion, including the introduction of related topics. The facilitator may also play the devil's advocate during these discussions to encourage participants to fully consider the consequences of the plans they are discussing or to see how the plans may affect various stakeholders.

Finally, the broadest focus discussions are brainstorming sessions in which trainers do little if any pre-planning and simply encourage spontaneous participation and interaction. Although the facilitator may introduce a process such as a fishbone diagram to help stimulate thought, the main role is to encourage creativity and to document the ideas as they are generated from participants. Although brainstorming is less used in training settings than content discussions, it is widely used in process improvement and problem solving sessions. In a training setting, brainstorming may be useful to get learners to think about how to apply skills in new situations or how to solve specific problems they may encounter on the job.

The typical content-focused discussion used most widely in training situations should be carefully pre-planned to achieve maximum results. The following model illustrates the training discussion process:

Figure 19-2:     ***Training Discussion Process Model***

| |
|---|
| **Choose Appropriate Topic** |
| **Prepare the Environment** |
| **Direct and Monitor the Discussion** |
| **Use Questioning Techniques to Deepen the Discussion** |
| **Use Summarizing Techniques to Solidify Learning** |

Appropriate topics for discussion include virtually any content that is subject to multiple interpretations. To hold effective discussions, trainees need to know enough about the topic to have a solid factual base and to have formed opinions. They also should be interested in the topic to stimulate participation. If learners are unfamiliar with a topic, it may be introduced using reading materials, videos, lectures, guest speakers or site visits.

Once learners have been introduced to the topic, the proper environment must be created. This usually calls for seating everyone in a circle or U-shape, so that participants can see each other and direct comments to each other. The facilitator needs to set a supportive tone by introducing the purpose of the discussion, the ground rules and encouraging everyone to participate. Rewarding the first few volunteers with praise helps to keep comments coming. Avoid passing judgment on opinions or allowing participants to do so, at least until the discussion is over and is being debriefed. Otherwise, the discussion can be side-tracked or participants may clam up.

The heart of facilitating discussion is directing and monitoring the conversation so that it achieves the goals it was designed for. Typically, the facilitator begins the discussion with an open-ended question, perhaps provocative in nature, which invites the group to offer opinions. In a performance management course, such an icebreaking discussion starter might be:

*What do you think really motivates your employees to perform at their best?*

Questions that start with 'how' and 'why' are also excellent discussion starters:

*How can managers get more results out of their employees?*

*Why do some employees become peak performers while others are just average?*

The trainer then stops and waits, however long it takes, for someone to offer a reply. Once the first person has broken the ice, encourage others to share their views, by agreeing, disagreeing or taking a whole different perspective on the question. The discussion then ensues following a communication pattern of ask-listen-respond. The communication pattern of ask-listen-respond is a hallmark of facilitated discussion. The trick that experienced facilitators learn over the years is how to listen for real meaning and intent and how to respond in a way that leads to learning or at least to further discussion of the topic.

One key strategy used by facilitators is the types of questions they pose during a discussion. As mentioned above, open-ended questions are used to stimulate discussion, or introduce a new discussion topic. Sometimes, the facilitator wishes to clarify a point in dispute or close out the discussion, sensing that the group has said what it wants. In these cases, closed-ended questions of the 'Yes/No' or one-word answer type are used. To clarify a point, a facilitator might say:

*What principle helps to maintain self-esteem?* Or:

*Did you say the first principle helps maintain self-esteem?*

To end a discussion, one might say:

*Does anyone have anything else they want to say before we close this discussion?*

In addition to open and closed-ended questions, facilitators frequently use six other discussion question variations. These are listed below with an example of each.

**Overhead Question:** [Posed to the entire group]
*What are the functions of an internal audit department?*
**Direct Question:** [Directed to an individual]
*John, what is the function of an internal audit department?*
**Combined Question:** [Use an overhead question and then direct it to an individual]
*What are the functions of an internal audit department? [pause.... No answer.] John?*
**Relay Question:** [Relay a learner's question directed at the trainer back to the group.]
*John: What do you mean by internal audit?*
*Trainer: Can someone tell us what internal audit departments do?*
*Jane: I think they make sure that companies and employees are honest and doing things according to the rules.*

*Trainer: That's certainly one of their major functions, Jane. We'll learn about more later in the course. Does that help answer your question, John?*

**Review Question:** [An overhead question designed to review previously-covered material.]

*What are the four functions of an internal audit department again, class?*

**Rhetorical Question:** [A question that the questioner answers himself or that does not require an answer.]

*Do you know what is the only dumb question? It's a question that someone doesn't bother to ask.*

Besides developing a repertoire of question types, good facilitators also make sure that everyone participates in discussions and that they stay focused on topic and continue to elicit new responses from participants. The following tips can help make discussions more effective.

*Table 19-4:*  **Discussion Questioning Techniques**

| |
|---|
| ☐ Distribute questions equally and randomly among the group. |
| ☐ Use easy overhead questions to get discussion started or restarted. |
| ☐ Use a direct question for an inattentive/uninvolved/disruptive participant. |
| ☐ Use relay questions to stimulate discussion and check for understanding rather than answering all the learner's questions for them. |
| ☐ Rephrase questions that do not elicit a response or appear to be confusing. |

The final step in leading discussion is to conclude in a way that reinforces the learning that the discussion has produced. One thing that helps is to summarize the discussion for participants, with or without the aid of notes or flipcharts. For complex or lengthy discussions, note taking is recommended, both for summary purposes and as a record that can be distributed to participants later. The summary should focus on the following points:

- topics discussed
- summary of views and schools of thought expressed
- areas of agreement and disagreement
- areas for further study or discussion
- ways to apply what has been discussed on the job

Mastering discussions is a key training skill. Once a trainer is good at facilitating discussions, they can move on to use discussion techniques along with case studies and role plays, the topics of the next section.

### Using Case Studies and Role Plays To Simulate Reality

Although it is desirable to simulate the work environment as much as possible when training employees, it is not always possible to do so. This is particularly a problem for management training, since a manager's work involves all aspects of a firm's business. In these circumstances, the best alternative is to simulate job conditions using case studies or role plays.

A case study is a real-life or fictional scenario which is used to give learners practical knowledge about an event or subject. Case studies have been used for over 100 years to teach managers how to solve complex business problems. A role play is an activity in which learners act out the roles of real-life individuals in order to gain personal experience dealing with a subject that involves interpersonal relations. Role plays have evolved from rather stilted, scripted mini-dramas into a flexible method of simulating many types of business situations and interpersonal interactions. Although these two learning methods are quite different in form, they serve a similar function in a training setting – to simulate the reality of the job in a way that allows learners to practice skills in a safe environment.

Both case studies and role plays have certain key advantages over other learning methods. These are summarized below:
- supports transfer of learning by simulating the job
- encourages an exchange of ideas and experiences among learners
- promotes self-discovery and critical thinking
- actively involves trainees in the learning process

Like any activity, these are not perfect. One common complaint is that they take too long and indeed well-run case studies and role plays can be time-consuming activities. A second complaint is that they may result in tunnel vision – a rather narrow view of issues based on the collective wisdom of the group, or in some cases, the lack thereof. These disadvantages can be managed and overcome if the case study or role play is well-planned and facilitated. A key feature of both techniques is the incorporation of a discussion phase that is designed to help participants learn from their experiences.

Case studies should be organized around the three-step process listed below.

Figure 19-5:  **Case Study Facilitation Process**

| 1. | Present the situation. |
|----|------------------------|
| 2. | Prepare questions. |
| 3. | Facilitate discussion. |

To present the case, written descriptions have traditionally been used, but video case studies are becoming increasingly popular due to the realism they add. Whether written or visual, case studies typically include the following key details:

1.  company background – markets, financials, history
2.  personal profiles of key characters
3.  description of the problem/opportunity

The case should contain sufficient details to make it life-like without adding too much complexity or making it too long.

The second element of a case study is a series of questions designed to establish the facts of the case and to stimulate thought and discussion about what the key players should do to resolve the case. The questions should be handed out with the case so that learners can focus on the key issues to be discussed later. The third, and most critical part of the case study, is the discussion that follows. This is where the real learning occurs, as participants wrestle with the issues raised and exchange ideas about the best way to resolve the case. When facilitating a case study discussion, focus on the objectives of the case study and the skills being learned. If the case study's purpose is to examine marketing strategy, focus the questions on this topic and not extraneous areas of the business. The discussion should proceed from facts to options to solutions to applications. Thus, a discussion of a case study of an international retailer's marketing strategy could include the following questions:

1.  *What was the company's market response to increased global competition? (fact)*
2.  *What were the possible marketing strategies that the company could have pursued? (options)*
3.  *Which marketing strategy do you think they should pursue and why? (solutions)*
4.  *How might these strategies work at our company? (applications)*

Role plays also require careful planning to obtain successful results. Too many role plays are little more than diversionary entertainment rather than serious learning events. To avoid this tendency, follow the process listed below to plan and conduct role plays.

*Figure 19-6:*          ***Role Play Process Model***

| | |
|---|---|
| 1. | Present the situation. |
| 2. | Identify roles. |
| 3. | Enact the role play. |
| 4. | Debrief the role play. |
| 5. | Discuss significance and learning points. |

In presenting the situation, give enough background information on the characters, setting, issues, and objectives of the role play so that participants can realistically play their roles. Depending on what learners already know about the issue, this may require only a brief introduction or a more detailed handout that can be reviewed in advance. Once the goals and the situation have been presented, identify the roles to be played, using handouts for more complex role plays. The roles should include the characters' names, positions, relationships to each other, points of view, and likely responses to the issues at hand.  Providing detailed role information helps participants play their roles accurately, a key factor in a successful role play.  Of course, some role plays involve participants playing themselves in a hypothetical situation, while others require participants to assume the roles of other people.  It is the latter case where detailed role identification is most necessary.

Once participants know the situation and their role, it is time to enact the role play. This may be done in small groups or in front of the whole group, although the latter is much riskier for participants.  Using small groups also involves more people, since the trainer can ensure that everyone is involved in the role play that way.  The only difficulty of small group role plays is monitoring them.  For a lone trainer with several role plays going on simultaneously, it is necessary to rotate around the classroom, eavesdropping on each one for brief periods to get a flavor for how things are going.  A good role play can be conducted in about 10-15 minutes. Anything beyond that begins to tax the imagination of participants and probably does not add much extra value to the process.

Once the role play is over, the learning really begins.  This is when the trainer should debrief the role play and lead a discussion about what was learned from it.  Failure to follow up role plays with discussion is one of the biggest weaknesses of role plays.  Too often, participants have  a few laughs playing some fictional actor and then the class moves on, without any clear idea of why the role play was conducted or what it means to participants' real life jobs.  The debriefing portion of the discussion should focus on how participants felt about their experience and how they would assess their performance.  Getting participants to share this information helps them reflect on their own learning and recognize personal insights that might otherwise be missed.  Once everyone has had a chance to express their feelings and personal insights, discussion should then turn to the key issues and learning points raised by the role play.  This is where the link to the content of the lesson should occur and where participants begin to see how to take what they learned in the role play and apply it to their own situation.  Some of this discussion can take place in small groups, especially for larger classes, but at least a summary of the discussion ought to be conducted with the whole group to avoid the tunnel vision syndrome mentioned earlier as a drawback of role plays.  If a particular group had an unsuccessful role play or got themselves off on a tangent, the group discussion can help refocus them on the key learning points that the role play was designed to accomplish and integrate their experiences with the rest of the class.

Additional training delivery techniques are included in Appendix Two, p. 302.

*Summary*

In this chapter, we have examined the key skills and techniques of successful classroom trainers. These include: a basic model for classroom lessons and strategies for using demonstrations, discussions, case studies and role plays to enrich the learning process. With this foundation and lots of practice, you will be ready to deliver training with impact. For more in-depth treatment of classroom facilitation, consult the following authors in the bibliography in Appendix One, p. 264 (Baird, Schnier and Laird, 1984; Bentley, 1994; Craig, 1996; Knowles, 1984; Smith and Delahaye, 1987; Pike, 1997).

Even if your role is only to design training, it is important to appreciate how training programs are delivered in classroom settings in order to prepare training programs that are easy and effective to deliver.

In the next chapter, we will consider the growing and exciting world of learning outside the classroom, a world that will play a dominating role in the training profession in the years to come.

# Discussion Questions and Exercises

1. Apply the Classroom Delivery Model to this class or the most recent one you have attended. How did the instructor implement each step?

2. What are the best ways to teach:
   a. Leadership skills
   b. Manufacturing skills
   c. Financial skills
   d. Computer skills
   e. Communication skills

3. Compare and contrast the following instructional methods: Case study, role play, discussion.

**Case Study: Lesson Planning**

Develop a lesson plan for a course you will teach in the future or for this chapter. Use the Lesson Plan template (tool 13) in Appendix 2 on p. 301.

# Chapter Twenty :
# E-learning Delivery Techniques

The fastest growing area of training is e-learning technology. It has increased from less than 5 percent of training delivery to over 30 percent in the past 20 years and is expected to continue to increase in the 21st century. Learning technology includes several delivery mediums, the most popular of which are:

- computer-based training (CBT – graphics and text delivered via computer)
- multimedia training (MMT – combinations of video, audio, graphics, animation and text delivered via computer or hand-held device)
- web-based training (WBT – training delivered over the Internet or company Intranet).

Though these delivery systems do not require a human instructor, they do not obviate the need for humans altogether. Someone must administer technology training, someone must facilitate trainees' use of the systems, someone must maintain and troubleshoot finicky systems, and someone must collect and report data regarding usage and learning. These skills and a good understanding of the technology used to deliver training must be taught to those who assist in the delivery of non-classroom learning. This chapter will cover these issues as well as other forms of non-classroom delivery, including: on-the-job learning.

A model of e-learning delivery was introduced at the beginning of section four. This model is expanded in Figure 20-1 below.

This model is similar in form to the classroom delivery model, with the exception of an extra step up front for set up. The specifics of implementing technology are quite different, however, and deserve some explanation. The set up phase is needed for technology-based learning because of the unique requirements for establishing suitable facilities, installing hardware and software and arranging technical support. These requirements can be quite elaborate, if technology is being deployed for the first time. It typically requires the involvement of several departments besides training, including information technology, purchasing and facilities. Information technology professionals should be consulted about hardware and software platforms, network capabilities, data security issues and technical support, especially for hardware. Purchasing departments get involved with large-scale purchases of hardware and software. It is important to understand purchasing procedures to avoid lengthy delays. Finally, facilities departments provide the space for technology learning, and take care of the physical security issues.

*Figure 20-1:*        ***E-learning Technology Implementation Model***

| Set Up |
| --- |
| • Facilities |
| • Hardware |
| • Software |
| • Tech. Support |

| Orient |
| --- |
| • Market |
| • Motivate |
| • Assess |

| Present |
| --- |
| • Demonstrate |
| • Simulate |
| • Inform |

| Practice |
| --- |
| • Drill |
| • Trial & Error |
| • Activity |

| Evaluate |
| --- |
| • Test |
| • Feedback |
| • Remediation |
| • Report |

| Apply |
| --- |
| • EPSS |
| • OJT |

Once the set up phase is complete, the next phase is orientation. Unlike classroom delivery, learning technology requires a concerted marketing effort to get employees to try out something new. A good marketing plan should include extensive publicity, a signature event to launch the effort and constant reminders. Besides a good marketing plan, attention must be given to motivating employees to use the system. Too many companies assume that if they put learning technology in the work environment, employees will naturally seek it out. This may not occur for several reasons:

- lack of time
- lack of interest
- lack of management support
- fear of failure
- difficulty using learning technology
- preference for social forms of learning

To overcome these barriers, incentives must be put in place to encourage employees to use the resources provided to them. Some companies opt for mandatory usage, and agree to pay employees to take lessons on company time. In this case, line managers must be willing to support such a policy and ensure compliance among their employees. Most companies eschew mandated attendance, preferring to encourage employees to take training on their own time. This is where utilization problems can crop up. Although employees may have the best intentions, time constraints and heavy workloads often prevent them from devoting the time to learning. Leading companies have experimented with a number of different incentives, including: cash bonuses, gifts and prizes, public recognition, certificates of completion, compensatory time off, etc. in order to motivate employees to make the effort to learn on their own time. Another key to building enthusiasm for learning technology is to provide an orientation and assistance to employees who are just beginning to use the technology. One company had great success with its multimedia learning labs after they hired a part-time facilitator who visited labs periodically and assisted new learners in logging on to the system, setting up individual learning programs, and getting comfortable with the user interface. The presence of a live human being helped new users overcome their fears and solved many problems that had been driving employees away.

The third task of orientation is to assess the learner's current knowledge and skill and place them in the appropriate level for their needs. Most good CBT/MMT programs include a diagnostic function that tests new learners, determines their current knowledge level and automatically places them at the right level. One of the true strengths of learning technology is its ability to individualize instruction to fit the unique needs of each learner. The assessment should not be skipped, even though employees sometimes prefer to explore and navigate the system on their own, without regard for recommended placement.

The next phase of the learning technology model is the presentation of content. This is typically accomplished in one of three ways:
1. Demonstration
2. Simulation
3. Information

Demonstration relies on providing role models and real-life examples to illustrate how a skill should be performed. An example is a sales training course that features video clips of successful sales people demonstrating the selling techniques taught in the lesson. By watching these individuals in real-life situations, the learner can see how the sales techniques are applied. Simulations also rely on real-life examples, but go beyond demonstrations in that they allow learners to manipulate objects and events in a simulated cyber-environment that approximates the real-world. A famous example is flight simulators used to train airplane pilots. These simulators include realistic cockpit controls and computer-generated scenarios that appear to the learner to be real, even down to the motion of the airplane and the readouts on displays. Simulations are the best current state-of-the-art for learning technology, since they come closest to job performance, but they are also the most difficult and expensive forms of technology learning to design and develop.

Finally, many programs rely on information for the bulk of the presentation. This includes screens of text, graphics, images, video and audio clips that essential provide the same role as a classroom lecturer. Although information presentations can be made to look very pretty with today's technology, they are the least effective presentation method for the same reason that lecture is the least effective classroom teaching method. Short presentations of content are fine, but subjecting learners to screen after screen of text does little to help them learn new skills that can be readily applied on the job.

The next phase of the model is practice. Arguably, this is what computers do best. They are incredibly patient tutors who will provide endless drill and practice to the willing user. The most common forms of practice are drills consisting of questions posed to the learner about the content of the presentation. These may be in many forms, including: multiple choice, matching, fill in the blank, true/false, etc. Though drill and practice is essential for building proficiency and fluency, it become dull in a hurry for most learners. As an example, a course on technical writing includes many drills on punctuation and syntax. Although these help learners build skill in correct grammar usage, learners quickly became bored with these endless drills. Another approach to practice, trial and error, allows the user greater control over the practice exercise by allowing them to manipulate objects and events to see what might happen. They can then try out another approach and experiment like this until they find a solution that yields the best result. An example of trial and error is a basic electronics course that includes a simulated printed circuit board that allows learners to add and remove various components and then see the result. This type of practice helps learners to develop higher-level thinking skills about how circuits are designed and how various components interact to produce different electrical currents and effects.

The third type of practice is activity-based. The learner is introduced to a topic and then asked to participate in an activity designed to build their skills. The activities may range from writing a report, preparing for a meeting, interacting in a role play, trying out a psychomotor skill or troubleshooting a technical problem. Activity-based practice has the advantage of engaging learners in ways that can be easily applied to the job, but like simulations, they are more difficult and costly to develop.

The next phase of technology learning is evaluation. This is another area where technology has a clear advantage over classroom delivery. The system allows for individual evaluation, feedback and remediation, and provides information in real time. Most multimedia training includes sophisticated testing routines that ensure that learners master objectives before being allowed to move on. After completing a test or exercise, learners receive immediate feedback on their results, including praise and reinforcement for doing well and corrective feedback when they do not fare well. The corrective feedback often includes specific remediation, based on an analysis of the errors made. For example, a basic skills course in shop math tests learners at the end of each module of instruction. After completing a module on converting fractions to decimals, learners take a 10-item test, receive their score, and if they get less than 80 percent, are automatically returned to the presentation again for additional tutoring and practice. The program even analyzed learners' wrong answers to determine precisely where they were having problems and offered additional help in those areas.

Finally, learning technology often includes sophisticated record keeping and reporting capabilities to enable trainers to track usage and each learner's individual progress. As an example, the basic skills course cited above kept track of each learner's initial reading level, how many lessons they had completed, their scores on tests, the number of times they had to repeat a lesson, their gains in reading level, the time spent on the system and the estimated time to complete the course. This information could be reported by individual, department, or the entire user population. Furthermore, the system had preprogrammed weekly and monthly reports that were automatically run and forwarded to the training department for review.

The final phase of technology learning is to apply newly-acquired knowledge and skill on the job. This is not always addressed in CBT, MMT or WBT courses, and is a clear weakness of much commercial courseware today. Those that do provide application support typically rely on one of two methods:

- electronic performance support systems (EPSS)
- on the job training (OJT)

EPSS is one of the more exciting applications of computer technology that is particularly effective at support application of skills. These systems, typically embedded in users' desktop PCs, offer a variety of contextual, real time job aids, reference materials, help files and resources to assist users in applying skills and solving problems while working. Though they can be quite expensive to build at this time, the pay off can be enormous in terms of increased productivity and reduced training costs. The most sophisticated EPSS are wedded with tutorials and other learning aids so as to provide a seamless learning and performance support system for employees.

A second type of application is OJT. In this case, the learning technology prepares learners to apply skills on the job by providing printed reference materials, additional exercises, job aids and the like that the learner takes with them back to the job and uses to refresh their memory. The materials may also be made available to learners' supervisors, along with instructions on how to reinforce new skills on the job. Although the OJT approach is not as robust as EPSS, it is much cheaper to create and can work in any environment, especially field environments where PCs may not be available to provide on-line support.

### Technology-Based Learning

Having examined the learning technology implementation model in detail, let's turn to the variety of learning technologies available today and how these have developed over time. Although many of the most exciting developments have occurred in just the past few years, instructional designers have been trying to harness the power of technology for many decades. At the turn of this century, the typewriter was introduced to business training with great fanfare. In the 1920's, trainers discovered film as a medium. In the 1960's, they tried to build teaching machines, an early forerunner of the computer. In the 1980's, they began to use the PC and videotape. These early efforts were always hampered by the limitations of the technology in allowing user control, interactivity and accurate simulations of the content. The cost of these systems was often prohibitive, both for development and delivery.

With the advent of the personal computer in the 1980's, computer-based training became a viable reality. These early CBT programs allowed an interactive dialogue between the learner and the machine that individualized the learning experience. Sophisticated computer programming enabled branching from one topic to related ones, user control over the pace and sequence of content, error detection and remediation based on the user's answers, and record keeping systems that provided detailed tracking of learners' progress.

The systems lacked the capability to display sophisticated visuals, video or sound, however, since they had limited processing and data storage capability. Some of the programming for early CBT was also lacking in interactivity. In many cases, textbooks were simply converted to digital form and CBT became little more than electronic page-turning or rote drill and practice.

In the 1990's, more sophisticated hardware and software has allowed true multimedia training to become a reality, including the use of Laserdisc, Compact Disk Read Only Memory (CD-ROM), CD-Interactive (CD-I), and Digital Video Disk (DVD) to deliver full-motion video, colorful graphics and stereo sound. In the near future, the computer and television will merge into a single digital medium capable of delivering the quality of television images along with the interactivity of computers. This allows designers to simulate almost any training content at a level of realism that has coined the term 'virtual reality'. While the quality of the medium has grown, the cost has plummeted, allowing widespread use of computer technology for the first time.

A third development of the past few years has been the creation of the World Wide Web (WWW), enabling billions of people to connect to each other and share text, images, voice and video in a standard form. Though the Internet has been used as a research tool for decades, its use for training is in its infancy. In the past few years, most companies have established a presence on the Internet with home pages on the World Wide Web. They also began to build Intranets, or internal web pages geared to their own employees. At first, these were repositories of reference materials and forms, but they have evolved into useful tools to distribute information and learning company-wide via the medium of the employees' computer. As the technology evolves and bandwidth increases, more sophisticated applications will be found for web-based learning systems. Some predict the web browser may even become the standard desktop interface, replacing existing Windows and Mac-based operating systems. Today, WBT is largely confined to providing background information and direct performance support in the form of electronic job aids or electronic performance support systems (EPSS), but the future of the medium promises much more than that. Already, attempts have begun to use the medium for teleconferencing, videoconferencing, distance learning, learner support groups, action learning teams and organizational learning. As the technology improves, and especially bandwidth increases to allow greater speed, the Internet may yet completely revolutionize the way people learn and interact.

Why is there a movement toward learning technology? Is it just our fascination with high tech, or is it grounded in something more substantial? Those who have worked with learning technology insist it is not just a passing fad, but a better way to learn. That's because technology enables a truly learner-centered and controlled training environment with a focus on improving job performance. Among the advantages of this approach, proponents cite the following (Howell and Silvey, 1996):

- provides individualized learning by tailoring content to many levels of expertise and allowing users to control the pace and sequence of learning.
- reduces the student-teacher ratio to one, since each learner has his own computerized tutor.
- offers simulations of the work environment and a variety of presentation media for different purposes.
- provides learning wherever needed, especially bringing training to employees' own desktops.
- speeds the learning process by focusing on essential knowledge and appealing to multiple senses.
- eliminates travel-related training costs and reduces the need for training facilities and labor-intensive classroom administration.
- provides a mastery-based learning approach and incorporates evaluation of learning and on-line training management record keeping.

With all these advantages, it is no wonder that learning technology is growing at a rapid clip. Yet, to deploy this technology successfully, careful, detailed planning is essential. Otherwise, companies can end up spending a lot of money on hardware and software and getting little from their investment.

### Key Delivery Issues with Learning Technology

To deploy learning technology effectively, it is imperative to have a well-designed implementation plan. The plan should actually begin with the original need for training and the decision to adopt a technology-based delivery system. A cost-benefit analysis should be done that compares the costs of a technology-based course to the cost of traditional classroom training. Some experts advocate that comparisons should be based on costs per learner over the life-cycle of the training program to arrive at an accurate estimate (Howell and Silvey, 1996). Situations where technology-based training can have a significant cost advantage include the following:

- the learning population is geographically dispersed or cannot easily be brought to a central training facility.
- the learning population is relatively large (hundreds or more).
- the learning population is familiar with the technology being used to deliver training.
- the content of the training is relatively stable, with a shelf-life of 1-5 years.
- the technology infrastructure exists to deliver training, including hardware, software, networks, and technical support.

When these conditions are present, the chances of a successful technology-based delivery system are greatly enhanced. These things alone will not guarantee success, though. Companies have found that it takes more than appropriate use of technology to make these training systems work.

Consider the example of a large telecommunications firm with over 20,000 employees scattered across six western states. They decided that their environment was well-suited to deploying computer learning labs in each of their major field locations so that employees could learn right at their work site and management could schedule training around production needs. After spending more than $5 million on hardware and a library of off-the-shelf courseware, the training department was dismayed to discover that less than 200 employees bothered to use the new labs in their first year of operation. Most of the time, the labs sat empty.

What went wrong with this implementation? The company thought that if they put learning technology in front of employees, they would embrace it wholeheartedly. It was the old "build it and they will come" philosophy. They offered virtually no incentives for employees to try the new labs and did not build support for them among the supervisors who controlled employees' time. Furthermore, the company miscalculated regarding the on-going maintenance and up keep of the labs. They assumed these labs would be larger self-regulating, with little or no human facilitation required. Instead, they found that hardware and software required on-going maintenance that the local PC specialists were unable to provide, and that many learners wanted to have a live human being around to help them get started on the system and to coach and assist them when they encountered difficulty. This company had no one on-site to assist learners, instead requiring them to call the central training department for telephone support that was often unavailable. Thus, the first time learners needed assistance, they found it was not readily available and so they gave up using the labs. Finally, the company found that the off-the-shelf courseware it had purchased at great expense was not particularly popular with employees. Some of the content was not directly applicable to employees' jobs and other courses did not make the most effective use of the technology. When the Vice-President who authorized the original $5 million investment found out so few employees were actually using the labs, he blamed the training department for its poor implementation plan and refused to authorize any more expenditures for technology-based learning. To avoid these kinds of mistakes, trainers should develop an implementation plan that ensures a successful launch and on-going incentives and support for learners. The table below summarizes the key elements of a technology-based implementation plan.

*Table 20-2:* Key Elements of Implementation Planning for Learning Technology

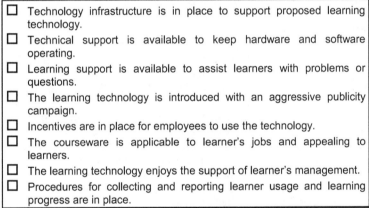

| |
|---|
| ☐ Technology infrastructure is in place to support proposed learning technology. |
| ☐ Technical support is available to keep hardware and software operating. |
| ☐ Learning support is available to assist learners with problems or questions. |
| ☐ The learning technology is introduced with an aggressive publicity campaign. |
| ☐ Incentives are in place for employees to use the technology. |
| ☐ The courseware is applicable to learner's jobs and appealing to learners. |
| ☐ The learning technology enjoys the support of learner's management. |
| ☐ Procedures for collecting and reporting learner usage and learning progress are in place. |

If one or more of these elements is lacking, the implementation can easily go awry, leaving everyone with a negative impression of learning technology. Conversely, successful launches of new learning technologies tend to have a solid implementation plan that includes the necessary technical and learning support systems, appropriate incentives to use the technology (whether mandatory or voluntary incentives are used is a matter of choice), and appealing courseware that focuses on improving employee job performance.

### On-the-Job Training (OJT)

A second major category of non-classroom training is actually the oldest training strategy known to man – OJT. People have learned skills on the job for millennia. Most of this learning has been unstructured, essentially a "sink or swim" philosophy. Typically, it involves pairing a new employee with an experienced one and letting the trainee follow the employee around or sit and watch what the experienced employee does. After a while, the trainee is expected to have "picked up" enough skill to perform the task unassisted. Though such unstructured OJT has severe limitations, it is still probably the most widely-used training technique in the world today. Ultimately, it usually works, although it is not a very efficient learning mechanism and it is impossible to monitor the quality of the learning with such an informal system.

Another form of OJT has emerged in the past four decades that takes the advantages of on-the-job learning, like providing just-in-time training in a practical, easily applied environment, and adds more formality to eliminate some of the disadvantages described above. The result is structured OJT, a method of on-the-job training that uses custom-designed training materials and a trained facilitator to ensure consistent learning that will meet the performance standards of the job (Rothwell, 1996b).

Like any good training, structured OJT starts with a thorough analysis of the training need, focusing on the needs of the learners and a complete job task analysis that clearly specifies the skills that learners must master to be successful in their jobs. Once the analysis is completed, the design phase consists of preparing an OJT plan, determining the content and delivery method and how learning will be measured and recorded. The development phase includes creation of formal training materials, instructor lesson plans, evaluation instruments and creation of props or other visual aids that can help learners quickly master the skills. The delivery plan should include train the trainer for those chosen to instruct the training, a roll-out schedule for reaching the target audience and on-going support and monitoring of delivery to ensure it proceeds according to plan. Finally, the evaluation plan should include ways to measure learning, such as performance tests, measures of learner satisfaction, job performance and business results. The plan should also look at ways of improving structured OJT based on feedback from participants and trainers. Table 20-3 summarizes the key activities involved in putting together a successful structured on-the-job training program (adapted from Nolan, 1996).

By following a systematic approach to on-the-job training, companies are able to enjoy all the benefits of this practical approach while minimizing its drawbacks. One aircraft manufacturing company that uses a structured OJT program to train thousands of its assembly workers found that such a system saved it several hundred thousand dollars in training costs by cutting down on training-related travel, eliminating waiting time for classes to form and be scheduled, avoiding the use of expensive classroom facilities and flexibly training employees when it would least impact production schedules. Furthermore, the company found that structured OJT led to higher levels of learning and skill transfer, since employees were learning as they worked, and ultimately to higher levels of teamwork on the job as employees became used to sharing knowledge and skill with each other and carried this over into collaborative learning in the workplace. Even supervisors benefited by sharpening their technical and coaching skills through delivery of structured OJT lessons to new employees.

## Summary

In this chapter, we have briefly examined the major issues that trainers face in implementing non-classroom delivery systems such as those that use learning technology or structured on-the-job training. We have seen that the use of these alternative delivery systems is increasing due to their lower overall cost and better on-the-job results. Such systems must be carefully designed, however, to avoid implementation pitfalls like a lack of technical and learning support, lack of management support and underutilization by the intended learning population. Through careful planning and attention to marketing, incentives, quality content, effective delivery and timely evaluation, many companies are finding that non-classroom delivery of training is the key to training more employees faster than ever before.

*Table 20-3:* **Structured On-the-Job Training Checklist**

| Phase | Item | Activity |
|---|---|---|
| Analysis | ☐ | 1. Define the scope of the proposed training. |
| | ☐ | 2. Conduct a job task analysis of the tasks to be trained. |
| | ☐ | 3. Conduct a learner analysis to determine current skill levels and identify the skill gap. |
| Design | ☐ | 4. Prepare training objectives from the job task analysis. |
| | ☐ | 5. Write content outline and have it approved. |
| | ☐ | 6. Determine delivery method, including who will deliver, when, and where. |
| | ☐ | 7. Determine teaching methods and learning activities. |
| Develop | ☐ | 8. Create learner materials. |
| | ☐ | 9. Create an instructor guide/lesson plan. |
| | ☐ | 10. Create props, job aids and visuals. |
| | ☐ | 11. Create tests and other learning evaluation tools. |
| Deliver | ☐ | 12. Train the trainers. |
| | ☐ | 13. Develop a delivery schedule. |
| | ☐ | 14. Provide support to trainers and monitor delivery. |
| Evaluate | ☐ | 15. Determine how learning will be measured. |
| | ☐ | 16. Determine how satisfaction will be measured. |
| | ☐ | 17. Determine how skill transfer will be measured. |
| | ☐ | 18. Determine how business results will be measured. |
| | ☐ | 19. Create a system to monitor delivery and results and to take corrective action when needed. |

# Discussion Questions and Exercises

1. What are some advantages and disadvantages of e-learning?
2. Go to the Internet and locate an e-learning course on a subject of interest to you. Analyze how the course addresses the steps of the e-learning model in this chapter.
3. What are some good examples of OJT that you can think of? How could you use structured OJT to improve training results?

## Case Study: The Field Sales Force

A large cosmetics manufacturer has a field sales force of 1000 across the U.S. and Canada. They require periodic training on new products, new marketing programs, updated sales techniques, sales campaigns and management strategies and goals. All have laptops that connect to the company intranet, but not all are computer savvy.

*Using the Trainer Delivery Techniques Matrix (Tool 14 in Appendix 2), develop a viable e-learning strategy for this client.*

## Conclusion of Section Four: Results from Implementation

In the previous three chapters, we have considered the key issues for successful implementation of training. First, you learned about the importance of preparing trainers through train the trainer programs. Second, you learned the rudiments of effective classroom delivery of training, including the application of a general teaching model that can be applied to any type of knowledge or skill-based training. You also learned about the use of specific techniques like: demonstration, discussion, case studies and role plays to enhance the learning experience. Finally, in the chapter on non-classroom delivery, you were introduced to the key implementation issues that must be addressed to make effective use of learning technology and on-the-job training.

Looking back on the original premise of this book – that business results must drive training – we can see that this is certainly true for the implementation phase of training. By this stage, instructional designers have already determined the training need and crafted a training solution that will effectively address the need. But the best-laid plans will not succeed without equal attention to the implementation phase, since this is truly where the rubber meets the road. Unless training is properly implemented by trained professionals, the quality of the learning experience may not live up to trainees' expectations, resulting in underuse of the skills taught or worse yet, the complete breakdown of learning. Conversely, when implementation goes well, the entire training endeavor is seen as a success and the organization reaps the benefits of higher-skilled employees who are capable of enhancing the quality and quantity of their labor for the good of themselves, customers and company stakeholders alike.

## Section Five  **Evaluation**

The final phase of the Instructional Design process is also historically the most neglected and underdeveloped.  Except for a quick reaction check with trainees, most training programs are still not evaluated in any systematic way. This is despite repeated calls from professionals within the training field and from business executives for more attention to the evaluation of training, especially its business results.  This section will address the need for evaluation and discuss the most common techniques currently in use to evaluate training on five different dimensions  reactions of participants, learning of participants, transfer of skills to the ob, business results produced by training and the return on investment from training. These topics will be addressed in four chapters: The Role of Evaluation, Evaluating Trainee  Reaction and Learning,  Evaluating Transfer of Training,  and Evaluating the Results of Training.

In chapter twenty-one, we will explore why evaluation is a key component of training and how it has developed over time.  In the second chapter, we will look at techniques to evaluate trainee reactions and learning, including the use of post-training surveys, pre-post tests and other learning assessments. In the third chapter, we will examine the evaluation of skill transfer, or the application of learned skills on the job.  In the final chapter of this section, we will discuss the evaluation of business results, including cost avoidance, cost savings, revenue and profit growth, strategic growth and the return on investment from training.

This section is based on a model of training evaluation adapted from Donald Kirkpatrick(1996).  The adapted model is presented below.

*Figure 21-1*

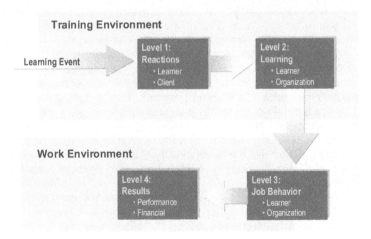

# Chapter Twenty-one :
# The Role of Evaluation in Training

Training evaluation has two primary purposes: to improve the effectiveness of training and to demonstrate its results. Over 40 years ago, these twin purposes were described as formative and summative evaluation (Scriven, 1967). Formative evaluation focuses on improving the training process and the effectiveness of training. It is primarily an internal evaluation process initiated and used by trainers to assess their own work and discover ways to make continuous improvements to the training process. It is also used to help monitor the quality of on-going instructional design projects and assure that they achieve their stated objectives. Summative evaluation is results-oriented. It focuses on assessing the impact of completed training programs to determine if they have met their goals and if the programs should be continued or curtailed. It is concerned with "go/no-go" decisions about training, as when a company must decide whether to offer a particular seminar again or whether to scrap it.

Originally, evaluation as a separate field of education and training was born in the federal government programs of the "Great Society" era of the 1960s. These programs contained a mandatory evaluation clause that required fund recipients to show that the program had had the intended impact in order to receive additional funding. Thus, the focus of evaluation was exclusively on summative issues like results and impact. Over time, evaluators found that many programs which had met the summative criteria for continued funding could nevertheless be markedly improved by making adjustments and improvements based on evaluation data. From this experience was born formative evaluation, which sought to improve on-going programs by determining what they did well and what they were weak in, so as to replicate strengths and improve weaknesses.

As the outside mandates to conduct summative evaluation waned along with government funding for education and training, the focus of evaluators shifted more to formative approaches. This is especially true of corporate training, since few training programs face a budget ax like that wielded by the federal government. Instead, companies were interested in achieving maximum efficiency and effectiveness from their on-going training function, resulting in a bias in favor of formative evaluation instead of summative. Recently, the emphasis has shifted back to summative evaluation, with exhortations to demonstrate the financial benefits of training (Phillips, 1997).

The twin purposes of formative and summative evaluation were expanded by Kirkpatrick and other training evaluators to cover the unique needs of corporate training evaluation. The result was four distinct, yet related, levels or phases of evaluation:

Level 1: reactions

Level 2: learning
Level 3: on-the-job behavior
Level 4: business results

Trainers are encouraged to evaluate programs on all four levels, at least some of the time. Furthermore, the four levels are seen as building blocks which demonstrate the success of training. The first step is to assess learner reactions. If learners are satisfied with the learning experience, they are more likely to learn. Second, an assessment of learning occurs. This demonstrates whether trainees have learned the knowledge and skills embodied in the learning objectives of the program. If trainees have demonstrated mastery of the objectives, then the third step is to determine if their job behavior changes as a result of learning new skills. This behavior change is investigated after employees have returned to their jobs and is often characterized as transferring skills from the classroom to the job. If skill transfer takes place, then the fourth step is to determine if the newly learned skills are contributing to the business' overall objectives and results. This is where the summative impact of training is measured in terms of lower costs, higher revenues and profits, strategic growth and the return on investment from training. These four steps logically build on each other, most especially the last three. One cannot talk about business results from training unless trainees have demonstrated new skills on the job. And one cannot talk about demonstrating new skills unless learning has occurred. The only weak link in this logic is reactions to training, since research studies have demonstrated that trainees sometimes have very positive reactions to training despite not learning anything of use, and that trainees may also have a negative reaction to training, and yet learn a great deal from it and use this knowledge to produce measurable results.

The role of training in evaluation can be summarized as having four major components, as listed below:

1. Improvement of the instructional process (formative).
2. Determination of the extent to which learners are mastering the learning objectives (formative).
3. Determination of whether training has produced the impact and results it was originally designed to achieve (summative).
4. Demonstration of the effectiveness of training to stakeholders such as: senior management, customers, clients and others (summative).

Despite a well-developed theoretical basis for evaluation, surveys indicate that few companies evaluate their training systematically. We need to understand why trainers often neglect evaluation and identify the problems this causes trainers. This will set the stage for detailed discussion of the techniques presented in the following chapters in this section.

### Why Evaluation is Neglected

Evaluation seems to be the poor orphan step-child of training. Despite years of repeated clarion calls to pay more attention to it, most training departments still spend precious little time looking at the results they achieve. One would expect, in the bottom-line, justify-your-existence business world of today that trainers and managers alike would place a very high priority on evaluation, but in most cases it just hasn't happened. Why not? It appears that both trainers and organizations are guilty of failing to put their effort where their rhetoric is.

Because of the fact that reaction and learning evaluations (levels one and two in Kirkpatrick's model) occur in the classroom, it makes them the easiest and consequently the most popular forms of evaluation to conduct. The ASTD Benchmarking Forum reports that up to 95 percent of companies surveyed conduct evaluations of participant reactions and 70 percent evaluate student learning, at least some of the time.

It is behavioral and results-based evaluation that has been slow to develop. The same study cited above found less than one-third of companies conduct any behavioral or skill transfer evaluation and a paltry 5 percent conduct results-level evaluation studies. For trainers, evaluation of behavior and results, which take them outside the comfortable confines of the classroom, has always been fraught with problems. The work environment is controlled by management, not trainers, and it is a place of busy schedules and heavy workloads. In such an environment, trainers seeking to discover proof of their work's impact have not been welcomed with open arms.

Then, too, it is a strange world to many trainers who have spent a professional lifetime in training positions. Outside their comfortable realm, they are uncertain what to do and often fail to collect meaningful information that will answer key results-based questions, like: did productivity increase or did costs decrease or did revenues grow or did the organization open a new market or position itself for future growth? If trainers could regularly link their programs to affirmative answers to these questions, they would be a much more valued corporate resource and even have a greater impact on the world at large. Yet most trainers don't have any clear idea how they would go about answering these questions systematically and accurately, since the answers require research, analytical and business skills they do not possess.

Finally, trainers do not conduct on-the-job evaluations because some of them continue to believe it is not their responsibility to do so. They claim that they are accountable for learning and managers are accountable for performance. If managers want to evaluate the results of training on the job, let them do so themselves, or perhaps with the assistance of the training department.

The notion that trainers are not responsible for the work environment of their learners is certainly true. Ultimately, management must ensure that training gets used on the job and that results are achieved. But those who hold that training's work is done at the classroom door fail to understand the powerful shift occurring from learning to performance. If we do not take ownership of the learning process all the way up to performance, then we will forever struggle on the fringes of organizations and have little impact. But taking ownership does not mean taking control. Evaluations of job results should be done as a joint project of managers and trainers. In this way, both sides share ownership for the results and ensure that they are acted upon for the good of the organization. Clearly, though, waiting for management to take the lead in training evaluation is a little like waiting for Godot. Some trainers argue that they'll postpone results-level evaluation until management demands it. If you wait that long, you probably won't survive anyway.

It is up to trainers to take the lead and initiate a complete learning performance evaluation system that takes both the formative and summative forms of evaluation to heart and practices them as fundamentally as one follows instructional system design and adult learning theory.

### How to Design Evaluations that Work

To effectively evaluate training, one needs a plan. The planned procedures and conditions chosen by trainers to collect and analyze evaluation data are known as an evaluation design. It needs to answer three basic questions:

1. What data should be collected?
2. Under what conditions should it be collected?
3. What decisions will be made with the data?

Answers to these three questions help to shape the basic framework of the evaluation plan. In answering these questions, additional issues come up. One paramount issue is the accuracy and relevance of evaluation data. This refers to the validity of the evaluation design. The second major issue to be considered is the reliability of the data and the instruments used to collect it. Evaluations must possess both reliability and validity to yield useful data about training programs. Otherwise, we could not trust that the data was a true reflection of reality.

To ensure reliable, valid evaluation designs, we should minimize the factors that can threaten an evaluation's validity. Basically, these factors are anything that may lead us to an incorrect conclusion about training outcomes. The biggest threats to validity occur in two basic areas: the instruments used to collect data and the conclusions reached after analyzing data. Let's consider each of these in turn.

Instruments like surveys, tests, interviews and observation worksheets are the tools evaluators use to collect data about training outcomes. If these instruments are fundamentally flawed, the data collected with them will also be tainted. Consider the example of a test for a computer software programmer that measures the wrong things. Let's say we are training a programmer to write Java applications for the company Intranet. If the test we give at the end of the class asks questions about network hardware instead, then the programmer would probably score poorly on the test, but this would not be an accurate reflection of the training he attended, since the questions were on a completely different subject.

Another example is a participant reaction survey that only asks participants to share positive feedback, but makes no attempt to seek constructive feedback on the course. If we conclude from this survey that 100 percent of participants enjoyed the class, we are making a false conclusion since we never asked participants if there was anything about the class they didn't like, or if they have any suggestions for improvement. The key point about evaluation instruments is that we can only expect to collect data about things that we directly seek. Thus, we must carefully word the questions we ask to ensure that the answers will give us useful and accurate information.

Other common problems with instruments are listed below:

- changing an instrument in the middle of an evaluation will result in inconsistent data being collected.
- using the same test over and over with a group of learners may result in the learners becoming test-wise, e.g. learners may simply memorize the right answer without really knowing the subject.
- distractions during administration may cause invalid data, e.g. trainees taking a test just before a major company layoff may do worse because of anxiety.

To avoid problems with instruments, make sure they are carefully designed and tested before using them in an evaluation. Have experts review them for clarity and accuracy and try them out with a pilot group of learners. Once the instruments are finalized, don't change them until an evaluation study is completed and additional information suggests that they should be improved. A second technique for assuring good tests is to develop an alternative form that contains slightly different questions but drawn from the same set of learning objectives. This alternative form helps assure that trainees will not be able to simply memorize test questions and answers. Finally, instruments should be administered in a consistent fashion, with everyone having equal time to complete them in an atmosphere free of distractions.

A second major validity problem with evaluations is drawing erroneous conclusions about training. Most of the errors in evaluations occur because the evaluator attributed a positive outcome to training when in fact something else caused the outcome. A number of factors can cause positive change in job performance besides training. Among the most common causes of performance change are the following:

- experience – over time, individuals get better at a job through repeated practice.
- management or organizational interventions – a change to the job, the incentives for doing it, the people assigned to do it, the leadership of the group, competition in the marketplace, economic problems and the like can all cause job performance to improve or suffer, depending on the nature of the change.
- changes to the composition of those included in the training evaluation study – participants who drop out of training, or those who are forced to

attend or chosen based on factors like: seniority, perquisite, favoritism, etc. may not be truly representative of the workforce in general.

To minimize these threats to validity, evaluators suggest doing two things:
1. use control groups to make certain that changes are really due to training and not other factors.
2. use random groups or at least matched groups to make certain that the employees being studied in an evaluation are truly representative of the larger population.

When we use control groups and randomly assign participants, we have a much better chance of isolating the true effects of training and reaching valid conclusions about training's impact.

In the following section, five of the most common types of evaluation designs will be described and illustrated. Some of these designs are better than others, because they control for more threats to reliability and validity. The least valid designs are presented first with a description of why they are weak. More robust designs are presented last.

The first design we will consider is by far the most commonly used. It's called a 'one-shot case study', because evaluators get only one shot at collecting data. The diagram below illustrates this simple design.

Figure 21-2: **One-Shot Case Study Design**

**T -------------------------------- M**
T = Training
M = Measurement

In this case, a single group of learners attends training and then a measurement occurs afterwards. This is the way participants' reactions to training are typically measured and the way much testing takes place, with a final exam at the end of a course. Though this design is simple and easy to implement, it is limited by the lack of a pre-measure to determine what trainees knew or thought before they started training and also by the lack of a control group who do not attend training, but complete the same measurement to provide a valid comparison. Of course, for reaction data, the one-shot case study is often adequate. Typically, we assume that trainees have no set opinion about training until they have attended a class. For learning data, however, the one-shot case study is limited by the lack of a pre-test to measure baseline data. Rarely do trainees take a class without having at least some knowledge about the subject matter. If a trainer only gives a final exam, and never determines what trainees already knew before they started the class, the trainer may erroneously conclude that everything a learner knows on the final exam is a result of the training, when in fact the learner may have known most of this before ever setting foot in class.

To avoid some of the problems with the one-shot case study method, a second common evaluation design adds a key third step in the process, as the diagram below illustrates:

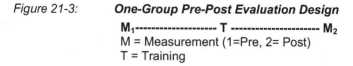

Figure 21-3: **One-Group Pre-Post Evaluation Design**

$M_1$-------------------- T ---------------------- $M_2$
M = Measurement (1=Pre, 2= Post)
T = Training

In this design, the critical third step is to add a pre-measure before training. This establishes a baseline so that the post-training measure can be compared and the effect of training can be better isolated. As an example, a class on computer programming could start by having all trainees complete a brief pre-test that measures their current knowledge of the programming language they are about to study. After they complete a one-week class, they take a post-test, or final exam. Their scores can then be compared to see how much progress was made. If the average score on the pre-test was 60 percent and the average score on the post-test was 90 percent, then evaluators could confidently conclude that the training class boosted learners' knowledge by 50 percent (30/60 = .5 X 100 = 50%). By adding a pre-test, we have eliminated the possibility that trainees may have already known the content of the training and learned nothing new. We have thus been able to isolate the specific effect that training had on learners, and can claim with a degree of confidence that the training program caused trainees to learn new skills. This design is much better than the first, but it still has one problem: we don't know if the trainees in the class are really typical of the entire population of programmers or are an idiosyncratic group.

The third evaluation design adds another element to the process to help assure that the trainees we are studying did indeed do something significantly different than other employees doing the same job. This element is a control group, which is a group of individuals like the trainees who do not receive training or receive a different kind of training so that a comparison between the two groups can be made. This is illustrated below:

Figure 21-4: **Non-Equivalent Control Group Design**

Group 1: $M_1$ ---------------- T -------------- $M_2$
Group 2: $M_1$ -------------------------------- $M_2$
M = Measurement (1=pre, 2=post)
T = Training

In this design, we have added a second group. This group is called the control group, because they are used simply to control for errors we might otherwise make about the performance of group one, which is our target or experimental group. An example of this would be a computer programming class in which only half of the programmers are chosen to attend, while the other half simply continue working. We measure the knowledge and skills of both groups before and after the training and then make two kinds of comparisons:

- within group comparisons of each group's scores on the pre and post-test
- between group comparisons of the performance of group 1 versus group 2

The addition of a between group comparison helps us further isolate the effects of training and to rule out other factors that might cause an increase in ability to program. Let's say that after testing both groups we arrive at the following group averages:

Figure 21-5:    **Experimental and Control Group Test Scores**

|  | Group One (experimental) | Group Two (control) |
|---|---|---|
| Pre-test | 50% | 55% |
| Post-test | 90% | 60% |
| Percent Increase | 80% | 9% |

This information allows us to draw some interesting conclusions about the training program. First of all, if we look at the performance of each group separately (within group comparison), we see that the experimental group made some pretty dramatic gains as a result of attending training while the control group only improved slightly. This suggests that the training was indeed effective in teaching new skills. Next, if we compare group one to group two (between group comparison), we find that their scores on the pre-test were nearly identical (50% versus 55%). This suggests that the two groups started out roughly equivalent in their knowledge of computer programming. By the end of the class, however, their knowledge is quite different, with the experimental group outperforming the control group by 30 percentage points (90 to 60%). We could use further statistical techniques like a t-test to determine if the difference between the two groups on the post-test was large enough to be statistically significant, or was merely a result of normal test measurement error or random chance.

We have now controlled for most of the problems that might threaten the validity of the evaluation study. There is still one last problem that the non-equivalent control group design does not eliminate, and that is the possibility that the two groups are not equivalent in background and knowledge. Although their scores on the pre-test suggest that they have roughly the same knowledge to start with, we could add one other safeguard to ensure that the two groups are really equivalent. We could first randomly assign programmers to the two groups. This would yield the evaluation design in Figure 21-6.

The addition of randomization ensures that the two groups are truly equal, and thus the comparisons between them valid ones. Of course, in the real world, randomization is often a luxury. Typically trainers just get who they get, with little control over the selection process. But, sometimes random groups can be formed when a large population must be trained and it doesn't matter who goes first. In this case, those chosen to be among the first attendees could be chosen from the population at random, thus creating a true experimental design. The scores of the first group to complete training could be compared to the control group that had not yet attended.

Figure 21-6: **Pre-Post Control Group (Classic Experimental Design)**

Group 1:  R – $M_1$ ---------------- T ------------ $M_2$
Group 2:  R – $M_1$ ------------------------------- $M_2$
R = randomize
T = training
M = measurement (1=pre, 2=post)

Another use of control groups in evaluation involves comparing two or more methods of training to determine which is superior. Let's say, for example, that a company is considering moving most of its classroom training to the Internet. Before it makes this multi-million dollar decision, management decides to conduct an evaluation of the effectiveness of the two mediums. One group is assigned to attend classroom training and the other takes the new Internet-based training. Their performance is then compared to determine which method results in better learning. This is illustrated in the diagram below. Variations on this approach include adding more options to be compared, and a corresponding number of groups, and adding a true control group who receives no instruction to see how much any of the groups are learning.

Figure 21-7:        **Comparing Two Training Options**
                    **Using Pre-Post Control Group Design**

Group 1:  R – $M_1$ ---------------- $T_1$ ------------ $M_2$
Group 2:  R – $M_1$ ----------------$T_2$ ------------ $M_2$
R    = randomize
$T_{1\&2}$ = 2 different training systems being compared
M    = measurement (1=pre, 2=post)

One final evaluation design especially helpful for level three and four evaluation is the interrupted time series design. This is unlike any of the others mentioned before, because it takes a longitudinal approach to looking at training's impact on key performance indicators over a longer period of time. Time series designs have long been used to identify trends and predict future events. Basically, they begin with historical data on a variable of interest, like company revenues. This may be tracked and charted over a period of years. Based on the patterns of the past and the likelihood of these patterns persisting into the future, the company is able to create a forecast of what revenues may look like in the future, assuming conditions remain constant. If an event comes along that interrupts the normal pattern, such as a world war, then future revenues are likely to go down substantially, thus altering the previous trend. Training evaluators can use this same methodology to look at the long-term impact of training on organizations.  In this case, they predict that training will "interrupt" the normal trends of the organization and alter them in a positive way.  The basic design model is presented in the diagram below:

Figure 21-8:        ***Interrupted Time Series Design***

$M_1$ --------- $M_2$ -------- $M_3$ -------- T --------$M_4$ --------$M_5$ -------- $M_6$
$M_{1-6}$ = Measures at regular intervals
T    = Training

As an example, consider a safety training program designed to prevent accidents at work.  A large furniture manufacturer had been experiencing a growing number of injuries, especially back injuries from improper lifting and slips and falls from a cluttered, dirty work environment.  The company decided to launch a major safety training and awareness campaign focused on safe lifting and housekeeping techniques.  To evaluate the business results from this major training effort, requiring the attendance of every employee in the company, the training department decided to use accident rates as a measure and to determine if the training program had made any demonstrable impact on the number of accidents.

The Training Manager obtained the following accident statistics from the Safety Department for the six months prior and the six months following a major one month safety training program.  The data are displayed in the table below:

Figure 21-9:       **Accident Statistics Before and After Safety Training**

| Month | Total Number of Accidents | Accidents Involving Lifting, Slips or Falls. |
|---|---|---|
| January | 10 | 5 |
| February | 12 | 7 |
| March | 11 | 8 |
| April | 14 | 9 |
| May | 18 | 10 |
| June | 19 | 11 |
| **Training Begins** | | |
| July | 17 | 9 |
| August | 14 | 6 |
| September | 11 | 4 |
| October | 12 | 4 |
| November | 10 | 3 |
| December | 11 | 3 |

From this table, we can see that the number of accidents peaked in June, just before the training began.  In the following month, as training was rolled out throughout the company, accidents fell by two, both of which were in the category that the training targeted.  Over the next four months, accidents fell every month, led by a sharp decline in lifting and falling accidents.  The fact that everyone had training on these two safety areas appears to be the cause of the drop.  When the Training Manager shares this information with the Safety Manager and the Vice-President of Human

Resources, they agree that the training had a positive effect on accident rates and rewarded the training department with a bonus.

In Chapter 24, we will learn additional analytical techniques that can be used with interrupted time series designs to gain even greater precision about training's impact. Now that you are familiar with the standard designs used to evaluate training, let's consider the questions of when to evaluate training and at what level.

### Determining When to Evaluate

The evaluation of training has suffered in part simply because it is the last step in the training process. Like anything occurring last, be it the final chorus of a song or the letter 'Z' in the alphabet, the tendency is never to get around to it. By the time trainers get to the evaluation phase of a program, the resources are exhausted and so are the trainers. So, one key factor to good evaluation practice is not to wait until the end of training to evaluate. Instead, evaluation should be built in at the design stage, when the rest of the course is being planned and laid out. When evaluation is an integral part of the design, it is much more likely to be accomplished.

The second thing to know about when to conduct evaluations is that at least some of the data that will be needed should be collected before any training takes place. If one waits until the training is over to begin the evaluation process, there is no baseline data against which to compare learner progress. This can be illustrated by Figure 21-10, which shows typical evaluation points for the four levels of evaluation.

As the chart shows, data about pre-existing knowledge, skill and performance levels need to be collected before training starts so as to have a baseline against which to compare learning and performance gains that occur as a result of training. Trying to extrapolate this data after the fact can be impossible, and without it, there is little hope of isolating the effect that training has had on learning and performance.

Based on this realization, the following guidelines should help to determine when to conduct various levels of evaluation. For reactions to training, the ideal time is immediately after the training has concluded, when the experience is fresh in the minds of learners. This is the best time to collect client reactions, too. For learning, data should be collected twice – once before learners attend training and again immediately afterwards. In this way, trainers can compare the amount of learning before and after the training and confidently attribute any gains in learning to the training program, rather than extraneous events. Often, pre-testing is done at the first class session with the post-test occurring at the last session. For one or two day classes, it may be advisable to collect pre-test data ahead of time, since such a short amount of time will have expired between pre and post-tests, if both are done in class. Alternatives to collecting pre-test data will be discussed in the next chapter.

For level three skill transfer data, the best time to collect is two to three months after trainees return to the job. This allows sufficient time for the newly learned skills to be practiced and applied and for the skills to make a noticeable difference in the workplace. Some far-sighted companies also follow up 6-12 months later to see if trainees are still using the new skills, but attributing performance gains to training that has occurred up to a year ago can be very difficult to prove, given the host of intervening events that may have influenced trainees' performance.

*Figure 21-10*:

# Typical Evaluation Points

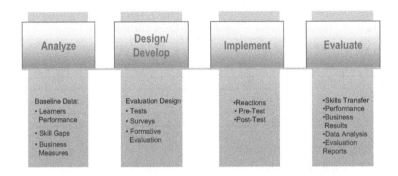

Results-oriented evaluation data needs to be collected pre-post, like learning data. Before trainees enter a new training program, data about their department's current productivity, financial and strategic performance should be collected to establish a performance baseline. Then, several months after the training, the same data should be collected again to determine if any improvements have occurred. It may also be helpful to sample performance data over a longer period of time to determine if gains occurring after training are sustainable over time or limited to a one-shot, or Hawthorne, effect caused by the fact that the company is paying attention to trainees and sending them to training.

Finally, we should discuss the extent to which companies should evaluate training at each level. Previously, we described how trainees typically evaluate nearly every class for reactions, and hardly any classes for business results. Although there is no fixed percentage of classes that should be evaluated, the following guidelines are based on companies that do an excellent job of evaluating training.

These guidelines are based on two considerations: the importance of evaluating training at each level and the pragmatic reality of the time and resources available to devote to evaluation. Based on this, learning should be evaluated most often, because it is critical that training produce measurable learning and because it is the basis of all other claims of training's impact. Reactions should be gathered for all new and pilot programs, as a customer satisfaction measure, but once programs are in place, sampling half of them is adequate. For behavior change, following up on half of all training programs gives an excellent picture of how much skill transfer is occurring without overburdening trainers and line managers with excessive data collection. Naturally, this total should include 100 percent of high stakes, high impact programs. Finally, with regard to level four evaluation studies, even the most ardent advocates recognize that such in-depth evaluation is not appropriate or realistic most of the time. Instead, it is best to choose about one-quarter or less of an organization's most significant training programs to evaluate for business results. Even this many may be too ambitious for those just embarking on results-based evaluation, but it is a good goal to aim for.

*Table 21-11:* **Training Evaluation Percentage Guidelines**

| Evaluation Level | Percentage of Programs to be Evaluated |
|---|---|
| Reactions to pilot classes | 100% |
| Reactions to regular classes/programs | 50% |
| Learning new knowledge and skills | 90% |
| Skill transfer/ job behavior change | 50% |
| Business results/ Return on Investment | 25% |

### Reporting Evaluation Results

When it comes time to publish the results of training evaluation, it is essential to keep in mind the audience for the report and their needs. This will ensure that the report focuses on key issues of interest to decision makers and is presented in ways that make it easy to understand the conclusions and lessons learned. Typically, decision makers are interested in answers to one or more of the following questions:
1. Are learners satisfied with the training they received?
2. Did learners master the objectives of the training?
3. Are learners better able to perform their jobs after receiving training?
4. Did the training help the company achieve its goals?

Once it is clear which of these questions the evaluation needs to address, the next step is defining the audience for the report in greater detail. This includes discovering the following information about the audience:
1. What is the level of knowledge about the training program, its objectives and content?
2. What is the level of knowledge about the evaluation methods and data collection process?
3. What do they need to know about the evaluation results?
4. What media are available to deliver the report?
5. How much time is available to present the report?

After answers to these questions have been determined, you can proceed to define the content and presentation method of the report. The report should include two versions – a complete report which includes the design, data analysis, statistics, conclusions and recommendations, and an executive summary that focuses on conclusions and recommendations only. You may end up presenting both versions, if executives request a separate briefing. Also, don't miss the opportunity to publicize training successes in newsletters and company publications, and for truly significant achievements, get the results published in a training trade journal so that others can learn from your experience.

When drawing conclusions from evaluation studies, err on the conservative side rather than risk overstating accomplishments. This is particularly true of claims involving business results. If you report astronomical gains in productivity, you may well be met with skepticism. Instead, focus on solid gains that can be proven easily. These may be less spectacular, but far easier to defend.

### *Summary*

In this chapter, we have examined the role that evaluation plays in improving the instructional design and training process and in demonstrating the results of training. We have examined five common evaluation design models, discussed when to evaluate training programs and how to write evaluation reports that communicate clearly to decision makers. Now that you understand the vital role evaluation plays in the training process, we will turn to specific techniques for conducting various levels of evaluation, starting with reactions and learning in the next chapter.

# Discussion Questions and Exercises

1. How does Kirkpatrick's model help us evaluate training programs? What does it leave out?
2. Compare and contrast several of the evaluation designs covered in this chapter. What are the advantages and disadvantages of each?
3. When should evaluation be conducted?

### Case Study: Designing an Evaluation Plan

Returning to the case originally presented in Chapter One: You've just received an e-mail from the Senior Vice-President of a consumer electronics company's largest division to request training for all of his 2,000 employees. His reason is that the company is about to launch a new line of wireless products and services and he fears employees will not be able to deliver these successfully without being retrained. Training needs to start in six months. The content must include: product features and benefits, sales techniques, customer service and a new customer information system being developed by the IT department. *Design an evaluation plan for this program, including evaluation questions, evaluation designs data collection and analysis and reporting.*

# Chapter Twenty-two :
# Evaluating Reactions and Learning

The most commonly conducted evaluation is an assessment of learner reactions immediately following training.  Usually conducted by anonymous surveys, this so-called level one evaluation provides a rough indication about how well trainees liked the training they received and any suggestions they might have to improve it.  Its value is primarily in giving the instructor immediate feedback on his/her performance and providing ideas for continuous improvement of the training design.

The second most popular way to evaluate training is to assess participant learning, typically through an end-of-course examination.  This type of evaluation is useful to demonstrate that learners have mastered the knowledge and skills of the course and to provide feedback to the instructor and designer about which objectives of the course were mastered and which might require rework to  achieve their intended results.  A number of techniques for creating level one surveys and enhancing their effectiveness will be presented in this chapter.  The second part of the chapter will outline a brief treatise on testing and learning assessment, picking up on this topic from the discussion on testing begun in Chapter 16.

### Evaluating Reactions to Training

As indicated in the last chapter, the most common form of evaluation by far is assessment of learner reactions to training.  This is typically done by using a survey distributed at the end of training.  Besides surveys, the other common methods for evaluating reactions include focus groups and word of mouth.  Focus groups allow the training department to explore learner attitudes in greater depth, and are useful to gauge interest in new training programs, methods and delivery systems before they are launched.

Word of mouth is probably the oldest form of evaluation.  After employees attend training, they invariably form impressions of their experience which they share with co-workers, supervisors and friends.  When enough people speak highly of a training program, it develops a positive image that encourages more people to enroll.  Conversely, when a training program develops a poor image, word travels quickly and enrollment may well suffer unless the program is mandatory.  The unfortunate thing about relying on word of mouth is that the squeaky wheel usually sounds loudest.  One disgruntled employee can do more damage to a training program's reputation than dozens of satisfied learners.  The complainer can do irreparable harm if they have the ear of someone in authority.  Although word of mouth will always play a role in learners' reactions to training, it is important to collect data representing a more balanced view of a course to counteract the negative buzz that may be created by a few disgruntled employees.

Learner reaction surveys typically fall into one of three types:
1.  Report card surveys
2.  Opinion surveys
3.  Open-ended surveys

The report card approach treats training events like traditional education and asks participants to assign a grade or rating to various elements of the course.  The elements most often included are:
1.  Instructor
2.  Materials
3.  Training aids/ audio-visuals
4.  Facilities/ logistics
5.  Relevance to the job
6.  Overall effectiveness

Each of these categories may be further sub-divided to determine exactly what aspects of the course were effective.  For instructors, as an example, the following categories are often evaluated:

*   Knowledge of the subject matter
*   Presentation skill
*   Organization of the class
*   Management of the class
*   Relationship with learners
*   Answers to questions
*   Use of specific teaching methods, such as: demonstration, discussion, lecture, role play, case study, hands-on practice, etc.
*   Use of audio-visuals

For each of these elements, the report card approach offers several categories, such as the letter grades A-F or the descriptors, 'Excellent,' 'Good,' 'Fair,' and 'Poor.'  Below is an example of this approach to collecting reactions.

*Figure 22-1:*      **Sample Report Card Reaction Survey**

| Instructor's Performance | Excellent (A) | Good (B) | Fair (C) | Poor (D) |
|---|---|---|---|---|
| Knowledge of subject | | | | |
| Presentation of content | | | | |
| Management of class | | | | |
| Use of media/equipment | | | | |
| Relationship with participants | | | | |
| Answers to questions | | | | |

A second type of survey used to collect reactions is an opinion survey that uses a Likert scale to assess agreement with a series of statements about a training program.  The scale may use 5-9 points, ranging from strongly agree to strongly disagree.  Proponents of opinion surveys argue that they result in more reliable information and a wider range of opinion than the grade card approach, which typically yields scores in the 'good-excellent' range, even for mediocre training programs.

An opinion survey approach to assessing an instructor's performance might look something like the example below.

Figure 22-2: **Sample Opinion Survey for Learner Reactions**

| Instructor's Performance | Strongly Agree 5 | Agree 4 | Neutral 3 | Disagree 2 | Strongly Disagree 1 |
|---|---|---|---|---|---|
| The instructor was knowledgeable about the subject. | 5 | 4 | 3 | 2 | 1 |
| The instructor presented the content in an interesting manner. | 5 | 4 | 3 | 2 | 1 |
| The class was very well-organized. | 5 | 4 | 3 | 2 | 1 |

Notice that all these statements are written to be positive. Negative statements like, "The instructor appeared disorganized." can be included, too, though care must be taken to score these items correctly (in reverse order of those written positively).

I will not add to the debate about which of these survey methods yields better results. I believe both can work well, if the questions are carefully worded and the responses allow a wide range of views. Of the two types, the opinion survey is the harder to construct, so that may tip the scales in favor of the report card approach. More important than the survey methodology is what trainers do with the information collected from participants.

### Analyzing and Applying Reaction Data

The main purpose of collecting reaction data is formative evaluation of the design and delivery phases of training. It provides instructors, in particular, with instant feedback about learner satisfaction with the training experience. It can also help the designers of the program learn how to improve materials, activities, and audio-visuals.

Aside from formative purposes, reaction data gives a general sense of customer satisfaction with training that can be used in conjunction with data about learning and results to demonstrate the effectiveness of the training function. Relying on reaction data alone will not suffice for this end, however, even though most training departments continue to seek their organization's support with reaction surveys.

One way to strengthen the customer satisfaction angle is to conduct a periodic training customer satisfaction survey that seeks a broader range of opinion about the training function overall. One organization sent an annual training survey to a random sample of 200 employees (about 10% of the total workforce). The survey asked the following questions:

1. When was the last time you attended a training program? What was the title?
2. How often do you attend training programs?
3. How satisfied overall are you with the training programs you've attended?
4. How useful was the training to you in performing your job?
5. How would you rate the quality of the training?
6. How would you rate the timeliness of the training?
7. What kinds of training programs would help you do your job better?

The results of the survey were tabulated and published each year, with yearly trends tracked as time went by so as to compare satisfaction levels longitudinally. After a while, the organization looked forward to the latest training customer satisfaction report and both the training department and management put a great deal of importance in its findings.

To get the most out of reaction data, it should be analyzed in ways that ensure the information is fed back to those who could benefit from it. Most organizations do little with the data except have the instructor review it immediately after class and then file it away somewhere. If that's all an organization plans to do with reaction data, it is hardly worth the effort entailed in collecting it. To get more out of the information, reaction data should be entered into a database and stored for later analysis and review. One innovative approach that a few companies have adopted is to conduct comparative analysis of reaction data by course topic and instructor to determine which courses and instructors are generating the greatest and least amount of customer satisfaction. This can easily be done using a database that allows data to be input sorted by course and instructor. Typically, participant entries are converted to numbers which are input for each question and each participant who completes a survey. A database can then calculate the mean average score for each question, sorted by course and instructor. These averages can then be compared against other courses and instructors by sorting them in rank order. Those who consistently receive high marks for design and delivery should be rewarded, while those consistently receiving low marks should be coached on ways to improve their performance. Used in this way, reaction data can be a powerful tool for continuous improvement and provide a modicum of objectivity to the otherwise notoriously subjective process of evaluating trainers.

Appendix Two, p. 303 contains an example of an opinion survey style participant reaction survey.

### *Evaluating Learning*

A far more important task than evaluating reactions to training is determining the amount of learning. Since learning is one of the key results promised by training, and the only one completely under the control of the training function, it is imperative that the majority of evaluation resources be devoted to learning evaluation, not reactions.

You have already learned about the role of testing for individual assessment in Chapter 15. Aside from determining whether individuals are learning the objectives of training, it is also important to establish whether groups of learners are mastering objectives and to use this information both to improve the training process and to demonstrate the learning results of training to clients and stakeholders.

Formal evaluations of learning rely on five primary methods:

1. Standardized, published tests
2. Criterion-referenced tests
3. Learning contracts/action learning
4. Self-assessment
5. Class quizzes, games and homework assignments

Each of these methods provides some concrete evidence of learning, but of the five, criterion-referenced tests offer the most valid information about learning, since they are custom-made to measure precisely the skills being learned in a given course.

Published tests may be of use in introductory courses or those geared to a particular craft or occupation. Care must be taken in selecting such tests, though. The test and the class it will be used to evaluate must have matching content and objectives, or else the test will not be valid for evaluating learning.

Learning contracts and self-assessments are popular alternatives to formal testing. Adults especially like the idea of assessing their learning by means of contracts. These are performance-based agreements that the learner and instructor negotiate in advance and to which the learner is held accountable. As learning occurs, evidence of achieving the terms of the contract must be presented by the student and evaluated by the instructor. This may be in the form of portfolios, work samples, reports, projects or any other useful evidence of achievement. A learning contract is completed when the learner has satisfactorily finished all the items in the contract. Self-assessments are sometimes used in courses where a formal grade is not required. They may take the form of a survey, project or other tool that allows the learner to reflect upon and assess their own learning. Sometimes, self-assessments are administered pre and post-training, like tests, so that changes in perception can be measured.

Finally, class quizzes, exercises, games and homework assignments may be used to evaluate individual learning and to some extent the group's learning as well. Though these methods are very useful to trainers to monitor learning progress in class, they rarely are tracked or recorded for later use by evaluators. For this reason, they are not frequently used for formal learning evaluations. Homework assignments are the one type of classroom assessment that may be kept and used to assess learning performance later on.

### Analyzing and Reporting Learning Data

The evaluation of learning is one area that has a long history and a highly developed methodology. (Bloom, Hastings and Madaus, 1971; Mager, 1973; Popham, 1975; Coscarelli and Shrock, 1989) Much of this work has been done in educational settings, however, so one must modify it somewhat to apply to a corporate or work environment. The basic theory behind criterion-referenced testing was presented in Chapter 15. Here, I will describe some of the practical considerations in using learning evaluations to measure training effectiveness.

The assessment of learning has two primary purposes: to determine if individual learners have mastered the objectives and to determine if training is effective. The first purpose is served by creating an assessment that each learner must pass in order to be considered competent in the objectives and skills taught. The assessment is often a paper and pencil examination, but it does not need to be. In fact, performance assessments in which learners must actually perform the skills they have learned for a trained observer are a better measure of learning than multiple choice tests.

To determine if training is effective, we can also use tests of various types. But the purpose of the test changes from a focus on individual achievement to examining group achievement. In evaluating group learning, we are seeking evidence that the training resulted in significant learning for the vast majority of participants. We are also concerned with the amount of learning and the specific knowledge and skills learned. This information can help judge whether the training was effective or not, and pinpoint problem areas that require improvement.

To evaluate learning, we first need to establish a baseline. This can be accomplished by having learners take a pre-test before the start of training. The pre-test should be an assessment of all the objectives of the training, so we have a solid baseline against which to measure progress through the course. The pre-test may also be used by those who believe that they already possess sufficient knowledge of the subject. They may attempt to 'test out' of the class by taking the pre-test and achieving a passing score. For those who will attend the class, the pre-test simply indicates how much they already know about the subject. Some training departments do not bother to pre-test every participant. Instead, they gather pre-test data from a sample of learners, and then extrapolate these results to the whole population. This saves time and resources, but you must make certain that the sample truly reflects the learning population as a whole to avoid erroneous conclusions.

Once pre-test data has been collected for each learner, this can be analyzed to determine the following:
- overall mean average score for the group
- mean scores for each learning objective tested
- range and variation of scores about the mean

This information tells us how well the group as a whole did on the pre-test, which specific areas participants are good and weak in, and the amount of variation within the group of learners.  Such information can be used diagnostically to adjust the training to suit the audience. Although this rarely happens with classroom training, most computer-based training programs include the ability to individualize instruction based on pre-test performance.

Once we have established a baseline, the next step is to instruct learners in the knowledge and skills they need.  The learning process should be tailored to the needs of individuals as much as possible, while ensuring that everyone gets consistent instruction on the learning objectives of the program.  The third step is to administer a post-test at the end of training that measures the objectives and skills learned.  This is usually done at the last class session, and may take the form of a written final exam, a performance exam or other assessment method devised by the trainer.

The final step in the evaluation process is to compare the pre-test scores to the post-test for the entire group and draw some conclusions about the effectiveness of the training program.  When post-test scores increase over the pre-test, we would conclude that significant learning occurred.  When post-test scores do not improve, we would conclude that little learning occurred, and would examine the training more closely to discover why it did not produce more learning.

The process for evaluating learning is summarized in the figure below.

*Figure 22-3:*      ***Learning Evaluation Process Model***

| **Develop Criterion-Referenced Test** |
|:---:|
| **Administer Pre-Test** |
| **Conduct Training** |
| **Administer Post-Test** |
| **Analyze Pre-Post Test Scores** |
| **Draw Conclusions about Training Effectiveness** |

To illustrate this, let's assume that you are asked to evaluate learning in an introductory computer database course.  Learners must pass this course before they are allowed to assume a position as customer service representative, since the reps use the database to look up customer account information and provide service to customers.   A performance test is created around the following course objectives:
1.   Access a customer's account information.
2.   Make a change to a customer's basic account information.
3.   Process a customer payment.
4.   Print out a customer bill.

The test consists of four tasks, one each for the objectives listed above.  To pass the course, participants must achieve a passing score of 70 percent or more on each of the tasks.

To evaluate learning, 20 participants took a pre-test before starting training. The mean scores for each of the tasks are listed below:

Figure 22-4: **Mean Pre-Test Scores**

| Task One | Task Two | Task Three | Task Four |
|----------|----------|------------|-----------|
| 60% | 40% | 45% | 55% |

After the training was completed, participants were tested again on the same four tasks. Their post-test results are displayed below:

Figure 22-5: **Mean Post-Test Scores**

| Task One | Task Two | Task Three | Task Four |
|----------|----------|------------|-----------|
| 90% | 75% | 65% | 85% |

To analyze these results, we should start by comparing pre-post performance on each task. We could use a statistical test such as a t-test to determine if the difference between pre and post-test scores is statistically significant. We could also use an informal method to measure learning by simply taking the average percentage gain from pre to post-test. Another area of interest is what percentage of learners achieved passing scores for each task. Let's look at the results, using these methods. We could use a computer statistical program to calculate the t scores for us and determine their probability (the chance that the difference is not significant). These results are displayed below:

Figure 22-6: **Three Ways to Measure Learning**

|  | Task One | Task Two | Task Three | Task Four |
|--|----------|----------|------------|-----------|
| Percent Increase (Post-Pre/ Pre) | 50% | 88% | 44% | 55% |
| t score | 2.2 | 3.3 | 1.5 | 2.8 |
| Probability | <.05 | <.01 | <.10 | <.05 |
| Percentage of Learners at Mastery | 95% | 60% | 45% | 85% |

What do these results tell us? The first row shows that learners made gains on all four tasks, ranging from a high of 88% on task two to a low of 44% on task three. Notice that the percentage gain is a factor of where learners started and where they ended up. When pre-test scores are very low, like they were for task two, learners are more likely to make large percentage increases, whereas when pre-test scores are fairly high, as they were on task one, the percentage increase is necessarily lower.

Regarding the statistical t-test, the raw t scores and probability for each task indicate that statistically significant learning occurred for at least three of the four tasks. We would likely question the learning gains for task three, since the probability of these occurring by chance alone is .10 or ten percent. That's a pretty high chance, and calls us to question whether significant learning really occurred on this task. Typically, evaluators look for probability scores of .05 or less, indicating the chances of the difference being due to random error is less that 5 percent.

Finally, if we look at the percentage of learners achieving the 70 percent mastery level, we see that learners did very well on tasks one and four, but much worse on tasks two and three. Task three appears to be a real concern, since less than half the group achieved mastery on this, even after attending the training.

To interpret these findings, we would need to reexamine the original instructional design and the way it was delivered to discover why participants performed more poorly on task two and especially task three. We might find that the training materials were weak or confusing in these two areas, or that the instructor's presentation and demonstration was flawed. We might simply discover that these tasks are so much more difficult than one and four that additional practice time needs to be devoted to them before learners achieve mastery. Whatever the cause of the deficiency, the learning data we have evaluated has pointed us in some likely directions to search for continuous improvement. This is one of the key uses of learning evaluation data.

A second key use of the data would be to inform the managers of these learners that their performance on tasks one and four is excellent, but they will need additional coaching and practice to fully master tasks two and three. Alerting managers of this situation will help them prepare to support learning transfer on the job and focus their efforts where they will do the most good. Of course, admitting to management that learners did not achieve everything the training intended can cause some public relations problems for training, but it also opens a dialogue about how to best meet the needs of learners and the department they work in. This dialogue engages both trainers and line managers in an important conversation about how to boost performance on the job, and should lead to a corrective action plan that may include on-the-job training, more classroom training, supervisor coaching or other interventions.

### Summary

In this chapter, we have examined how to conduct evaluations based on reactions to training and participant learning. We have explored some useful techniques to measure these variables and to use the information to improve the training process and communicate to clients and stakeholders about the results. Although these are important issues to evaluate, especially learning, we cannot stop here. Instead, we must press ahead and look at how to evaluate changes in job behavior and bottom-line results in order to determine the full impact of training. We will start with behavior change in the next chapter.

# Discussion Questions
# and Exercises

1. What are some of the best ways to use reaction data?

2. What are three ways to analyze test data? Compare and contrast each method.

**Case Study: Designing a Learning Evaluation Plan**

Returning to the case originally presented in Chapter One: you've just received an e-mail from the Senior Vice-President of a consumer electronics company's largest division to request training for all of his 2,000 employees. His reason is that the company is about to launch a new line of wireless products and services and he fears employees will not be able to deliver these successfully without being retrained. Training needs to start in six months. The content must include: product features and benefits, sales techniques, customer service and a new customer information system being developed by the IT department.

*Design a learning evaluation plan for this program, including evaluation questions evaluation designs and instruments, data collection and analysis and decision made based on the results.*

# Chapter Twenty-three :
# Evaluating the Transfer of Training

The third level of training evaluation is determining whether knowledge and skills taught in the classroom are transferred back to the job and whether they result in meaningful behavior change. This is an area of evaluation receiving increased attention these days, due to numerous studies that show as much as half of all training content is never applied at work, resulting in a waste of training resources. This chapter will give the theoretical foundation for level three evaluation and practical guidance in how to assess the transfer of training both subjectively and objectively. Numerous examples will illustrate these techniques, including empirical evidence from the author's own research.

### What is 'Level Three' Evaluation?

Donald Kirkpatrick coined the term 'Level Three evaluation' to refer to the assessment of changes in behavior on the job that occur as a result of learning new skills. He favored the term "behavior" for this level (Kirkpatrick, 1996), but others have come to call it "skill transfer" (Broad and Newstrom, 1992). Regardless of its name, the basic notion behind level three evaluation is that skills learned in training must be applied on the job in order to do the organization any good. If skills are never applied, or transferred, from the classroom to the job, then the training that produced those skills is useless to the organization that paid for it. Even the learners themselves will eventually not benefit, since research clearly indicates that skills which are not used eventually atrophy. So, once learning has occurred, the critical next step is to apply these skills, and the sooner the better, in order to reap the benefits in higher job performance.

Skill transfer is a highly complex area of evaluation, since it depends on a number of factors, most of which are not under the control of trainers. Kirkpatrick identifies five requirements for successful job behavior change:
1. Desire to change
2. Skill to change
3. Hospitable job climate
4. Support to apply new skills
5. Rewards for behavior change

Let's examine each of these requirements in more detail. The desire to change refers to the performer's motivation. We have previously discussed motivation as it relates to learning. Motivation to change one's behavior mirrors learning motivation, but also goes beyond it in some ways. Like learning motivation, the motivation to change one's behavior rests on two fundamental tenets:
1. Believing in a need to change

2. Making sufficient effort to change

The two are directly connected, since effort is a function of whether we believe in something enough to make the necessary exertion, as well as our own sense of self-confidence about our ability to succeed. Psychologists have found that behavior change is predicated on a belief that some future state is desirable enough to convince us to let go of a current behavior pattern. Since we are naturally creatures of habit and seek stability in our lives, we loathe change instinctually. In order to overcome this natural aversion to change, we must be convinced that the benefits far outweigh the discomfort and uncertainty that change brings. What convinces people to make change? It typically requires several of the following:

- learning new sets of behaviors to replace the current ones
- realization that the present behavior is not working
- having a supportive environment to try out new behaviors
- having a compelling desire to make change
- having an extrinsic reward for making change

The first requirement is to acquire new behaviors to replace the old. Unless people know how to act differently, they cannot make a significant change, even if they desire to do so. This is why training is critical in building new knowledge and skills. Since learning is fundamentally a change in the behavior of the learner, training is ultimately a matter of helping people change their behavior by acquiring new knowledge and skills and learning how to apply them.

We have already discussed how trainers should create engaging reasons for learners to change their behavior in the training environment. It is equally important that managers create engaging reasons for their employees to change their behavior on the job. The best way to do this is to create an intrinsic desire to change on the part of the performer. This can be done by pointing out both the personal and the organizational advantages of making a change and by creating the right climate to do so.

The job climate is primarily a function of the supervisor and co-workers, with the general management philosophy and organizational culture playing a supporting role. To enhance skill transfer, the job climate must support the behavior change or at least be neutral. This means primarily that the learner's supervisor must actively support the application of skills learned in training. This can be done by any of the following:

- model the new behavior on the job
- coach employees to apply new behaviors
- provide feedback on results of new behaviors
- reward new behaviors
- take corrective action when employees fail to apply new behaviors

Because the learner's supervisor is the key to supporting on the job behavior change, much of the strategy driving level three evaluation focuses on the supervisor. But the training department also has a key role to play in helping learners apply new skills on the job. We will examine how training can support skill transfer in the next section.

### How Can Training Support Skill Transfer?

When someone attends a training class, they do so expecting to learn new skills that will make them a more effective employee. This can only happen if the new skills are applied after they are learned. With this in mind, trainers can assist learners by starting the skill transfer process while the learner is still in class, and then continuing to support learners when they return to work. In Chapter ??, we discussed how trainers can use strategies like demonstrations, case studies and role plays to simulate the work environment and create learning activities and relevant practice that helps learners build skills that can easily transfer to the job. Aside from these strategies, trainers can assist learners by encouraging them to develop action plans to use new skills before they leave class, and by providing them with job aids and other support once they return to the job.

The action plan is a good tool to conclude a training module or lesson. Basically, a good training action plan contains the following elements:

- summary of the skills that have been learned
- list of ways in which the new skills can be applied
- identification of any obstacles or barriers to skill application
- identification of any enablers for skill application
- specific steps to be taken and deadlines
- follow up actions to be taken to review progress

The action plan can be introduced in class. Learners discuss the application of skills, and begin completing an action plan. This document can then be taken back to the job and shared with the immediate supervisor, who can then become a resource to help the learner achieve the action plan.

Action plans get the learner to think very concretely about what they have just learned and how they can use it to improve their performance. Some of this may seem very obvious to a trainer, but such is not the case to most learners, who are not experts at learning and who often are clueless about how they will go about using what they have learned. After completing this exercise, the learner has a specific plan of action that is realistic and definite. With the right climate and support back on the job, this learner is much more likely to fully apply what she learned in class than someone who simply shows up back at the job with no fixed plan to use newly learned skills. Figure 23-1 shows a sample action plan from a Customer Service training program for new call center representatives.

The other key action that trainers can take to support learning transfer to the job is to make use of job aids and other support systems that reduce the difficulty of applying new skills on the job. As we discussed in the development section of this book, job aids are any tool or reference material that can be used while performing a task which make the task easier. A job aid can be as simple as a list of commands and their functions, or even a list of frequently called telephone numbers. Job aids can also be highly complex flowcharts, tables, matrices and reference materials that are used in conjunction with performing a job. In the example above, the learner referred to two job aids: the Inquiry Matrix and the Customer Complaint Resolution Job Aid. Both of these are summaries of procedures learned in class, arranged in a useful way for performing tasks. They were both summarized on a single sheet of paper and then laminated for durability so that they could be used at the customer representative's desk while talking on the telephone with customers.

*Figure 23-1:* **Sample Action Plan for Customer Service Training**

---

**SUMMARY OF SKILLS LEARNED**
In this course, I learned the following new customer service skills:
How to greet customers. How to identify customer needs. How to locate customer account information in the customer database. How to make simple changes to an account, like updating the customer's name, address, applying payments, waiving late charges and fees. How to handle customer complaints and problems

**WAYS THE NEW SKILLS CAN BE APPLIED**
Once I return to work, I can apply these new skills in the following ways:
Use the standard customer greeting I learned in class with every customer. Ask questions of the customer, following the Inquiry Matrix I learned about in class. Listen actively to identify the customer's real needs. Use the Customer Database (CD) to access account information, either by looking up the customer's name, social security number or account number in the system. Use the system features to update the customer's account. Handle any complaints by using the Customer Complaint Resolution Job Aid.

**OBSTACLES OR BARRIERS TO SKILL APPLICATION**
Barriers include: lack of time to practice on the job, waiting time for system to access account information, some customers do not speak English well and are hard to understand, some customers are already so upset by the time they call that it is difficult to solve their problem.

**ENABLERS FOR SKILL APPLICATION**
Enablers include: My supervisor wants me to succeed and is willing to give me time to learn the new skills. My co-workers are willing to help me and answer questions when they have time. I like helping people and will try hard to satisfy upset customers. The computer system is being improved to speed up access time.

**SPECIFIC STEPS TO BE TAKEN AND DEADLINES**

| Step | Deadline |
|------|----------|
| 1. Use standard greeting on all calls. | Tomorrow |
| 2. Begin using the Inquiry Matrix on all calls. | Tomorrow |
| 3. Practice looking up customer information. | Tomorrow |
| 4. Become proficient on the Customer Database system. | One Month from now |
| 5. Use the Customer Complaint Resolution Job Aid to resolve all customer complaints. | One Month from now |

**FOLLOW UP ACTIONS TO BE TAKEN TO REVIEW PROGRESS**
Meet with my boss to discuss this action plan within one week.
Begin using the job aids immediately to help me.
Ask co-workers for help when I need it.
Register to attend another customer service class next month.

---

A second type of job aid is the electronic performance support system (EPSS). This is simply an electronic, or on-line version of a job aid that can be accessed on an employee's desktop PC or terminal whenever needed. The best of these systems provide contextual help as needed, meaning that the EPSS is intelligent enough to know where the performer is encountering difficulty and offers assistance in that particular area. A good example of this is newer software programs developed by Microsoft that include a 'Wizard', or intelligent on-line support contextualized to the software program. If someone is trying to create a table in Microsoft Word, the 'Wizard' offers tips and menu navigation assistance on tables when the performer requests help. The growth of PCs and new processors has allowed the development of innovative EPSS applications in many disciplines that use computers.

### Evaluation Methods for Skill Transfer and Behavior Change

Once we have done everything possible to increase skill transfer through training and support, we should measure how well we are doing, to identify areas for further improvement and to ultimately determine the results achieved by training. A number of different methods may be used to evaluate job behavior change. Among the most common are the following:

- management surveys
- learner surveys
- peer surveys
- job observation
- interviews
- records of work output, attendance, tardiness, performance reviews and other performance documentation

Survey research is the most popular method and one that easily lends itself to the task of measuring behavior change. The most popular group to survey is the learner's own supervisor, since this person is presumed to have the best first-hand knowledge of an employee's job behavior and performance. Sometimes, the learners themselves are also surveyed to see if their self-perceptions have changed as a result of training. For management personnel, inclusion of their subordinates gives a 360 degree perspective to the data. Finally, learners' peers and co-workers may be included to provide an objective third-party source of data. Of course, none of these sources is completely objective; all have personal biases and feelings about the learner that can color their opinions.

To move beyond opinion research, it is necessary to go into the work environment and observe employees first-hand. This approach yields the most complete evidence of behavior change, but is also the most time-consuming and intrusive, making it a less popular methodology. One other common source of data for level three evaluations is records of work performance such as: work output, productivity, attendance and tardiness records, performance reviews, quality assurance reports, scrap and rework reports, and customer feedback. All of these can provide benchmarks against which to compare individual performance, but few companies keep the kind of detailed individual performance records that are needed to measure the impact of training on the job.

### Evaluation Models for Measuring Behavior Change

The most common model used to measure behavior change is the one group pre-posttest design presented in Chapter 21. Occasionally, a more rigorous nonequivalent control group design is used to better control for the effect of training. The two models both require a pre-training measurement of learner performance. This is usually done during the analysis phase, when evidence of the performance problem or opportunity is gathered as part of the needs assessment. This assessment may consist of a survey sent to both the prospective learner and his/her supervisor, asking them to rate the employee's current level of skill and job performance. Once this baseline of data has been collected for each individual slated to attend training, or at least a representative sample of the target audience, the training can begin.

After learners have successfully completed training and returned to the job, a post-training survey is sent to the same audience as the pre-training survey to measure the differences, presumably caused by training. There is usually a wait from one to three months after training to allow the employee some time to begin applying the newly learned skills and make an observable difference in their performance. If a control group is added to the evaluation design, it should also be surveyed pre and post-training. For this group, we would expect little or no improvement in work performance. If this is the case, and the trained group exhibits a change in performance, then we have solid evidence that training caused a change in job behavior.

The key to getting valid results from this approach is to design a reliable and valid survey. The survey should be carefully designed and tested before using it to evaluate training. Although skill transfer surveys vary considerably due to differences in organizational culture and training subject matter, they should contain the following kinds of questions:

- Demographic information: course, date, time frame of the evaluation, job title of trainees, job title of person evaluating, location, department, work experience, etc.
- Ratings of specific skills covered in training, including: current skill level, frequency of use, importance and change from previous time period.
- Job climate, including performance support systems, coaching, management support, obstacles to skill transfer, enablers, motivation factors, etc.
- Overall satisfaction with training, usefulness and relevance of training topics, additions and deletions to training topics, etc.
- Open-ended questions inviting more detailed responses on the topics listed above.

An example of a survey used with trainees' supervisors is included in Appendix Two, p. 306.

### Examples of Level Three Evaluations

Let's now consider several real-world examples of behavior change evaluation studies, drawn from different industries and training topics. The first one is an evaluation of beginning computer software training offered to employees by a large electronics company. The company had been introducing PCs into its office work environment over a period of five years, but had done little formal training to help new users gain proficiency with the software and operating system. As a result, the expected productivity gains from office automation were not materializing. The training department was asked to design and deliver a series of beginning PC software classes focused on the three programs most widely used throughout the company – word processing, spreadsheets and presentation graphics. The introductory courses were each 20 hours in length. Those who attended all three received 60 hours of instruction spread over a 15 week period (4 hours per week).

To measure the behavior change caused by PC training, the training manager designed a 10 question survey that asked trainees' managers to rate the extent to which the trainee was using a PC on the job and the perceived impact of the PC on work quantity and quality. Among the questions asked were the following (with pre and post-training mean scores):

*Figure 23-2:* **Sample Skill Transfer Survey for PC Skills**

| Question | Mean Pre-Class Score | Mean Post-Class Score | Percent Improvement |
|---|---|---|---|
| Performs assigned job tasks using a PC | 4.0 | 5.1 | 27% |
| Gets more work done when using a PC | 4.5 | 4.8 | 8% |
| Produces better quality work when using a PC | 4.8 | 5.3 | 9% |
| Performs new tasks using a PC | 3.6 | 4.8 | 33% |
| **Averages** | 4.2 | 5 | 19% |

Note: Scale used was 6=Always, 5=Usually, 4=Frequently, 3=Infrequently, 2=Rarely, 1=Never

In this case, managers reported higher frequencies of PC usage and better results after training than before. When these findings were presented to management, they responded by approving an expansion of the PC training program, a clear sign of support.

A second example of the pre-post survey approach to evaluating skill transfer and behavior change is from an introductory supervision course offered by a mid-sized computer manufacturer to its factory supervisors. Most of the supervisors attending were new to their positions, having been promoted from skilled assembly or technician positions within the last six months.  To measure the extent of job behavior change, the training department developed a custom survey, based on the objectives of the eight week, 64 hour supervision training course.  The survey was administered one week before the start of training and again three months after participants completed training.  The following four groups were surveyed:

- training participants (self-rating)
- participants' managers (middle management)
- participants' employees (assemblers and technicians)
- participants' colleagues (other supervisors)

This gave the evaluation a 360 degree perspective, which helps to control the biases of any one level.  A sample of the survey and the results obtained is presented in Figure 23-3.

The results of this survey were further analyzed using Analysis of Variance, a statistical technique for examining data involving two or more groups or variables to determine if any differences are statistically significant.  Further statistical techniques allowed evaluators to pinpoint which groups were statistically significant.  The results of the analysis showed that the post-training survey results were significantly higher than the pre-test for all groups surveyed as well as for the overall group average.  Participants made statistically significant progress in eight of the ten objectives measured.

*Figure 23-3: **Sample Skill Transfer Survey Results for Supervisory Training***

| Question | Self | | Mana-ger | | Em-ployee | | Col-league | | Ave-rage | | % Gain |
|---|---|---|---|---|---|---|---|---|---|---|---|
| This Supervisor: | Pre | Post | Pre | Post | Pre | Post | Pre | Post | Pre | Post | |
| Communicates effectively with employees | 3.5 | 4.5 | 2.4 | 3.0 | 2.1 | 2.9 | 3.0 | 3.3 | 2.8 | 3.4 | 21% |
| Establishes clear performance expectations and goals | 2.7 | 4.1 | 1.9 | 2.7 | 3.1 | 3.9 | 3.5 | 3.6 | 2.8 | 3.6 | 29% |
| Provides coaching and on the job training | 3.2 | 3.8 | 3.0 | 3.3 | 2.5 | 2.9 | 3.7 | 3.7 | 3.1 | 3.4 | 10% |

This information was shared with the training staff responsible for the supervisor training program, the participants, their managers and senior management.  As a result of this evaluation study, the training department won approval to expand the supervisor training program to other departments at the company and to make it mandatory for all newly-promoted supervisors.  The training department also used the data to improve the sections of the course devoted to two objectives that participants had not demonstrated significant progress in achieving on the job.

The final example uses a different approach to measuring job behavior change – direct work output measures. An electronics manufacturer with a polyglot workforce was experiencing quality and communications problems in its factory due to the large immigrant workforce and low level of basic skills among some of its assembly workers. To combat these problems, the company engaged with an outside vendor to provide custom basic skills and Vocational English as a Second Language (VESL) courses for 60 of its hourly assemblers, including those who had the lowest communication skills in English. The 18 week, 72-hour program focused on teaching the vocabulary, language and mathematics used in the factory. To evaluate the behavior change of employees enrolled in the course, the training department used the factory's own computerized labor cost and accounting system data. This factory built electronic sub-assemblies for many industrial customers. To accurately bill customers for work performed, every assembler used a bar code system to record the amount of time they spent on each assembly operation. This data was then fed to the company's accounts receivable department for proper billing of customers. The training department learned of this system from conversations with factory managers, who suggested it might provide a way to accurately measure productivity gains. The training department was able to obtain productivity data for the 60 people enrolled in the program over a one year period, including the five months before the program began and three months after the program ended. The monthly productivity figures were compared, using the interrupted time series evaluation design described in Chapter 21. As a control, the overall factory productivity was also tracked over the same period.

The results are presented in the chart below (Ford, 1994).

*Figure 23-4:***Productivity Gains Caused by Workplace Literacy Training**

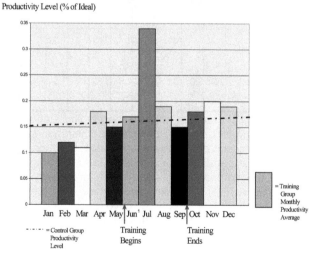

Productivity Level (% of Ideal)

While overall factory productivity rose a scant 5 percent during the period studied, the productivity of participants in the basic skills training rose an impressive 45 percent. These results were widely publicized throughout the company and subsequently published, resulting in the training department gaining greater respect in the organization and winning approval to expand the basic skills program.

These three examples, involving very different training programs and evaluation designs, illustrate the possibilities for evaluating skill transfer and behavior change. Although it requires some effort and skill, level three evaluation paid off in a big way for the trainers in these examples. It really isn't too hard to understand why. Management is far more interested in how training impacts job performance than in whether trainees are happy about training or even whether they learned something. When trainers can deliver hard proof of a positive impact on performance, they are likely to be greeted with praise and support.

### *Summary*

In this chapter, we have examined evaluation methods for skill transfer and job behavior change. You have learned why it is important to extend evaluation to the work environment, ways that training can support skill transfer through job aids and electronic performance support systems and methods for evaluating behavior change. You also examined three real-world examples of level three evaluation that illustrate innovative ways to measure skill transfer.

In the next chapter, you will learn about one more reason to evaluate skill transfer, and that is to be able to measure the business results of training.

# Discussion Questions and Exercises

1. What are some ways that training can promote skill transfer to the job?
2. What are some data collection methods for level three evaluations?
3. How can we best isolate the effects of training on job performance?

### Case Study: Employee Productivity

A hospital is introducing quality and critical care training to improve employee productivity and cut costs at the 110-bed facility. All nurses, nursing support staff, lab staff and housekeeping staff are scheduled to attend the training. The Vice-President has aksed for a plan to evaluate the impact of this training on product ivy and cost of care.

*How would you create a level 3 evaluation plan for this project? What are some likely productivity measures you could use?*

# Chapter Twenty-four :
# Evaluating the Results of Training

The ultimate purpose of training is to help organizations achieve their results. Yet the link between training and business results has always been a tenuous one at best. Business executives have largely been asked to make a leap of faith with regard to training their employees, while they would obviously prefer hard data, just as they expect data to justify other business decisions they make. This chapter will present the latest research on evaluating training results, including linking training to objective measures of success in the workplace and calculating the return on investment from training. Numerous examples and empirical research conducted by the author will illustrate the techniques discussed in this chapter.

### Results-Based Evaluation Defined

In Donald Kirkpatrick's original four-level evaluation model (Kirkpatrick, 1975), the fourth level was devoted to results. He defined this rather broadly to include any tangible benefits to an organization arising from training, including: increased productivity, better quality and quantity, reduced costs, and increased revenues and profits. Although he did not specifically cite return on investment, this too falls under the rubric of results. Subsequently, other researchers, notably Jack Phillips, have argued for a fifth level of evaluation, namely the return on investment from training. (Phillips, 1997) Whether ROI should be considered a separate level or part of level four results is a debate that will not be resolved any time soon. For our purposes, ROI will be considered as a part of results-level evaluation, since it is a logical extension of the kind of analysis typically done at this level.

The kind of results that training seeks to create is not merely an academic debate, however. It is a critical point in defining the very purpose of training and development activities in organizations. In the Introduction to this book, I argued for four levels of results that bottom-line training produces:
1. Learning
2. Performance
3. Financial
4. Strategic

In Chapter 22, you examined how to evaluate learning results using pre-post tests and other assessment techniques. Learning is the foundation for all other training results, which are dependent on learning new knowledge and skills. In the last chapter, you learned techniques for evaluating job performance, including management surveys, 360 degree surveys and work documentation. After employees learn new skills, they must apply them on the job to create higher levels of performance. Only after learning and performance results have been demonstrated can we turn to examine financial and strategic results. These are the legitimate areas of study for level-four evaluations. The study of bottom-line results typically centers on one of four areas of impact. These are shown in the diagram below.

*Figure 24-1*     **Bottom-line Training Model**

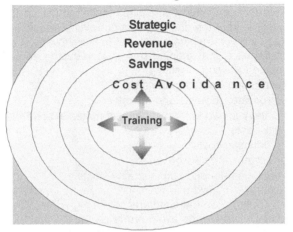

As the diagram illustrates, training creates a ripple effect on an organization s financial and strategic results, much like dropping a rock into the middle of a pond. The first three levels of impact are financial. The last is strategic impact, which is farthest from training s immediate influence and therefore the most difficult to link back to training.

Closest to training and easiest to tie directly to it is cost avoidance, or money saved that would otherwise be spent paying for the consequences of untrained employees. Examples of cost avoidance are easy to cite. Among the most common are the following:
- costs of turnover, absenteeism and tardiness
- costs of ob accidents and safety problems
- costs of retraining, or training using a more expensive method
- costs of hiring new employees instead of using existing ones more efficiently
- costs of customer service complaints and lost business opportunities

For this category of results, training does not directly reduce current expenses or produce greater revenues or profits, but it does enable an organization to avoid costs of business it would otherwise have had to incur without training. For example, a performance management training program may be able to cut the turnover and absentee rate by making managers more effective at motivating and leading their employees, thus causing employees to want to come to work and to stay with the firm longer. These benefits can be translated into avoided costs for recruiting, hiring and training new employees or for hiring temporary workers or paying overtime in order to cover for absent employees who might be away from the job because they are sick of the work, the company and their boss. Without the performance management training, the company could expect to pay a certain sum of money to replace workers that the training allowed them to retain instead.

The second category of financial results is cost savings. This is removed somewhat from the direct impact of training and so is a bit harder to link directly to a given training event, but in many cases, it is possible to isolate the contribution that training makes in reducing an organization's costs in any of the following areas:

- reduced scrap and wasted materials
- reduced error rates, defects and rework
- reduced outlays for worker's compensation, health and other insurance and benefits costs
- reduced production costs
- reduced warranty and service costs
- reduced management and administrative costs

For example, consider a training course on Quality Improvement designed for an automobile manufacturer with a high defect and scrap rate. If the training helps employees avoid errors on the job that lead to defects and scrap, the training will have saved the organization the money it now must expend to fix defects or replace scrapped material. Of course, the quality training would not occur in a vacuum. Chances are the company would also undertake other initiatives to improve its product quality, perhaps including better quality control measures, better management oversight and selection of better vendors. Taken together, all of these things would positively impact the quality problem and result in cost savings. The trick is figuring out which part of any savings can be directly attributed to training as opposed to the other measures taken to combat the problem. In some cases, it may be possible to isolate the effects of training, while in others it is only possible to say that training contributed, along with other factors, to reducing costs.

The final financial impact of training is also the hardest to prove: growth in revenues and profits. While training is often a contributing factor in allowing companies to boost revenues and profits, it is rarely the sole factor responsible for profit growth. Thus, the ripple effect of training on profitability is usually indirect and hard to isolate from other factors that impact profits. Nevertheless, the following are some of the ways that evaluators have tried to tie training to revenue and profit growth:

- increasing revenues per employee
- increasing profits per employee
- increasing sales
- increasing market share
- increasing customer satisfaction and retention
- increasing stock price, earnings per share and return on equity

In each of these cases, training can play a supporting role, but rarely is the leading cause of these changes. Thus, evaluation of training's role in a firm's profitability is generally limited to identifying specific training programs as contributing to revenue or profit growth, rather than the more ambitious claim that training alone caused this growth to occur or assigning a specific percentage of growth to training's impact.

One area of training where direct links to revenue can be demonstrated is sales training, since sales people directly impact revenues in most organizations. A new sales training program for a financial services company's outside sales force could be evaluated by measuring participants' average monthly sales before and after attending training. Any growth in sales revenues occurring after training could be attributed to the training if a clear link can be established and if other intervening factors like market forces, product mix or organizational changes can be eliminated as potential causes for revenue growth.

Aside from financial results, training can also aspire to create strategic results for organizations. This level of results refers to building competencies in an organization for future growth and expansion. Some training programs are aimed more at strategic goals than immediate financial ones. Some examples of strategic results that training can achieve include the following:

- introducing new products and services to the market
- creating new ways to serve customers
- expanding into new business ventures
- expanding to new markets and locations
- acquiring and merging with other firms

In these cases, training's impact is one of several enabling factors that would need to be in place in order for the business to grow. It is rarely possible to isolate training's contribution from that of other departments and events. But it is possible to explicate the specific contributions that training can make in reshaping the strategic direction of organizations.

One example of this involves the merger of an insurance company and a financial services company. One of the strategic goals for the merger was to position the new company to compete in both insurance and financial services markets, and to offer a one-stop, financial resource for customers. To accomplish this, the new firm realized it would have to retrain virtually its entire workforce. The insurance side needed to learn the financial services business, and the financial services employees had to learn insurance. The training department played a key role in designing and delivering tens of thousands of hours of training in new knowledge and skills needed to make the merged organization function as envisioned. A year after the training was completed, the company could boast that it was offering customers the fullest range of insurance and financial services in the industry and that its best employees were able to handle the entire breadth of the company's services, thanks in no small part to the training they had received. As a result, the company announced record revenues, up 20 percent from the previous year.

## How Training Contributes to Business Results

As you have seen throughout this section on evaluation, training is part of a series of events that results in financial or strategic gains. The process is akin to a nuclear chain reaction, where one isolated event provides the catalyst for another and so on until a critical mass is formed and results can be seen. For training to impact an organization's bottom-line, it must start with the bottom-line firmly in mind. As I argued in Chapter One, training should start with results, end with results and never let results out of its sights. Only by being obsessed with achieving results can trainers overcome the obstacles and challenges that prevent so many training programs from reaching their full potential.

At each stage of the training process, results must drive the effort. In the analysis phase, attention should be paid to analyzing performance issues in a way that clearly identifies what the problem is, what the solution is and how training will achieve it. Trainers should also look at business results up front to determine how organizations measure results and to plan for how training can impact them. During design and development, trainers must ensure that the performance issues discovered during needs analysis are properly addressed with an instructional strategy and learning materials that are motivating and relevant and that can achieve the kind of learning needed to produce performance. During implementation, trainers must prepare themselves to deliver the content in a way that maximizes learning and that prepares learners to transfer what they have learned back on the job. Finally, during evaluation, trainers must commit themselves to continuous improvement of the instructional process and to helping the organization measure the impact of training on organizational learning, performance, financial health and strategic growth. By doing all these things right, and by working in partnership with management and employees for the greater good, trainers have the best opportunity to impact results. If one or more of these links in the results chain is missing, it jeopardizes the entire process.

## Methods for Evaluating Results

Now that we have established the need for results-level evaluation and the role that training must play, it is time to examine the methods available for evaluating financial and strategic results. Among the evaluation designs presented in Chapter 21, two are of particular value in evaluating results: interrupted time series designs and pre-post control group designs. To evaluate the return on investment from training, cost-benefit analysis is also used.

The interrupted time series design is ideal for measuring financial and strategic results because it is longitudinal in nature and captures results occurring over long time periods. To use it for bottom-line results evaluation, trainers choose business measures that are impacted by training and track them over a period of months before and after training takes place. Changes in the expected trend occurring after training are attributed to the training program's impact. As an example, consider the quality improvement training described earlier. The financial impact of this training could be measured by calculating the average scrap and rework rates before the training with the averages afterwards to determine how much the training saved in scrap and rework costs.

Pre-post control group designs allow for measurement of training's impact on quantifiable business results like: scrap, rework, errors, defects, warranty costs, revenues and profits. They are especially effective when a group or department has been singled out for training to correct a problem impacting business results. The targeted training group can be compared to a control group of employees in another department, division or company who are not attending training. Comparisons can then be made both within the two groups on a pre-post basis and between the two groups on the pre and post-training measures to better isolate the effect of training.

In the example cited above, a pre-post control group design would also examine the trends in business measures pre and post-training, but would introduce a control group to the process. The control group might be another department or even another factory that did not have the same quality problems as the one receiving training. Their performance on the same business measures would be tracked along with the training group's performance. This would allow between group analysis that could pinpoint differences between the two groups that would be directly attributable to training.

For example, suppose we had obtained the following scrap costs for the factory in which the trained group works and for another factory the company owns which makes a similar product line:

Figure 24-2:    **Scrap Cost Pre-Post Training**

| Group | Avg. Monthly Scrap Pre-Training | Avg. Monthly Scrap Post-Training | Avg. Amount Saved/Month |
|---|---|---|---|
| Training | $100,000 | $ 50,000 | $ 50,000 |
| Control | $ 60,000 | $ 55,000 | $ 5,000 |
| Difference (T-C) | $ 40,000 | $ -5,000 | $ 45,000 |

If we look at the group that received training alone, we see that the training resulted in a 50 percent reduction in scrap costs, totaling an average savings of $50,000 per month, or annual savings of $600,000 (12 x 50,000). If we consider the control group as well, we see that they had a much lower scrap rate to begin with, but it went 8 percent lower during the same period, for a savings of $5,000 per month or $60,000 annually. Finally, if we consider the differences between the two (the between group comparison), we see that the trained group went from generating $40,000 more in scrap per month than the control group to generating $5,000 *less* per month after training. The difference in the amount saved between the two groups is $45,000 per month, or $540,000 annually. This figure is a more accurate calculation of the real financial impact of training on scrap costs, since it discounts savings that probably would otherwise have been achieved anyway. By reporting the lower figure, the training department demonstrates that it understands how the factory operates and recognizes that other factors besides training have an impact on scrap costs.

### Bottom-Line Results Evaluation Process

To properly prepare to conduct evaluations focused on results, it is best to follow a systematic process. The figure below outlines an effective process that has been used by many training evaluators seeking to link training to the bottom-line (Halprin, 1995).

Figure 24-3:     ***Bottom-Line Results Evaluation Process***

| |
|---|
| 1.  Select Appropriate Training |
| 2.  Focus the Evaluation |
| 3.  Design the Evaluation |
| 4.  Collect Data |
| 5.  Analyze Data |
| 6.  Report Results |
| 7.  Apply Results |

The first step is selecting appropriate training programs to evaluate for business results. As indicated in Chapter 21, it is not feasible or desirable to evaluate every single training program up to level four. It simply takes up too much time and resources to be able to afford 100 percent evaluation of all training. Instead, a more realistic target is evaluating about 25 percent (or one in four) training programs for bottom-line impact. This immediately raises the question of how to select the one in four to be evaluated. One approach is to randomly select a sample of programs to evaluate, or to agree to evaluate all programs of a certain type (say those targeted at key performers or groups within a company). This approach makes the choices easy and the results more scientific (in that they represent a larger population of training events), but it is also a strategy likely to result in some inappropriate selections.

A better approach is to develop a strategy for selecting training programs based on the following criteria:
- criticality to the business
- feasibility of obtaining quantifiable results, given the content and business measures intact
- frequency and duration of training
- high cost training programs
- high visibility training programs involving large numbers
- problem-plagued training that is under scrutiny or criticism

One organization created a decision matrix that listed these factors and others of interest and asked key stakeholders, including clients and line management, to rate the desirability of evaluating various training programs. Those receiving the highest votes were selected for financial evaluation.

A second key question about selection is who gets to participate. The training department should not make this decision alone, since they will need to work in partnership with line managers to effectively conduct a level-four evaluation. It is much better, in fact, if bottom-line evaluation is initiated by clients or management, since they will have a higher stake in it and will support it better than if training is the initiator. Nevertheless, trainers should not sit back and wait for clients to demand evaluation services, but should proactively look for opportunities to market these to the people they serve.

The next step is to focus the evaluation. This involves answering the following questions:

1. What is the purpose of the evaluation?
2. Who is the audience for the findings?
3. What bottom-line results will be evaluated?
4. What knowledge and skill learned in training can be linked to business measures?
5. Which groups, departments, divisions, companies, etc. benefited from training?

The answers to these questions will go a long ways toward defining the evaluation design.

The purpose of bottom-line evaluation is typically one or more of the following:

- training's impact on a specific business factor, like customer satisfaction
- return on investment from training (cost/benefit ratio)
- which new skills are having the biggest impact
- compare results obtained in various parts of an organization
- benchmark results with other companies
- identify causes of problems with ineffective training programs

The purpose should drive which business results and skills will be evaluated. The other major driver is the audience. An executive-level audience will want highlights of the findings and a focus on recommendations and follow up action. Line managers will be interested in how they can better support and reinforce training on the job, and on the capabilities and limitations of training as a solution to skill and performance problems. Training and human resource audiences will be much more intrigued by design and methodology issues, and less so with outcomes. The time frame also dictates the level of detail, although this can be compensated for in part by writing up the results in a report to be read and referred to later, along with a brief oral presentation for findings and recommendations.

One thing we know for sure about training programs is that they create both measurable and unmeasurable results. It is important to focus on what can be measured, and weigh this along side the intangible benefits in assessing the true worth of a training program. The business results should have been identified during needs analysis and addressed during design. Key additional questions to answer at this point include:

1. What quantitative data is available to measure results?
2. Is there historical data to use for a pre-training baseline?

3. Is there any trend data available for time series evaluation?
4. Can data be translated into dollars?
5. What new data might be needed that currently doesn't exist?

Once the data sources have been identified, the next step is to clearly link training outcomes to these results. This is where the creative aspect of bottom-line evaluation comes into play. It takes some imagination at times to find the links, but it can be done. The starting point should be the training's objectives, framed as statements of skills and tasks that learners will be able to perform upon successful completion of training. These outcomes will produce the performance of new skills in the work place, if the skills are transferred through practice and support. The better performance will then impact results like: productivity, quality, reliability, customer service, sales, etc. These results in turn enable financial results like profit growth and strategic results like new markets. This is shown in the diagram below:

*Figure 24-4:* **The Links Among Learning, Performance and Results**

LEARNING ——————▶ PERFORMANCE ——————▶ RESULTS

To illustrate the linkage, consider the following examples in the table below:

*Table 24-5:* **Sample Links in the Performance Chain**

| Occupation | Skill Learned | Performance Outcome | Bottom-Line Results |
|---|---|---|---|
| Trainer | Authoring CBT | Increased learning flexibility and training volume | Saved $100,000 in learning time and travel costs |
| Engineer | Rapid Prototyping | New Designs created faster and with fewer engineering changes | Company launched a new product in half the time, boosting market share by 20% |
| Customer Service Representative | Handling irate customers | Irate callers decline, fewer problems escalated | Customer satisfaction index improves 10%, customer retention improves 20% |
| Department Manager | Budgeting and financial management | Budget variances decline, cost overruns reduced | Department saves enough to cut its annual budget 10% |

In each of these cases, the skill learned is one that can be readily traced to a performance and financial outcome. Not every training program is so easy to link to quantifiable results. And yet, if too many of a training function's programs have no visible link to performance and bottom-line results, then it is time to stop and reconsider priorities. There are too many crying performance needs in organizations today to spend scarce resources on nice-to-have extracurriculars.

Once the evaluation is focused on the purpose, audience and measures, the design planning can begin. This includes framing the questions of the study, determining data needs, identifying sources of information and data collection methods. An implementation strategy should also be charted at this point, especially if data collection will be obtrusive.

It is advisable to state evaluation questions, like research questions, as yes/no hypotheses to be tested. Here are a few examples from actual bottom-line evaluation studies:

- Did the contract management training program result in contract cost savings?
- Did the relationship selling training program increase sales revenues?
- Did the computer software training increase office productivity?
- Did the sexual harassment training decrease the amount of money spent defending the company from sexual harassment lawsuits?
- Did the basic skills training reduce scrap and rework costs in the factory?

Once the question has been framed appropriately, the next step is deciding what information is needed to answer the question. You should think of a variety of ways to answer the question and choose the one that seems most feasible and credible. A key factor in level four evaluation studies is using credible data accepted by the audience for the evaluation. Among the sources of credible data to consider are:

- key business indicators and results
- work performance measures and documentation
- company budgets and accounting systems
- management information systems and databases
- standard and ad hoc company reports
- training records
- opinions of learners, their supervisors, colleagues, employees, customers and experts
- direct, first-hand job observation

The key to using these sources is to be sure that the data is reliable and that it accurately answers the question at hand. If the question cannot be measured directly, such as whether a leadership training program has created a more empowered organization, then the use of indirect measures like opinion surveys, interviews or focus groups can at least give a sense of the magnitude of training's impact.

Data collection methods must be tailored to the methodology and design chosen. The four most common methods are:

1. Analysis of Company Documents and Databases
2. Surveys
3. Interviews
4. Observation

Starting with existing documentation is wise, since many answers can be found there. Companies collect, store and report vast amounts of information about their daily activities and results. Tapping into this information can yield a treasure trove. It is especially useful for establishing baseline measures, spotting trends and conducting time series studies. Performance and cost data are among the two most useful pieces of information for level four evaluation. If we can measure an improvement in performance, we can use the company's accounting methods to calculate what that improvement is worth in dollar terms.

Other data collection methods primarily rely on opinion to judge results. Surveys are frequently used to collect self-reports and management feedback, while interviews, focus groups and observation allow for in-depth exploration of the impact of training. The problem with these methods, of course, is that they yield secondary evidence of training's impact, not the primary evidence we seek. It is also difficult to translate opinions or other qualitative data into financial results. One technique that some evaluators use is to extrapolate opinions about performance improvements into estimated cost savings, using standard labor rates and accounting methods (Phillips, 1994). For example, if a quality improvement training program was being evaluated to see how it impacted factory productivity, the participants and their managers could be surveyed and asked to estimate the amount of improvement they have observed in productivity from before training till afterwards. They might further be asked to assign a percentage of that improvement that could be attributed to training. This improvement could then be converted to monetary values by multiplying the percentage improvement times the total payroll of those participating in training. The resulting figure represents the productivity gain, stated in labor dollars, attributed to the quality improvement program. As an example of this approach, consider the sample data in the table below:

*Table 24-6:* **Sample Method for Converting Opinion Data to Monetary Data**

| Self-Rating % Improvement | Management Rating % Improvement | Percent of Improvement Caused by Training | Total Payroll of Participants | Estimated Productivity Savings |
|---|---|---|---|---|
| 20% | 10% | 60% | $500,000 | $30,000 |
| (avg. pre-post gain in productivity) | (avg. pre-post gain in productivity) | (60% of total gain due to training = 10% X 60%= 6%) | (total payroll for 20 employees participating in training) | ($500,000 X 6% = $30,000 savings) |

The estimated labor savings of $30,000 is based on a conservative estimate by managers of how much productivity was boosted by training. If managers accept the original premise of the survey, they are likely to also accept the resulting monetary savings, even if this is not precise.

The final issue to address in the evaluation design is the implementation strategy. This includes deciding who will develop any evaluation tools, such as surveys, that are needed, who will actually collect data, when the data will be available and who will be providing it. If data collection includes participants and managers, permission to do this will need to be arranged in advance to avoid disrupting work.

The next step in the process is to actually collect data, using the tools and methods previously specified. Persons assigned to data collection should be thoroughly trained in the methods to be used to ensure reliable data. If qualitative methods are used, like interviews or focus groups, skilled facilitators should lead these efforts to maximize the amount and quality of information received. If company records are being used, verify that the data is accurate, current and comprehensible to those who will be analyzing it. It may help to have an expert on the data source brief evaluators on the nature, source and limitations of the data, so that these can be considered in drawing conclusions based on it.

Once data has been collected, the next step is to analyze the data. Analysis includes the following issues:

- analytical methods and tools
- data interpretation

The methods and tools available to analyze level four data include a variety of software programs, such as spreadsheets, statistical software, databases, and specialized survey and questionnaire data analysis software. Presentation software can be used to create descriptive statistics, charts and graphs. Manual tools like tally logs, observation checklists, interview logs, etc. may be employed. Sometimes, the addition of an outside evaluator can help bring objectivity and expertise to the effort.

The key to analyzing bottom-line data, once again, is to look for valid links among learning, performance and results. Once a link has been established, you must isolate the effect of training on the results. Sometimes this will be 100 percent, but very often it is something less than that. Part of the interpretation effort is to make judgments about training's impact, including estimates of the contribution of training and non-training factors on the results achieved. In interpreting data, the evaluators should take the lead, but they should also consider the views of line managers, participants, subject matter experts and others who can help to identify key factors and trends in the data.

Once the data analysis is completed, the next step is reporting the results, using both a written and oral report geared to the audience. Advice on how to do this was presented in Chapter 21.

The last step of the evaluation process is to apply the findings of the evaluation to improve training and boost bottom-line results. Sometimes, this simply means reporting a success story to the organization to reward those responsible for it and to encourage others to use training as a resource. Other times, the findings of bottom-line evaluations suggest ways to improve the training, the transfer of skills to the job, or the way results are being achieved. Findings that require change should be put in an action plan that clearly specifies how the change will be made, by whom and by when. Someone should then be appointed to monitor the action plan and ensure it is followed through. By taking a systematic approach to the evaluation of business results, trainers have a much greater chance of identifying training's true impact and of building greater support for training from those who participate in evaluation studies.

## Methods for Calculating Return on Investment

Return on investment is a standard formula for stating the monetary benefits to be derived from an investment. It is generally calculated as follows:

*Figure 24-7:*  **Return on Investment Formula**

$$ROI (\%) = \frac{\text{Net benefits (Costs-Benefits)}}{\text{Costs}} \times 100$$

For example, if a quality improvement training program cost $100,000 to design, develop and deliver, and it produced $200,000 in reduced scrap and rework costs, the ROI would be:

ROI = (200,000-100,000) / 100,000 = 100%

That is, for each dollar invested in the training, the company received a dollar back in net benefits. ROI is usually calculated on an annual basis. Results may accrue for more than one year, but to be conservative, training should probably limit its focus to one year after a training program is implemented. After that time, so many other intervening variables come into play it is difficult to isolate the contribution of training alone.

As an example of ROI calculation, let's consider the case introduced in the last chapter of an electronics firm that conducted basic skills training to improve the quality of its products. Recall that a study of the performance of employees enrolled in the program found a 45% average increase in productivity after training as compared to before, using an interrupted time series design that looked at changes in actual factory productivity over a period of a year. To calculate the ROI for this program, evaluators had to do two things:

1. calculate the total costs of the program
2. calculate the total monetary value of the benefits

The total costs were the easier part to calculate, since these were already known or easy to collect. Costs were broken into two categories: direct and indirect. Direct costs included the following:

- testing
- needs assessment
- instructors' salaries
- computer hardware and software

Indirect training costs included:

- participants' wages while attending class on company time
- management steering committee's wages
- training management's wages
- printing, shipping and miscellaneous costs

Adding up all of these costs for the three month program totaled $38,000.

Now the evaluators had to calculate the monetary benefits of the training. They divided these into two types: cost savings from scrap and rework reductions, and labor savings from increased productivity, which resulted in less labor expended per product built (and hence a higher profit margin on the products). The total annual benefit from reduced scrap and rework was easy to figure, because the factory kept monthly records of this and these were simply added up for one year to arrive at a total value of $27,000. Figuring out the labor savings from increased productivity was a bit trickier. The formula in Figure 24-8 was used to estimate labor savings:

The monthly labor savings was multiplied times 12 months to arrive at an annual savings figure of $294,000 ($24,500 X 12 = $294,000).

*Figure 24-8*: **Labor Savings Formula**

| % Productivity Increase | X | Average Wage/Hr. | X | Average Hrs/Mo. | X | # Employees Trained | = Monthly Savings |
|---|---|---|---|---|---|---|---|
| 45% | X | $11 | X | 165 | X | 30 | = $24,503 |

Now all these numbers can be plugged into the ROI formula to get the total return on investment from the basic skills training.

*Figure 24-9*: **ROI of Literacy Training**

$$ROI = \frac{(\$321,600 - 38,200)}{\$38,200} = \frac{\$283,400}{\$38,200} = 742\%$$

In this case, the training returned $7.42 in benefits for every dollar invested, a huge ROI. Typically, ROI from training runs in the range of 50 to 200 percent, but reports of ROI as high as 2,000 percent have appeared in the literature.

Reporting training results in these bottom-line terms has a powerful effect on executives and line managers. They not only see clearly, sometimes for the first time, how powerful investments in human capital really are, but they also gain new respect for the training function and its business acumen. Trainers who can regularly report these kinds of results, even on a small fraction of their total offerings, are bound to enjoy greater management support for their efforts.

### Training Balanced Scorecard

So far, we have discussed how to evaluate individual training programs to isolate the impact they have on performance and business. But what about the cumulative effect of many training programs over time on a business' financial and strategic results? To aggregate training results over time, we need another methodology. One that is gaining popularity is the training balanced scorecard.

Based on work by Kaplan and Norton (Kaplan & Norton, 1992), the balanced scorecard strives to measure intangible human resource assets by looking at how they create value for organizations. These notions have been applied to human resources (Bechler, Husled & Ulrich, 2001) and trainers are now taking an interest in this approach.

So what should a training scorecard measure? The sample scorecard below looks at three critical training areas: activity, efficiency and results. Training activity looks at the investment in training and the amount of training provided as critical inputs. Efficiency looks at how productively training departments use the resources provided to them. Finally training results looks at aggregate outcomes produced by training, using Kirkpatrick's four level evaluation model.

*Figure 24-10*:

# Training Balanced Scorecard

- Training Activity
  - % Payroll:_____
    Training budget/Payroll
  - Hrs./Empl._____
    Training hours/Employees
  - $/Empl. _____
    Training budget/Employees
- Training Efficiency
  - Cost/Hr. _____
    Training budget/ training hours
  - % Billable _____
    Billable hours/staff hours

- Training Results
  - % Positive Ratings
    Positive ratings/total ratings
  - % Learning Gain
    Post-pre / Pre-test scores
  - % Performance Gain
    Post-pre / Pre-performance
  - Revenues/Employee
    Total revenues/employees
  - Market/Book Ratio
    Total market worth/ total physical assets

*Figure 24-11*:

# Training Scorecard Results

- Training Activity
  - % Payroll
    US Avg.=1.9% ‡
  - $/Employee/year
    US Avg.=$569 ‡
  - Hrs./Empl./year
    US Avg.= 36 ‡
- Training Efficiency
  - Cost/Hour
    US Avg.=$28 ‡
  - % Billable Hrs.
    US Avg.=70% †

- **Training Results**
  - % Positive Course Ratings
    Avg.=91%†
  - % Learning Gain
    Avg.=45%†
  - % Behavior Change
    Avg.=25%†
  - Revenues/Employee
    Avg.=$100K†
  - Market/Book†
    Avg.=10:1

Each of these measures is a ratio, which economists and financial experts consider to be the most powerful measures of business performance. The ratios allow comparisons between firms of different sizes and longitudinal tracking of training over time. To calculate each ratio, identify annual totals for each category and then divide them to arrive at an average number. For benchmarking comparisons, the following data was assembled from the *ASTD Training Data Book* (ASTD, 2003) and from my own study of leading high tech companies conducted in 1993 and updated in 1999. The results appear in Figure 24-11.

## Summary

In this final chapter on evaluation, you have learned about how to evaluate training programs for bottom-line results, including both financial and strategic results. You have examined the role and importance of level four evaluation and explored a process to design, measure and report results obtained from bottom-line evaluations. You have also examined how to calculate return on investment from training, using techniques to calculate training costs and measure monetary benefits.

At this point, we have completed the full cycle of training design. We have now only one chapter left - a look back at how far we've come and a look forward at where we may be heading in the years to come.

# Discussion Questions and Exercises

1. What kinds of results does training produce?
2. Describe the process for determining bottom-line results from training.
3. Describe the method of calculating ROI from training.
4. Calculate a training balanced scorecard for your training organization. Compare to the U.S. average, how is your organization doing? In what areas should you make improvements?

**Case Study: Hotel Quality Initiative**
    A five-star hotel initiated a major quality and customer service training program after it experienced an increase in customer complaints and a loss of market share. After the training was conducted for the entire staff, the Training Department wanted to calculate the ROI. They assembled the following figures on key business and performance benefits and costs:

### Hotel Quality Initiative

| Measures | Pre-training | Post-training |
|---|---|---|
| Market share (each percentage point is worth $1 million in revenue) | 22% | 24% |
| Staff error rates (each error cost $160 on average to fix) | 1200/year | 850/year |
| Turnover (each new hire cost $4000 to recruit) | 110/year | 88/year |
| Cost of training | Needs analysis, design and development = $250,000 | Delivery and evaluation = $300,000 Indirect labor (trainees) = $250,000 |

    *Calculate the ROI of this training, assuming that all results and costs are included in the table.*

# Chapter Twenty-five :
# Where We've Been and Where We're Headed

The concluding chapter will look back at 60 years of training to understand where we are today and looks forward to the next 40 years to hazard a prediction on where the filed will be in 2050. Besides summarizing key themes of this book, I will highlight those activities that constitute the current state of the art and best practices in the field. I will also provide a glimpse toward emerging trends, such as continuous learning, learning technology and automated design that predict where the field is likely to move in the twenty-first century.

### Where We Have Been

The field of training, most particularly instructional design, has come a long way in 60 years form factory floors and vestibules of the past into the corporate boardrooms and on the desktops of virtually every employee in America in the twenty-first century. Originally conceived as a way to quickly train millions of new workers supporting the massive war effort, instructional systems design began as a systematic way to apply principles of behavioral psychology to programmed instruction and audio-visual media. The early teaching machines of the 1950's look laughable and quaint from the perspective of current multimedia training courses, but the roots of instructional design are present in both. The systems approach to designing training holds that learning is a complex human system that can be facilitated by instructional and learning theories. Instruction is seen as having three basic parts: input, process and output. Inputs to learning include the following elements: organizations' business needs, learners' prior experience and knowledge, training resources and instructional theory.

The process of learning is much better understood today than in the past, although there is still much to know about exactly what makes instruction effective. At its inception, instructional design was dominated by the views of behavioral psychologists like B.F. Skinner, whose stimulus-response operant conditioning theories dominated instructional methods and gave us the famous drill and practice routines many of us grew up with in school.

Today, we have discovered that learning occurs when courses are designed around the key tasks and skills needed to perform on the job, when learners are motivated to acquire new knowledge and skill, and when instruction is delivered by trainers who are knowledgeable in both the content and facilitation of learning. We also know that learning must be reinforced through appropriate practice and transferred to the job with management support. Thanks to contributions from cognitive psychology, we now better understand the mental processes behind learning, including the way knowledge is stored and used by the brain, the way memory functions and the role that both biology and environment play in shaping human learning and experience.

The outcomes of learning have expanded to include not only the traditional one of learning new skills, but also improving job performance, and ultimately boosting the financial and strategic results of the organization. The systems view of learning has helped us see that the real purpose of instructional design is to deliver to learners what they need, when they need it, in a form that they can readily assimilate and apply.

On the journey to better learning, trainers have expanded their capabilities to analyze problems, identify root causes that are both training and non-training related, design more sophisticated solutions using innovative learning activities and technologies, deliver training in consistent and effective ways, and evaluate the results of training, especially tying training to financial and strategic business results. Each of these developments has strengthened the field of training, and helped it occupy an ever-more important role in organizations and society at large.

### The Current State of The Art

In reflecting on all the elements that make training design effective, the following emerge as current best practices in the field.

*Figure 25-1:* **Current Best Practices in Training Design**

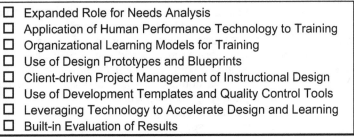

> ☐ Expanded Role for Needs Analysis
> ☐ Application of Human Performance Technology to Training
> ☐ Organizational Learning Models for Training
> ☐ Use of Design Prototypes and Blueprints
> ☐ Client-driven Project Management of Instructional Design
> ☐ Use of Development Templates and Quality Control Tools
> ☐ Leveraging Technology to Accelerate Design and Learning
> ☐ Built-in Evaluation of Results

Let's examine each of these best practices in more detail to see how they impact training design. The first two involve the analysis phase of training, which has grown enormously over the past decade. Traditional instructional design focused almost exclusively on behavioral job task analysis to determine the need for training and the specific objectives to be taught. Today, needs analysis has expanded to include consideration of competencies, as well as tasks, especially for knowledge or management work that cannot be easily observed using traditional task analysis. Secondly, needs analysis is often a team effort nowadays, with active participation by clients, key stakeholders and other areas of an organization like human resources, IT and quality assurance. The expansion of needs analysis now includes consideration of a host of non-training related issues, like employee motivation, reward and compensation systems, work design, performance management systems, leadership structure, organizational systems and culture, career systems and performance improvement theory. Training is seen as a part of a larger system of job performance that is influenced by many non-training variables. Instructional designers are increasingly becoming business consultants, helping organizations define the nature of work and build job models and organizational structures that will support continuous learning and improvement. They are also paying greater attention, thanks to cognitive psychology, to analyzing the needs of learners and the context in which learning will occur, so as to structure learning in ways that are compatible with learners' abilities and predispositions.

A second major force today is the advent of learning organizations and the philosophy of continuous learning advocated by researchers such as Peter Senge (Senge, 1990) and others. This has shifted focus from classroom mastery of skills to performance-centered development of employees in the context of their work and the organization's current and future needs. The focus on organizational learning includes both formal training and informal learning on the job, and the ways that organizations can enhance their human capital and core competencies in order to better compete in the marketplace. These trends have shifted focus from individual learners to the organization as a whole and the way in which it builds core competencies over time.

Instructional designers have wrestled with the implications of a continuous learning environment, including incorporating some of the principles of dialogue, reflection and systems thinking that drive organizational learning and finding ways to short cut the design process in order to keep pace with the rapid demands for new learning materials. Some experts warn that learning must accelerate due to the shrinking half-life of knowledge in an ever-changing world. In rapidly developing fields like electrical engineering and computer science, knowledge has a shelf-life of five years or less. This compels these professions to be constantly learning just to keep pace with technological change.

In the design phase of training, innovations include the widespread use of design blueprints and specifications to clearly spell out what training will look like and what it can be expected to accomplish. Rapid prototyping has enabled training designers to cut time from the design and development phase while allowing clients to directly influence the outcomes long before most of the resources have been expended. Secondly, training design has become much more complex, especially when technology is employed. This has given rise to increased use of project management theory and tools to successfully manage large-scale training design projects. The use of project management software, detailed work breakdown structure, cost and time tracking and customer consultation and input have greatly strengthened the design and development phase, making these much more efficient than ever before.

Another key development in design is the growing influence of cognitive psychology, and cognitive theories of learning. This can be seen in the focus on learner analysis, information processing, higher level thinking processes and instructional strategies and the sequencing of instruction to enhance learning. Although behavioral psychology continues to exercise great influence on training, the most recent and compelling developments in instructional design and performance technology have come from cognitive sciences.

In the development phase, the biggest changes have been in the use of computer technology to speed materials development, especially sophisticated word processing, desktop publishing and graphics software that enable designers to turn out higher quality work in less time than ever before. A related development is the use of templates to help standardize material development and the use of design libraries to speed development by reusing materials whenever possible.

The other major change in development is the increased use of technology to both develop materials and deliver them to users. Today, instructional designers are nearly as likely to produce materials in computer authoring languages or using Internet-based HTML (hypertext markup language) as they are to produce print materials with a word processor. The demands of technology have forced instructional designers, like their counterparts in information technology, to embark on life-long learning of new development and delivery technologies in order to stay current. Increasingly, we see instructional designers asked to create virtually instant materials that are quickly consumed and become obsolete. This forces designers to search for new ways to short-circuit the development process, and collapse the time required to produce usable learning materials.

Implementation of training has seen the greatest change in non-classroom delivery, including computer-based, Internet, distance learning, self-study, structured OJT and the like. These delivery methods allow trainers to reach employees where they work, rather than having them removed from the work environment and placed in an artificial training environment. As technology has developed, the options available to trainers have also expanded greatly. We are now on the threshold of an exciting new era of digital technology that will revolutionize the way we work, learn and live.

Even the low-tech classroom has not escaped these changes. Trainers no longer simply stand in front and lecture to groups of learners. Instead, they facilitate discussions, role plays, case studies, games, simulations and other innovative ways to get learners to open their minds and practice new skills in ways that make them easy to transfer to the real world. Increasingly, too, technology is an integral part of the classroom environment, as computers and audio-visual equipment become key tools to help trainers deliver effective instruction and provide relevant practice.

Finally, evaluation has matured from a weak afterthought of the instructional design process to an essential component of effective training. The focus of evaluation has also expanded from looking solely at learner reactions and learning outcomes to job behavior change, performance, financial and strategic results. We can now even determine the return on investment from some training programs, giving us a new currency with which to discuss training results and build support from executives.

The best training programs build evaluation in at the design phase rather than letting it be an afterthought. When this is done, key baseline measures are collected during analysis and the entire training focus shifts from internal concerns to business outcomes, thus strengthening the partnership between training and the organizations they serve. Evaluation is also seen by leading firms as a key method for improving the training process. They take evaluation results seriously and apply them to continuously improve the instructional design process, thus creating ever-better results from training.

### The Future of Training Design

Any attempt to gaze into the future and predict events and trends is perilous, given the rapid pace of change today. One thing about the future seems clear, however. Training designers will certainly be challenged to solve increasingly complex learning and organizational problems. To address these challenges successfully, designers must invent new ways to accelerate the design and learning process, and to use technology to help learners reach their full potential.

If we surveyed executives today and asked them what they would like to see changed about their training and instructional design functions, they would probably mention three things: we need training to be faster, cheaper and better. These three forces, once thought to be mutually incompatible, are likely to drive change in the future. Those who figure out how to deliver better training faster and cheaper than their competitors will win out in the ever-competitive global economy. Those who don't change are likely to be left behind on the scrap heap of history.

Among the most significant developments in the years ahead are likely to be those listed in Figure 25-2. The demand for continuous learning is putting tremendous pressure on traditional instructional design systems, which are often too slow to meet accelerated demand. The key to success in the future will be finding ways to speed up the design of training to keep pace with the demands of a learning organization. The other key is to anticipate training needs as they emerge so as to proactively plan future training to be available whenever needed. Trainers will need to streamline their own processes, using evaluation feedback to continuously improve, and will also need to better anticipate the future needs of their organizations by becoming active players in strategic planning and other future-oriented business planning activities. Trainers must display the same visionary skills that we currently demand of business leaders.

In the area of learning technology, training designers must constantly educate themselves about emerging technologies so as to be able to apply these in solving performance problems at work. Though the focus is on developments in computer hardware and software, trainers must also continuously improve the theory and practice of instructional design, incorporating new ideas like performance technology, artificial intelligence, cognitive science, systems theory, and the like which will produce the next generation of learning theory. We must embrace technology and learn to master it in the interests of learning and performance improvement. If trainers do not master the technology, they run the risk of allowing others in the organization to seize the initiative and move technology forward without the benefit of an instructional design perspective.

*Figure 25-2:* **Future Developments in Training Design**

Designers must focus on refining new theories of training such as human performance technology, learning organizations and social learning networks. Although these new perspectives offer the promise of solving many existing performance problems, the science and theory behind these movements are still underdeveloped. It is not clear yet whether performance improvement strategies represent a whole new way of designing and delivering training, or merely an expanded horizon and set of options for trainers. At this point, once performance analysis identifies a training issue, designers still rely on the instructional systems design model to guide their work. Though modified and expanded over the years, the ISD or ADDIE model remains the most complete theory guiding instructional design work despite many contending alternatives. Further research in the fields of learning and instruction may eventually result in a better model, but it hasn't happened just yet.

Ultimately, technology may exert the strongest force to revolutionize the design and development of training by enabling much of the work currently done humans to be produced automatically by computers instead. Already, sophisticated software tools enable designers to quickly plan and design training programs, and then develop materials with the aid of knowledge databases. In the future, an instructional design expert system, powered by artificial intelligence, may be able to take the design specifications fed into it by an instructional designer and automatically generate learning materials and activities that can be applied immediately. Perhaps, one day in the not too distant future, employees may be able to order their own custom training, delivered instantly to their desktop on any subject of need, without the intervention of human hands. If this sounds far-fetched now, imagine how today's personal computer would appear to the pioneers of computer science 50 years ago, who needed an entire building, and millions of dollars to house the computing power of a single microprocessor selling for less than $200 today.

If anything, our vision of technology is probably much too timid. Perhaps we will ultimately see combinations of technology and living systems that will require us to redefine what we mean by life itself. Recent advances in biotechnology, including genetic engineering and the infamous cloning of animals, will open new areas of science that could have a profound effect on learning. What if it becomes possible to alter the human genetic code to enhance our ability to learn? What if someday prospective parents get to choose the intelligence level of their off-spring? Won't they all opt for precocious geniuses? And what if someday medical science finally develops the 'smart pill' that trainers sometimes joke about, that gives the person taking it instant intelligence and the ability to learn at previously unheard of speeds?

All of this may sound a bit far-fetched now, but given the pace of change over the past 50 years, it is impossible to rule out any of these scenarios occurring over the span of the next 50 years as we live in a new millennium full of ambitions and dreams.

### The Training Professional of Tomorrow

If we hope to make the future of training come true, we must prepare to lead organizations into the age of knowledge. A recent competency study by ASTD revealed the latest thinking on what it will take for trainers to succeed in the future. Figure 25-3 shows the new ASTD Training Competency model (ASTD, 2004). The biggest departure from the past is the increased emphasis on business and management skills, which help trainers define and drive towards results. From this we see new technology-based areas of expertise and roles for trainers emerging. It is an exciting time to be in the training profession, if we are equal to the task that faces us.

### Summary

Whatever the future might bring, training designers must prepare themselves to deliver learning and performance in a world of constant change. Truly, as never before in our history, the future of training is full of challenge and hope. It is up to both theorists and practitioners today to work together in advancing the field of training and instructional design to meet the future demands placed upon it by society. If we can succeed in this grand endeavor, we will help humankind in significant ways, for our success as a species on this planet is a direct outgrowth of our incredible ability to learn and to change. While we help others, we will also help ourselves by ensuring the survival and growth of training as a profession worthy of admiration.

If this book moves us forward, in even the smallest ways, in the quest for better human performance at work, it will have been worth every cent spent in writing and publishing it.

*Figure 25-3:*

© 2004 American Society for Training and Development

# Discussion Questions and Exercises

1. Compare and contrast training in 1950 and today. What major changes have occurred? What is still largely the same?
2. Which of the current training best practices do you use? How could you apply the other best practices in your work?
3. What are the major challenges facing the training profession in the future? How can trainers best prepare to meet them?

**Case Study: Future Planet**

Imagine it is the year 2050 and you have been invited to work on a major training project to prepare a group of space colonists to live in a permanent colony on the moon. They must be prepared for the journey to the moon and for the tasks of growing food, building homes and creating a social and political environment for their biosphere.

*Assuming any technological breakthroughs that seem plausible by 2050, develop a high-level training design for this project.*

## Section Six:
# Appendices

The book ends with three appendices: an extensive reference bibliography, examples of instructional design tools and products (sample surveys, blueprints, templates, tests, checklists, etc.), and an index.


## Appendix One: Reference Bibliography

The following are sources used in the research and writing of this book.

Andrews, D. and Goodson, L. "A Comparative Analysis of Models of Instruction Design," *Journal of Development.* 19803(4), pp. 2-16, (ED EJ 228 351)

Baird, L.S., Schneier, C.E. and Laird, D. (Eds.) *The Training and Development Sourcebook.* Amherst, MA: HRD Press, 1984.

Baldwin, T., and Ford, J. "Transfer of Training: A Review and Directions for Future Research." *Personnel Psychology,* 1998, 41(1), pp. 63-105.

Bentley, T. Facilitation: Providing Opportunities for Learning. London: McGraw-Hill, 1994.

Biech, Elaine. *ASTD Handbook for Workplace Learning Professionals.* Alexandria, VA: ASTD, 2008.

Blalock. R. "Using Development 'Shells' for Fast and Creative Multimedia Development at American Airlines." *Journal of Instructional Delivery Systems,* Summer 1995, pp. 3-9.

Bloom, Benjamin, J. T. Hastings and G.F. Madaus. *Handbook on Formative and Summative Evaluation of Student Learning.* N.Y.: McGraw-Hill, 1971.

Broad, Mary and John Newstrom. *Transfer of Training*: Action-Packed Strategies to Ensure High Payoff from Training Investments. Reading, MA: Addison-Wesley, 1992.

Campbell, Donald and Stanley, J. *Experimental and Quasi-Experimental Designs for Research.* Skokie, IL: Rand McNally, 1966.

Campbell, J.P., R.J. Campbell, & Associates. *Productivity in Organizations: New Perspectives from Industrial and Organizational Psychology.* San Francisco, CA: Jossey-Bass, 1988.

Carkhuff, R.R. and Fisher, S.G. *Instructional Systems Design.* Amherst, MA: Human Resource Development Press, 1984.

Carnevale, Anthony, Gainer, L. and Villet, J. *Training in America: The Organization and Strategic Role of Training.* San Francisco: Jossey-Bass, 1990.

Chingos, Peter. *Paying for Performance: A Guide to Compensation Management.* New York, N.Y.: Wiley, 1997.

Cholofsky, N. and Lincoln, C.I. *Up the HRD Ladder: A Guide for Professional Growth.* Addison-Wesley, 1983.

Clark, Richard E.. *Training Design.* Los Angeles, CA: Atlantic Training, 1995.

Craig, Robert L.(Ed.) Training and Development Handbook: A Guide to Human Resource Development. (4th edition). New York, N.Y.: McGraw-Hill, 1996.

Dick, W. and Carey, L. *The Systematic Design of Instruction.* (3rd ed.) New York, N.Y.: HarperCollins, 1990.

Dubois, David. *Competency-Based Performance Improvement: A Strategy for Organizational Change.* Amherst, MA: HRD Press, 1993.

Dunnette, M.D. and Hough, L.M. (Eds.) *Handbook of Industrial and Organizational Psychology.* (2nd edition). Palo Alto, CA: Consulting Psychologists Press, 1991.

Edmonds, G., Branch, R. and Mukherjee, P. "A Conceptual Framework for Comparing Instructional Design Models." *Education Technology Research and Development,* 1990, 42(4), pp. 55-72.

Ellington, H. Producing Teaching Materials: A Handbook for Teaching and Trainers. East Brunswick, N.J.: Nichols, 1985.

Filipczak, Bob. "Different Strokes: Learning Styles in the Classroom", *Training.* March, 1995, vol. 32, no. 3, pp. 43-48.

Fitz-Enz, Jacques. *How to measure Human Resources Management.* New York, N.Y.: McGraw-Hill, 1984.

Ford, Donald J. "Evaluating Performance Improvement," *Performance Improvement.* January, 2004, vol.43, no. 1, pp. 36-41.

Ford, Donald J. *Training Needs Assessment.* Los Angeles, CA: ASTD-L.A., 1994.

Ford, Donald J. (Ed.) *In Action: Designing Training Programs.* Alexandria, VA: ASTD, 1996.

Ford, Donald J. "Benchmarking HRD", *Training and Development.* 1993, 47(6), pp. 36-41.

Ford, Donald J. "Toward a More Literate Workforce," *Training and Development.* 1992, 46(11), pp. 52-57.

Foshay, W., Silber, K. and Westgaard, O. *Instructional Design Competencies: The Standards.* Iowa City, IO: International Board of Standard for Training , Performance, and Instruction, 1986.

Gagne, Robert and Medsker, K. *The Conditions of Learning: Training Applications.* Fort Worth, TX: Harcourt Brace, 1996.

Gagne, Robert, Briggs, L. and Wager. W. *Principles of Instructional Design.* (4th ed.) Fort Worth, TX: Harcourt Brace, 1992.

Gery, Gloria. Electronic Performance Support Systems: How and Why to Remake the Workplace Through the Strategic Application of Technology. Boston, MA: Weingarten, 1991.

Gilbert, Tom. Human Competence: Engineering Worthy Performance. New York, N.Y.: McGraw-Hill, 1978.

Goodman, L. and R. Love. (Eds.) *Project Planning and Management: An Integrated Approach*. New York, N.Y.: Pergammon Press, 1980.

Greer, Michael. *ID Project Management: Tools and Techniques for Instructional Designers and Developers*. Englewood Cliffs, N.J.: Educational Technology Publications, 1992.

Halprin, Michelle. *Evaluating Business Results*. L.A., CA: Pacific Enterprises, 1995.

Hammer, Michael and J. Champy. *Reengineering the Corporation: A Manifesto for Business Revolution*. New York, N.Y.: HarperCollins, 1993.

Herrmann, Ned. *Creative Brain*. North Carolina: Brain Books, 1989.

Howell, Jeffery and Larry Silvey. "Interactive Multimedia Training Systems", in *The ASTD Training & Development Handbook*, 4th edition. N.Y.: McGraw-Hill, 1996.

Kaye, Beverly. *Up is Not the Only Way: A Guide to Developing Workforce Talent*. (2nd edition). Palo Alto, CA: Consulting Psychological Press, 1997.

Kirkpatrick, Donald. *Evaluating Training Programs: The Four Levels*. New York, N.Y.: Berrett-Koehler, 1996.

Kirkpatrick, Donald. (Ed.) *Evaluating Training Programs*. Alexandria, VA: American Society for Training and Development, 1975.

Knowles, Malcolm, *The Modern Practice of Adult Education: From Pedagogy to Andragogy*. New York, N.Y.: Cambridge Book Company, 1980.

Knowles, Malcolm. *The Adult Learner: A Neglected Species*. (3rd edition) Houston, TX: Gulf Publishing, 1984.

Laird, Dugan. *Approaches to Training and Development*. (2nd edition). Reading, MA: Addison-Wesley, 1985.

Lawler, Edward III. *Strategic Pay: Aligning Organizational Strategies and Pay Systems*. San Francisco, CA: Jossey-Bass, 1990.

Lee, W. and Mamone, R. *Handbook of Computer-Based Training: Assessment, Design, Development, Evaluation*. Englewood Cliffs, N.J.: Educational Technology Publications, 1995.

Likert, Rensis. *The Human Organization*. New York, N.Y.: McGraw-Hill, 1967.

Mager, Robert and Peter Pipe. *Analyzing Performance Problems: Or You Really Oughta Wanna*. Berkeley, CA: Fearon, 1970.

Mager, Robert. Measuring Instructional Intent, or Got a Match? Belmont, CA: Fearon Press, 1973.

Mager, Robert. *Preparing Instructional Objectives*. (2nd edition). Palo Alto, CA: Fearon, 1975.

McCormick, E. *Job Analysis*. New York, N.Y.: AMACOM, 1979.

McLagan, Patricia. *Helping Others Learn: Design Programs for Adults*. Reading, MA: Addison-Wesley, 1978.

McLagan, Patricia. *Models for HRD Practice*. Alexandria, VA: American Society for Training and Development, 1989.

Milkovich, George T. and Wigdor, Alexandra. (Eds.) *Pay for Performance: Evaluating Performance Appraisal and Merit Pay*. Washington,

D.C.: Committee on Performance Appraisal for Merit Pay, National Research Council, 1991.

Nadler, D.A., M.S Gernstein, R.B. Shaw & Associates. *Organizational Architecture: Designs for Changing Organizations.* San Francisco, CA: Jossey-Bass, 1992.

Nadler, Leonard and Zeace Nadler. *Designing Training Programs: The Critical Events Model.* (2nd edition). Houston, TX: Gulf Publishing, 1994.

Nadler, Leonard. (Ed.) *Handbook of Human Resource Development.* (2nd ed.) New York, N.Y.: Wiley, 1990.

Nolan, Michael. "Job Training", in *The ASTD Training & Development Handbook*, 4th edition. N.Y.: McGraw-Hill, 1996.

Noe, R.A. *Employee Training and Development.* Singapore: McGraw-Hill, 2007.

Otto, C.P. and Glaser, R.O. *The Management of Training.* Reading, MA: Addison-Wesley, 1970.

Overfield, Karen. "Non-linear Approach to Training Program Development," *Performance and Instruction*, July 1994, pp. 26-35.

Peters, Tom. Thriving on Chaos: Handbook for a Management Revolution. New York, N.Y.: Knopf, 1987.

Phillips, Jack J. *Handbook of Training Evaluation and Measurement Methods.* 2nd ed. Houston, TX: Gulf Publishing Co., 1997.

Phillips, Jack J. "Measuring ROI: Progress, Trends and Strategies," *In Action: Measuring Return on Investment,* Vol. I. Alexandria, VA: ASTD, 1994.

Phillips, Jack J. *Return on Investment in Training and Performance Improvement Programs.* Houston, TX: Gulf Publishing Co., 1997.

Piskurich, G.M., Peter Beckschi, and Brandon Hall. *The ASTD Handbook of Training Design and Delivery.* Alexandria, VA: ASTD, 1999.

Popham, W. James. Educational Evaluation. Englewood Cliffs, N.J.: Prentice-Hall, 1975.

Popham, W. James. *Modern Educational Measurement.* Englewood Cliffs, N.J.:Prentice-Hall, 1981.

Pucel, D. *Performance-Based Instructional Design.* New York, N.Y.: McGraw-Hill, 1989.

Reigeluth, C. Instructional Theories in Action: Lessons Illustrating Selected Theories and Models. Hilldale, N.J.: Erlbaum, 1987.

Robinson, Dana G. and James C. Robinson. Training for Impact: How to Link Training to Business Needs and Measure the Results. S.F., CA: Jossey-Bass, 1989.

Robinson, Dana G. and Robinson, James. *Performance Consulting: Moving Beyond Training.* San Francisco, CA: Berrett-Koehler, 1995.

Rock, Milton and Berger, Lance. *The Compensation Handbook: A State-Of-The-Art Guide to Compensation Strategy and Design.* New York, N.Y.: McGraw-Hill, 1991.

Rogers, J. *Adult Learning.* London, U.K.: Penguin, 1971.

Rosenberg, Mark and W.A. Deterline. *Workplace Productivity: Performance Technology Success Stories.* Washington, D.C.: International Society for Performance Improvement, 1992.

Rossett, Allison. *Training Needs Assessment: Techniques in Training and Performance Development.* Englewood Cliffs, N.J.: Educational Technology Publishers, 1987.

Rothwell, William and Cookson, Peter. *Beyond Instruction: Comprehensive Program Planning for Business and Education.* San Francisco, CA: Jossey-Bass, 1997.

Rothwell, William and H.C. Kazanas. *Mastering the Instructional Design Process: A Systematic Approach.* 2$^{nd}$ edition. San Francisco: Jossey-Bass, 1998.

Rothwell, William. *ASTD Models for Human Performance Improvement: Roles, Competencies and Outputs.* Alexandria, VA: ASTD, 1996.

Rothwell, William. *The Self-Directed On-the-Job Learning Workshop.* Amherst, MA: Human Resource Development Press, 1996.

Rummler, Geary and Alan Brache. *Improving Performance: How to Manage the White Space on the Organization Chart.* San Francisco, CA: Jossey-Bass, 1990.

Schank, Roger. *Tell Me a Story: A New Look at Real and Artificial Memory.* N.Y., N.Y.: Macmillan, 1990.

Shavelson, Richard. *Statistical Reasoning for the Behavioral Sciences.* New York, N.Y.: McGraw-Hill, 1980.

Smith, B. and Delahaye, B. *How to Be an Effective Trainer.* (2$^{nd}$ ed.) New York, N.Y.: Wiley, 1987.

Spencer, L., Jr. And Spencer, S. *Competence at Work: Models for Superior Performance.* New York, N.Y.: Wiley, 1993.

Stolovitch, Harold and E.J. Keeps. "What is Human Performance Technology?" *Handbook of Human Performance Technology.* San Francisco: Jossey-Bass, 1992.

Swanson, Richard A.. *Analysis for Improving Performance: Tools for Diagnosing Organizations and Documenting Workplace Expertise.* San Francisco, CA: Berrett-Koehler Publishers, Inc., 1994.

Thiagarajan, S. "Formative Evaluation in Performance Technology," *Performance Improvement Quarterly,* 1191, 4(2), pp. 22-34.

Tripp, S. and Bichelmeyer, B. "Rapid Prototyping: An Alternative Instructional Design Strategy." *Educational Technology Research and Development,* 1990, 38(1), pp. 31-44.

Tyler, Ralph. *Basic Principles of Curriculum and Instruction.* Chicago, IL: University of Chicago Press, 1949.

U.S. Department of Labor and U.S. Department of Education. *The Bottom-Line: Basic Skills in the Workplace.* Washington, D.C.: U.S. Government Printing Office, 1988.

U.S. Department of Labor. *What Work Requires of Schools: A SCANS Report for America 2000.* Washington, D.C.: Government Printing Office, 1991.

Ulrich, David and Lake, D. *Organizational Capability: Competing form the Inside Out*. New York, N.Y.: Wiles, 1990.

Vroom, Victor. *Work and Motivation*. New York, N.Y.: Wiley, 1964.

West, C. Farmer, J. and Wolff, P. *Instructional Design: Implications from Cognitive Science*. Upper Saddle River, N.J.: Prentice Hall, 1991.

Zemke, Ronald, and Kramlinger, T. *Figuring Things Out: A Trainer's Guide to Needs And Task Analysis*. Reading, MA: Addison Wesley Longman, 1982.

# Appendix Two:

# Instructional Design Tools

Here are assembled a collection of sample tools and products for each of the five phases of Instructional Design. These include things like sample needs analysis tools, design blueprints and prototypes, development templates, delivery techniques and checklists, and evaluation surveys, tests and ROI calculations. The digital version is available at trainingeducationmanagement.com.

## Listing of Design Tools and Products

*Tool One:*

# *Organizational Surveillance Worksheet*

*Directions:*

Scan the areas listed below and determine how many of them are relevant to your organization and job. Where would you obtain current information about relevant areas? What's the current state in your organization?

| Areas of Interest | Sources | Current State |
|---|---|---|
| Strategic Plans | | |
| Business Objectives | | |
| Policies and Procedures | | |
| Performance Standards | | |
| Job Descriptions | | |
| Organization Charts | | |
| Annual Reports | | |
| Performance Appraisal Results | | |
| Key Performance Indicators | | |
| Cost of Quality | | |
| Turnover | | |
| Absenteeism | | |
| Disciplinary Actions and Trends | | |
| Accident Rates & Costs | | |
| Labor Costs | | |
| Scrap/Waste Costs | | |
| Rework Costs | | |
| Marketing Plans | | |
| Competitive Analysis | | |
| Industry Trends | | |
| Engineering/Technical Forecasts | | |
| Legal Issues and Mandates | | |
| Other? | | |

# *Job Task Analysis Worksheet*

### *Directions:*

- Use this instrument formally or informally, according to the ability and motivation of the group you are working with.
- All questions should be answered by the employees who do the job.
- Those employees should answer all questions in respect to their present job.  For example, if they are now working as a welder but they worked as a crew assistant for years, they should still make their ratings only according to their present job as a welder.

### *Interview Questions*

1. What is your present job title?
2. How long have you held your present job title?
3. What department/division do you work in?
4. What are the major tasks of your job? (Use job description to verify)
5. How many people will be performing the tasks?
6. What is the time spent performing each task?
7. What is the time lag between training and performing the tasks?

*For the next series of questions, focus on each major task individually.  Use the Task Rating Form to help capture this information.*

8. What are the consequences of performing the task inadequately?
9. What is the probability of deficient performance of this task?
10. What are the requirements of this task?
    \_\_\_\_\_ Memory -- recall, report, identify, restate, explain, look up
    \_\_\_\_\_ Divergent Thinking -- Create, forecast, invent, state all the things that ...  What would happen if ...  Decorate, Modify
    \_\_\_\_\_ Convergent Thinking -- deductive reasoning, problem solving, hypothesize, organize, decode, find the rule
    \_\_\_\_\_ Evaluation -- Check, compare.
11. What is the current skill level required?
12. What is the future skill level required?
13. Are there any sub tasks related to this one?
Capture important ones.

## Task Rating Survey

*Directions:*

On the following pages are a large number of task statements. For each task statement do the following:

1. Read each task statement and think about your job.
2. If you perform the task, rate the task according to Importance (both current and future). If you do not perform the task, put a zero in the boxes for that task.
3. Finish all task ratings on Importance.
4. Do the same for the Difficulty, Frequency and Physical Effort scales.

In the blank spaces at the end of the list of tasks, write in any tasks you perform that are not listed. Be sure to provide information on Importance, Difficulty, Frequency and Physical Effort for all tasks you write in.

| Name of Job Task | Current importance: 5 - Essential 4 - Important 3 - Moderately Important 2 - Less Important 1 - Minor | Future importance: 5 - Essential 4 - Important 3 - Moderately Important 2 - Less Important 1 - Minor | Difficulty of the task: 5 - Most Difficult 4 - Very Difficult 3 - Moderately difficult 2 - Relatively easy 1 - Easy | Difficulty to learn: 5 - Most Difficult 4 - Very Difficult 3 - Moderately difficult 2 - Relatively easy 1 - Easy | Frequency: 5 - Daily 4 - Weekly 3 - Monthly 2 - Occasionally 1 - Infrequently | Physical effort: 5 - Very high level 4 - High level 3 - Moderate level 2 - Low level 1 - Very low level |
|---|---|---|---|---|---|---|
| 1. [List Job Tasks Here.] | | | | | | |
| | | | | | | |
| | | | | | | |
| | | | | | | |
| | | | | | | |
| | | | | | | |
| | | | | | | |

## *Task Rankings*

*Directions:*

Calculate the ratings for each task from the Ratings Survey by adding up the rows. List the top ten tasks here in rank order. Discuss with the client whether you should include lower rated tasks in the training.

1.

2.

3.

4.

5.

6.

7.

8.

9.

10.

*Tool Three:*

# Task Analysis Summary Report

JOB/COURSE:_____

FUNCTION/SECTION: _____

TASK/LESSON:_____

PREREQUISITES:_____

EQUIPMENT AND MATERIALS: _____

REASONS:_____

_____

STANDARDS:_____

_____

INITIATING EVENT:

**STEPS**

1.

2.

3.

4.

5.

6.

7.

**Concepts/Principles:**            **Examples:**

*Tool Four:*

# Learner Analysis Worksheet

**Learner Analysis for _____Course**

## Competencies

1.  What is level of students' current knowledge and skills in subject area? Check one:
    _____ None
    _____ Basic background
    _____ Intermediate
    _____ Advanced

2.  What aptitudes have been demonstrated/tested prior to attending this course?
    _____

3.  What major misconceptions are new students likely to have regarding the subject matter?
    _____

## Attitudes

4.  Are there topics toward which the students are likely to feel especially positive?
    _____

5.  Are there topics toward which the students are likely to feel especially negative?
    _____

6.  Are there any preferences the students have in instructional format or media?
    _____

## Language Skills

7.  What is the language level of the students?
    _____ English as a Second Language/functional illiterate
    _____ Native English up to high school
    _____ College educated
    _____ Specialized/technical vocabulary

8.      What style of language is preferred?
        _____   Colloquial/conversational
        _____   Formal


## Tool Skills

9.      Are there any sensory-perceptual deficiencies that will require special attention?

_____


10.     Are there any special skills students will bring to the course?

_____


## Motivation

11.     To what extent do the students value the training they will receive from the course?

                _____   Training is essential to obtaining the job.
                _____   Regard training as having little value to success on the job.
                _____   Regard training as having considerable value to success on the job.

12.     To what extent are students confident in their ability to succeed in the training?

                _____   They have little confidence in their ability to succeed in training.
                _____   They are confident in their ability to succeed in training.
                _____   They are overly confident in their ability to succeed in training.


## Complete the analysis

13.     List any subgroups within the target population to be trained.
        Include the location of various groups and any logistical issues regarding demographics.

14.     Identify how the subgroups are different. (For example different learning preferences, language skills, attitudes, competencies, etc.)

15.     List recommendations on how the training should respond to these differences. (For example, have special modules for specific groups, have the entire group take the same modules.)

# *Context Analysis Worksheet*

## Context Analysis for _____ Course

1.      What presentation equipment will be available?

_____ None
_____ Flip Chart/White Board
_____ Overhead projector
_____ Video system with DVD
_____ CBT workstation
_____ Multimedia workstation (incl. videodisk and/or CD-ROM)

2.      Will the course be offered to individuals or groups?

_____ Individuals only
_____ Groups only
_____ Individuals and groups

3.      If groups, how large will they be?

_____

4.      Will we be able to train the trainers?

_____ Yes
_____ No

5.      What other resources are available to support training delivery?

_____

6.      How frequently will the course be offered (per year)?

_____

7.    How long can this course be?


8.    How can learning from this course be reinforced once the course is completed?

_____


_____


_____


9.    Will the course be sold?

\_\_\_\_\_Yes
\_\_\_\_\_No

10.   Will people pay to come to the course?

\_\_\_\_\_Yes
\_\_\_\_\_No

11.   What secondary uses are there for the course?


**Complete the analysis**

12.   Recommend the facilities to be used.

13.   Recommend the equipment to be used.

14.   Recommend how to modularize the course according to the needs of different groups with varying needs.

15.   Recommend how frequently the course should be offered per year.

16.   Recommend a course length.

17.   Recommend a strategy for the transfer of training.

# *Objectives Matrix*

*Directions:*

Use this matrix to plan a course with multiple learning objectives. List the target behaviors in the columns across the top and the content topics next to the rows on the left. Place an X in boxes that represent a learning objective. Make sure you have at least one objective per content area.

Content Topics       Target Behaviors

| | | | | |
|---|---|---|---|---|
| 1. | | | | |
| 2. | | | | |
| 3. | | | | |
| 4. | | | | |
| 5. | | | | |
| 6. | | | | |
| 7. | | | | |
| 8. | | | | |

# *Design Budget Template*

*Directions:*
*Use this template to enter budgeted and actual costs for training projects*
*It may be recreated in a spreadsheet program with formulas to automatically calculate costs and tally totals.*

| Project Name: | | | | DATE: |
|---|---|---|---|---|
| Project No. | | | | |
| Staff Costs | $/Hour | Budget ($) | Budget(d) | Actual($) |
| | | | | |
| | | | | |
| | | | | |
| | | | | |
| | | | | |
| Total | | $0.00 | 0 | $0.00 |
| | | | | |
| Contract Labor | | | | |
| | | | | |
| | | | | |
| | | | | |
| Total | | $0.00 | 0 | $0.00 |
| | | | | |
| Non-labor & Video Cost | | | | |
| Graphics | | | | |
| Instructor binders & matls. | | | | |
| Video production | | | | |
| Computer programming | | | | |
| Printing/reproduction | | | | |
| Student materials (consumables) | | | | |
| Total | | $0.00 | | $0.00 |
| | | | | |
| 10% Contingency (contract/non-labor only) | | $0.00 | | |
| | | | | |
| Total | | $0.00 | | $0.00 |

# *Blueprint Template*

*Direcions:*

Using the data from the job task analysis, context analysis, learner analysis, and objectives matrix, complete the template by adding Content, Presentation, Media, Practice, Deliverables, Learning Activities, and Tests/Assessments.

Blueprint for _____ Course

Summary:

Job Analysis Findings:

Context Analysis Findings:

Learner Analysis Findings:

*Description of the module/lesson/course:*

*Time to complete:*

*Objectives:*

*Prerequisites:*

*Content:*

**Presentation Methods:**

**Media:**

**Practice Activities:**

**Pre-work/Homework/Projects:**

**Evaluation Plan:**

*Tests/Assessments:*

*Deliverables:*

*Budget:*

*Milestones:*

# *Training Manual Template*

*Directions:*

The following template may be used either as a participant workbook, a leader's guide or a combination of both. If used as a leader's guide, the left column should show instructor notes and the right column student material. If used only as a participant workbook, the left column may be deleted or used to display icons and headings.

# Course/Module Name

## Leader Notes

This area is for special leader notes and should be used for information such as reminders to the leader, special emphasis or tips.

This Leader Note Box can be modified in several manners:

☆ copied and pasted anywhere

☆ resized by pulling of the corners or sides

☆ text formatted as bulleted text

☆ anything you could do in in a regular text box

## Leader Notes

Special icons for leader/participants guide

☆ Leader Notes Bullet

☎ Telephone Bullet

▤ Flipchart Bullet

🖑 Exercise Bullet

🖳 Computer/Hands On Bullet

📖 Policy/Procedure Bullet

▤ Overhead Bullet

# Introduction/ Overview

# Learning Objectives

By the end of this module, you will be able to:

◆ Identify QUACK.

◆ Apply QUACK.

# Key Concepts

◆ What is QUACK?

# Content

**Sub Head**

# Activity

# Action Plan

# Learning Check

**Module Name**                                        **p. 2**

# *Sample Test Specifications*

## Purpose

The following test specifications are meant to provide uniform guidelines for the preparation of test items in all training programs which include testing. Two types of test specifications are included: paper and pencil (cognitive) tests and performance (psychomotor) tests. Cognitive tests are appropriate when evaluating the acquisition of new knowledge, attitudes or thinking skills. Psychomotor tests are appropriate for evaluating behaviors and physical skills.

The examples provided, from an introductory Field Service Representative (FSR) course of a power utility, may serve as a model for other courses.

## Cognitive Test Specifications

## General Description

> After attending a training session and reading the accompanying course manual, trainees will answer questions about factual details by selecting the one response from a choice of four which correctly answers the question. The objective of this test is to identify facts which correctly answer questions based on the content of training classes.

## Sample Item

> **Directions:** Read the text and question below. Then read the four possible answers and select the one choice which correctly answers the question, based on the content of the FSR training program you attended. Circle the letter of the correct answer.

```
┌─────────────────────────────────────────────────────────────┐
│            FSR GAS OFF TURN-ON PROCEDURE                     │
│                                                              │
│   1.    Arrival                                              │
│         A. Record arrival time.                              │
│         B. Go to meter and record meter number and read      │
│         C. Verify whether meter is ON or OFF.                │
│                                                              │
│   2.    Shutdown                                             │
│         A. Follow FSR Shutdown Routine                       │
│         B. Tell customer that you have to go outside to work on │
│   the                   meter and that you will return to light and │
│   adjust                        appliances.                  │
│                                                              │
└─────────────────────────────────────────────────────────────┘
```

1.    According to the text, what is the second step in the gas off turn-on routine?

    a.    Record the meter number and read. [correct]
    b.    Verify whether the meter is ON or OFF. [contradicted]
    c.    Go to the meter and follow the FSR shutdown routine. [inaccurate]
    d.    Be polite and courteous to the customer. [unsupported]

**Stimulus Attributes**

1.    The questions will be taken directly from the course manual or other participant handout. When appropriate, the material will be reprinted in the stimulus.
2.    The questions will cover content which is specified in the objectives of the course.
3.    The questions will include one of the following interrogative words: who, what, when, where, why, how, how many, how much, etc. The questions posed must be directly answered by material in the course manual or handouts.

## Response Attributes

1.    Trainees will be asked to circle the letter of one of four given response alternatives, or to mark the letter of the answer on a pre-printed answer sheet. The four choices will consist of one correct response and three distracters.

2.    Distracters will be of four types:

    a.    **Irrelevant detail**: the distracter contains a detail from the course, but it is irrelevant to the question posed.

    b.    **Contradicted detail**: the distracter directly contradicts information stated in the instruction.

    c.    **Inaccurate detail**: the distracter inaccurately states a detail in the instruction. It may be inaccurate because of different scope (too broad or narrow), because a detail is omitted, or because incorrect information has been added to the detail.

    d.    **Unsupported detail**: the distracter makes a statement about information in the instruction which is not directly supported by details in the instruction. The statement, however, is neither irrelevant nor contradictory.

3.    The three distracters for each question will be drawn from at least two of the types mentioned above.

4.    The correct answer will include all information required to completely and accurately answer the question.

# *Performance Test Specifications*

## General Description

After attending a training session and reading the accompanying course manual, trainees will demonstrate their ability to perform specific job skills by completing a series of directed tasks under the observation of the instructor or qualified subject matter expert. The objective of this test is to demonstrate competent performance of specified job skills learned in training classes.

## Sample Item (from FSR Training Course)

Trainees will correctly disassemble and reassemble a Fisher S-102 regulator with the aid of a cross-sectional drawing and an FSR tool kit.

**Directions to Instructor:**
Provide each trainee with an assembled Fisher S-102 Regulator, a drawing of the regulator, and a standard FSR tool kit.
Instruct the trainee to disassemble the parts of the regulator listed below in the stimulus attributes and then to reassemble these parts. Observe the trainees performing this task and rate their performance on the Performance Observation Checklist (attached). Tally the total score on the checklist and go over the results with the trainees.

## Stimulus Attributes

1.  Each trainee will be provided with an assembled Fisher S-102 regulator, a cross-sectional drawing and an FSR tool kit.

2.  Trainees will be instructed to perform the following tasks:
    a.  Disassemble flange union
    b.  Remove disc holder assembly
    c.  Remove stem guide
    d.  Remove closing cap
    e.  Remove adjusting screw and spring
    f.  Reassemble all the above parts

3. Trainees will be observed by the instructor or subject matter expert as they perform the six tasks above. They will receive no coaching or assistance while performing the tasks.

## Response Attributes

1. The instructor or designee will record whether the trainee performs each step successfully on a Performance Observation Checklist (below).

2. Successful performance includes all of the following:
   a. identifying the correct parts to remove
   b. removing the correct part without damaging it or the unit
   c. reassembling all the parts so that the unit is functional

   Partial credit (1/2 point) may be awarded for successful completion of one or two of the steps above.

3. A passing score will be awarded to trainees who perform all six steps correctly. Trainees who fail to achieve a score of 5 or more will receive additional instruction and be required to take the test again.

4. The following checklist will be used to record and score observations.

### *Performance Observation Checklist*

| ITEM | TASK | CORREC T (1 POINT) | PARTIALLY CORRECT (.5 POINT) | INCOR-RECT (0 POINTS) |
|---|---|---|---|---|
| 1 | Disassemble flange union | | | |
| 2 | Remove disc holder assembly | | | |
| 3 | Remove stem guide | | | |
| 4 | Remove closing cap | | | |
| 5 | Remove adjusting screw and spring | | | |
| 6 | Reassemble all parts | | | |
| TOTAL SCORE | | | | |

*Tool 11:*

# Training Quality Control Technique Checklist

| Design Phase | Quality Control Technique | Reviewed and Approved By |
|---|---|---|
| Analysis | 1. Create a reliable, valid assessment design. | ☐_____ |
|  | 2. Ensure reliable data collection and analysis. | ☐_____ |
| Design | 3. Ensure a creative training solution that solves the identified need. | ☐_____ |
|  | 4. Ensure that proposed training solution is feasible. | ☐_____ |
| Development | 5. Orient developers to the needs of the customer and the blueprint specifications. | ☐_____ |
|  | 6. Use a template to standardize training presentation. | ☐_____ |
|  | 7. Develop a prototype and review it for accuracy and fit. | ☐_____ |
|  | 8. Provide timely feedback about the quality of work. | ☐_____ |
|  | 9. Review work for consistency, accuracy and quality. | ☐_____ |
|  | 10. Ensure that needed changes are completed. | ☐_____ |
| Implementation | 11. Conduct Train-the-Trainer. | ☐_____ |
|  | 12. Transition materials and course maintenance to Implementers. | ☐_____ |

| Evaluation | | |
|---|---|---|
| | 13. Conduct a formal evaluation of the pilot. | ☐_____ |
| | 14. Ensure that any needed changes are completed. | ☐_____ |
| | 15. Conduct formal evaluation of reactions, learning, skill transfer and business results. | ☐_____ |
| | 16. Use evaluation results to refine the training design process and to improve the quality of training. | ☐_____ |

# *Production Evaluation Checklist*

| Production Media | Key Items to Check | Reviewed and Approved By |
|---|---|---|
| **Print Materials** | **Copy editing**<br>1. Grammar, punctuation, spelling, language and usage are all correct. | ☐_____ |
| | 2. Technical jargon and acronyms used appropriately. | ☐_____ |
| | 3. Masters include all edits identified in earlier drafts. | ☐_____ |
| | **Formatting**<br>4. Page layout is correct, including: margins, headers, footers, headlines, spacing, etc. | ☐_____ |
| | 5. Page breaks are correct, and do not leave any widows or orphans. | ☐_____ |
| | 6. Paragraph formatting is correct, including use of: fonts, paragraph styles, spacing, indentation, use of bullets, numbers, special characters, etc. | ☐_____ |
| | 7. Tables, job aids and reference materials are formatted correctly and read clearly. | ☐_____ |
| | **Graphics and Artwork**<br>8. Artwork is legible and clearly labeled. | ☐_____ |
| | 9. Artwork is technically accurate, including use of call outs, labels and sources. | ☐_____ |
| | 10. Graphics support the instructional message and do not detract from it. | ☐_____ |

| | | |
|---|---|---|
| **Visual Materials** | **Content** 11. Overheads, slides, computer displays, flip charts, etc. convey a consistent, technically accurate message. | ☐ _____ |
| | 12. Visuals properly support the instructional intent of the program. | ☐ _____ |
| | 13. Visuals are clear and useful to learners. | ☐ _____ |
| | **Impact** 14. Visuals express their messages clearly and powerfully. | ☐ _____ |
| | 15. Visuals are pleasing to the eye. | ☐ _____ |
| **Video Production** | **Video** 16. Actors are chosen who reflect the roles they are to play. | ☐ _____ |
| | 17. The sets support the instructional intent. | ☐ _____ |
| | 18. All equipment, props and backgrounds used are technically accurate. | ☐ _____ |
| | 19. Video properly matches the script and storyboard. | ☐ _____ |
| | 20. Final video output gives proper emphasis to people and objects depicted. | ☐ _____ |
| | **Audio** 21. Actors have followed the script. No omissions or additions that affect the message. | ☐ _____ |
| | 22. All technical jargon and company names have been pronounced correctly. | ☐ _____ |
| | 23. Sound is clear and understandable on the type of speakers that learners will be using. | ☐ _____ |

| Computer & Multimedia Production | **Screen Design** 24. Screen layout is suitable for the content and activities. | ☐_____ |
| | 25. Screen look and feel is inviting and user-friendly. | ☐_____ |
| | 26. Screens all use the same template. | ☐_____ |
| | **Interactivity and User Control** 27. Questions formats are appropriate for the content. | ☐_____ |
| | 28. Questions evaluate learning or require application of knowledge/skill. | ☐_____ |
| | 29. Learners can easily navigate through the course and choose entry/exit points. | ☐_____ ☐_____ |
| | 30. The user interface is simple and familiar to learners. | |

| | | |
|---|---|---|
| **Feedback and Evaluation** | 31. Learners receive frequent positive and corrective feedback. | ☐_____ |
| | 32. Feedback is individualized depending on the learner's responses. | ☐_____ |
| | 33. Remediation is provided for all learner errors. | ☐_____ |
| | 34. The program measures and tracks learning pre and post-instruction. | ☐_____ |
| | 35. The management system records learner progress and prints relevant management reports. | ☐_____ |
| | 36. An evaluation plan to measure skill transfer and results is implemented. | ☐_____ |

Tool 13:
# *Lesson Plan Template*

*Directions: The following template may be used to develop a lesson plan for an experienced instructor or for a designer who will also deliver training. The template may either be completed by hand or using a word processor, with a table format.*

**Program Title** _____

**Lesson Title** _____

**Total Lesson Time** _____

**Lesson Objectives** _____

**Materials Needed**_____

| Time | Content Outline Points | Method/Materials | Trainee Activities /Exercises |
|------|------------------------|------------------|-------------------------------|
| :00 | [List key content outline points] | [List methods and materials to be used] | [Describe what trainees should be doing] |
| | | | |
| | | | |
| | | | |
| | | | |
| | | | |
| | | | |

# *Training Delivery Techniques Matrix*

**Directions:**

*The following matrix shows a variety of methods for learning, presentation and distribution of training, using both classroom and non-classroom delivery systems. Although some methods naturally compliment each other, it is possible to select a methodolgy from each column and assemble a training delivery solution. (Adapted from ASTD, 2003)*

| Learning Methods | Presentation Methods | Distribution Methods |
|---|---|---|
| ☐ Action Learning | ☐ 3D Modeling | ☐ Audiotape |
| ☐ Apprenticeship | ☐ Art/Illustration | ☐ Cable TV |
| ☐ Case Study | ☐ Audio | ☐ CD-I (Interactive) |
| ☐ Demonstration | ☐ Classroom Trainer | ☐ CD-ROM |
| ☐ Discussion | ☐ Computer (CBT) | ☐ DVD (Digital Video) |
| ☐ Drill and Practice | ☐ Dialogue | ☐ Electronic Mail |
| ☐ Expert Panel | ☐ E-mail | ☐ Floppy Disk |
| ☐ Game | ☐ EPSS | ☐ Internet |
| ☐ Homework | ☐ Groupware | ☐ Intranet |
| ☐ Lecture | ☐ Interactive TV | ☐ LAN/WAN |
| ☐ Mentoring | ☐ Internet (IBT) | ☐ Laserdisc |
| ☐ OJT | ☐ Job Aid | ☐ Live Speech |
| ☐ Project | ☐ Learning Group | ☐ Mail |
| ☐ Role Play | ☐ Print | ☐ Satellite TV |
| ☐ Self-Study | ☐ Tele/Videoconference | ☐ Simulator/Tactile Gear |
| ☐ Simulation | ☐ Television | ☐ Telephone |
| ☐ Small Group Activity | ☐ Video | ☐ Videotape |
| ☐ Trial and Error | ☐ Virtual Reality | ☐ Voice Mail |

# *Sample Participant Reaction Survey*

*The following participant reaction survey may be used to assess participant opinions at the end of classroom or e-learning programs.*

## Training Evaluation Survey

Course Name: _____ Date: _____

Instructor(s):

_____

*Directions:*

*Please read each item carefully and place a check mark in the column which comes closest to how strongly you agree or disagree with the statement. Check only one column for each item. Write any comments or suggestions in the space provide on the reverse side of the form.*

| | Strongly Agree | Agree | Disagree | Strongly Disagree |
|---|---|---|---|---|
| **Course Administration** | | | | |
| 1. I was able to take this course when I needed it. | ☐ | ☐ | ☐ | ☐ |
| 2. The facilities and equipment were favorable learning. | ☐ | ☐ | ☐ | ☐ |
| 3. I had the skill and knowledge required to take this course. | ☐ | ☐ | ☐ | ☐ |
| **Course Content** | | | | |
| 4. I clearly understood the course objectives. | ☐ | ☐ | ☐ | ☐ |
| 5. The course met all of its stated objectives. | ☐ | ☐ | ☐ | ☐ |

|  | Strongly Agree | Agree | Disagree | Strongly Disagree |
|---|---|---|---|---|

## Course Design

6. The way this course was delivered (classroom, computer, video, self-study) was an effective way to learn.  ☐ ☐ ☐ ☐

7. I had enough time to learn the subject matter presented.  ☐ ☐ ☐ ☐

8. Participant materials (manuals, workbooks, job aids, handouts, etc.) were useful to me.  ☐ ☐ ☐ ☐

## Course Instructor(s)/Presentation

9. The instructor's presentation was well-organized and easy to follow.  ☐ ☐ ☐ ☐

10. The instructor(s)/presentation was knowledgeable about the content.  ☐ ☐ ☐ ☐

11. The instructor(s) created a positive learning atmosphere.  ☐ ☐ ☐ ☐

12. Overall, I was satisfied with the instructor/presentation.  ☐ ☐ ☐ ☐

## Course Relevance

13. My knowledge and skills increased due to this course.  ☐ ☐ ☐ ☐

14. I can apply what I learned in this course on my job.  ☐ ☐ ☐ ☐

15. Overall, I think this course was a valuable investment of my time.  ☐ ☐ ☐ ☐

**Overall Evaluation**

16. What did you like best about the course?

_____

_____

17. What did you like least about the course?

_____

_____

18. How do you plan to apply the knowledge and skill gained from the course?

_____

_____

19. What additional comments or suggestions do you have?

_____

_____

*Thank you for taking the time to complete this survey. Your opinions will help us improve the quality of training programs and measure their results.*

# Sample Supervisory Behavior Change Survey

*Directions:*

*The following is an example of a post training behavior change and skill transfer survey sent to learners' supervisors three months after completion of training. The cover letter explains the purpose and procedures for completing the survey.*

---

## Sample Cover Letter for Supervisor Survey

---

Dear [ Name]:

About three months ago, one or more of your staff attended [Name of Training Program]. The course taught your employee(s):
- [List terminal performance objectives]

The attached survey asks some questions about the behavior and skills you have observed since the training took place. The information you provide will help us measure how well newly-learned skills are being transferred to the workplace and how job performance improves as a result of training.

We are asking you to complete this because, as their supervisor, you are in the best position to observe and judge how well your employees are performing. Please answer the questions that follow as completely and accurately as you can. It should take you about 10-15 minutes to complete the survey.

Return the survey by [Deadline Date].

Thank you very much for your support of training. Let me know if you have any questions.

Sincerely,
[Training Manager]

# Training Behavior Change Survey

**Course:** _____  **Date:** _____

**Department:** _____

**Part One:**

1. How many of your employees attended this training?

   _____

2. How would you rate your overall satisfaction with the training your employees received?

   | Very Satisfied | Somewhat Satisfied | Neutral | Somewhat Dissatisfied | Very Dissatisfied |
   |---|---|---|---|---|
   | – | – | – | – | – |

3. What was your employees' average personal productivity before they started training?

   | Very High | Better Than Satisfied | Average | Worse Than Average | Very Low |
   |---|---|---|---|---|
   | – | – | – | – | – |

4. What is your employees' average personal productivity now that they have completed training?

   | Very High | Better Than Satisfied | Average | Worse Than Average | Very Low |
   |---|---|---|---|---|
   | – | – | – | – | – |

**Part Two:**

For each of the skills listed below, please estimate the following:
1. The current skill level of your employees (Very High to Very Low).
2. How often they use the skill (Always to Never).
3. How important the skill is for their jobs (Very Important to Very Unimportant).

Use the five point scale, with five being highest and one being lowest.

| Skill Learned | 1,Current Skill Level (5-1) 5 = Very High 4 = Better than Average 3 = Average 2 = Worse than Average 1 = Very Low | 2.Frequency of Use (5-1) 5 = Always 4 = Often 3 = Sometimes 2 = Infrequent 1 = Never | 3.Importance to Job (5-1) 5 = Very Important 4 = Somewhat Important 3 = Neutral 2 = Somewhat Unimportant 1 = Very Unimportant |
|---|---|---|---|
| 1. *[insert skills taught here.]* | | | |
| 2. | | | |
| 3. | | | |
| 4. | | | |

**Part Three:**

1. Please check ALL of the following ways that you support training in your department.

    ____ Supervisor Coaching
    ____ Peer Coaching
    ____ On the Job Training
    ____ Job Aids
    ____ Electronic Performance Support Systems
    (computer knowledge bases)
    ____ Other? (What?)

    _____

    _____

2. Please rate the effectiveness of the following training support activities in your department by checking the correct box below.

| Activity | Very Effective | Some-what Effective | Neutral | Somewhat Ineffective | Very Ineffective |
|---|---|---|---|---|---|
| Coaching by Supervisor | O | O | O | O | O |
| Coaching by Peers | O | O | O | O | O |
| On the Job Training | O | O | O | O | O |
| Job Aids | O | O | O | O | O |
| Electronic Performance Support Systems | O | O | O | O | O |
| Other (What?) | O | O | O | O | O |

3. What barriers or obstacles (if any) make it difficult for your employees to apply newly learned skills on the job?

_____

4. What enablers or motivators help employees to apply newly learned skills on the job?

_____

5. What changes to the training your employees took would help them to perform better?

_____

Thank you for completing this survey. Please return it to: [Name, Address].

# Training ROI Worksheet

## Directions:
Use the worksheet below to plan and calculate training ROI. Enter data in the spreadsheet and the totals are automatically calculated.

| Costs | Category | Calculation | Subtotal | Grand Total |
|---|---|---|---|---|
| Direct | | | | |
| | | | | |
| Indirect | | | | |
| Opportunity | | | | |
| Sub Total | | | | $ 0.00 |
| **Benefits** | **Category** | **Calculation** | **Subtotal** | **Grand Total** |
| Direct | | | | |
| | | | | |
| Indirect | | | | |
| Windfall | | | | |
| Sub Total | | | | $ 0.00 |
| | **ROI** | (B-C)/C x 100) | | % |

# Index

## A

Accelerating Training Design, 99
Action plan, 228, 231, 232, 233, 253
ADDIE model, 1, 262
American Society for Training and Development (ASTD)
    Models for Human Performance Improvement, 23
Analysis of Variance (ANOVA), 149
ASTD Benchmarking Forum, 88, 206
Authoring software, 88, 104, 125, 130

## B

Baird, Schnier and Laird, 190
Basic skills, 56
Bell Curve, 145
Bentley, 190
Best Practices in Training Design, 257
Bloom, Hastings and Madaus, 224
Brainstorming sessions, 185
Broad and Newstrom, 22, 229
Budgets
    examples of training design resources, 95
    Final Working Budget, 96, 98
    Preliminary Proposals, 95
    Sample Preliminary Proposal Budget, 97
Business results, 1, 4, 5, 32, 72, 80, 97, 108, 112, 119, 131, 155, 166, 200, 201, 202, 203, 205, 214, 216, 217, 218, 239, 240, 244, 245, 247, 248, 253, 257

## C

Case Studies and Role Plays To Simulate Reality, 187
Case study, 71, 76, 173, 187, 188, 209, 210, 220
Cause analysis, 23, 26, 31
CD-ROM, 163, 196
Change management, 24
Clark, 29, 31, 32
Classroom Delivery, 167, 173, 174
Cognitive psychology, 51, 174, 257, 258, 259
company organization chart, 36
Competencies, 39, 40
Computer programmers, 122, 128, 129, 160, 161
Computer-based training (CBT), 51, 53, 60, 62, 84, 86, 88, 100, 102, 119, 191, 196, 225
Context analysis, 9, 58, 59, 115
    Elements, 58
    Importance, 58
Context Analysis, 9, 58, 59, 115
    Elements, 58
    Importance, 58
Continuous Learning, 261
Corrective Action, 154, 156, 158
Correlation coefficient, 147
Coscarelli and Shrock, 137, 224
Cost avoidance, 120, 203, 241
Cost Estimation Techniques, 97
    Material Estimation Standards, 98
    see also Budgets, 97

# M

# N

# O

# R

# S

# T

training transfer strategies, 62
Training transfer strategies, 62
Transfer of Training, 203, 229
Transferring skills to the job, 63, 179, 181
Tyler, 74

# V

Validity, 135
    Construct Validity, 136
    Content Validity, 136
    Criterion Validity, 136
    Threats to validity, 208, 209

# W

Workplace Literacy Training, 239
World Wide Web (WWW), 196

9 780976 397403